Coaching Competitive Team Sports for Girls and Women

Hally B. W. Poindexter, Ed.D.

Professor of Health and Physical Education
Rice University and the University of Houston
Houston, Texas

Carole L. Mushier, Ph.D.

Associate Professor
Women's Physical Education Department
State University of New York
Cortland, New York

1973
W. B. SAUNDERS COMPANY Philadelphia London Toronto

W. B. Saunders Company: West Washington Square
Philadelphia, Pa. 19105

12 Dyott Street
London, WC1A 1DB

833 Oxford Street
Toronto 18, Ontario

Coaching Competitive Team Sports for Girls and Women   ISBN   0-7216-7271-X

Print No.:   9   8   7   6   5   4   3   2   1

"The one purpose of sports for girls and women is the good of those who play."

DIVISION FOR GIRLS' AND WOMEN'S SPORTS
AMERICAN ASSOCIATION FOR HEALTH,
PHYSICAL EDUCATION AND RECREATION

Preface

Competitive athletics for girls and women is a growing area of activity, interest and concern in schools, colleges and universities. It is to the philosophical and realistic concerns of such competition and to the development of competitive skill in five selected team activities that this book is directed. The undergraduate student participating in competitive sports and preparing for a career in teaching and coaching, the woman physical educator concerned with the total program of physical education and the coach directly responsible for girls and women in competitive athletics may find value in the contents.

The authors have had competitive team sports experience and have coached and administered competitive programs. We are convinced that positive educational and developmental results are possible through interscholastic, intercollegiate and other competitive experiences. For many years the needs of the highly skilled girl have not been fulfilled through customary programs of physical education. The highly skilled have been neglected for obvious reasons—philosophical differences among educators, financial limitations and limited leadership. Conferees at the Division for Girls' and Women's Sports Study Conference on Competition for Girls and Women in 1965 identified three major problems which persist as the greatest concerns in the conduct of competition for girls and women.[1]

1. Differences in philosophy as to what is appropriate for girls. Women tend to resist studying competition because of tradition, prejudice, or fear of the unknown.
2. Providing adequate facilities and finances (without relying on gate receipts).
3. Providing a sufficient number of women leaders or competent coaches and officials.

---

[1] Division for Girls' and Women's Sports, Guidelines for Athletic Programs, 1965.

Policies and standards considered basic for the conduct of athletic competition for girls' and women's sports are periodically reviewed and revised by the Division for Girls' and Women's Sports. *Philosophy and Standards for Girls' and Women's Sports*,[2] written with concern for the changing sports culture and expanding research dealing with women in competition, indicates standards and guidelines considered desirable for junior high school, senior high school and collegiate competitive programs. The broad standards are not intended to be the final nor ideal statement for specific local areas or districts — they are *guidelines*. Local, state and district groups are encouraged to develop their own specific policies for the conduct of competitive sports within the framework of the DGWS recommendations. Many high school, college, and recreational groups are presently developing and refining their own standards and working closely with the organizations responsible for rule development and the conduct of competitive events.

The expansion of programs of competitive sports is not an attempt to replace or displace the broader base of instructional and intramural programs. It is rather an attempt to complete the well-known pyramid of a total program of physical education — one that challenges all levels of skill and interest. Faced with the realities that there are girls and women who want and need competitive experience, and that there are concerns and difficulties in providing these experiences, it has become obvious that women physical educators and recreation leaders should accept the responsibility of exerting positive influence on the development and conduct of competitive activities within an educational setting.

The materials presented herein are intended to be at least a partial response to some of the needs expressed by persons interested and actively engaged in programs of competition for girls and women. These needs have existed for many years; and with an increasing number of programs and greater interest and concern, the book is most timely. The authors have limited their responses to the following areas:

1. Presentation of a point of view about athletic competition and the organization of such competition within the framework of educational and recreational programs.
2. Comments directed to the coach which may serve as "checkpoints" in her personal development as she leads a competitive program and team.
3. Presentation of suggestions for the organization of competitive experiences.
4. Presentation of specific information on advanced skills, strategy and coaching in five selected team sports.

---

[2] American Association for Health, Physical Education and Recreation, Division for Girls' and Women's Sports, *Philosophy and Standards for Girls' and Women's Sports*, 1201 16th St., N.W., Washington, D. C., 1969.

In discussing basketball, field hockey, lacrosse, softball and volleyball, the authors recognize the varying rules under which some of the sports are played. The rules are gradually becoming more universal through the co-operative efforts of the several ruling organizations. The merit of having a single set of rules is obvious to both coaches and players. For purposes of this book, the authors consider DGWS rules basic to competitive play, yet realize that consideration must be given the different advanced skills and strategy which naturally have evolved where there is general acceptance of other rules.

The materials in the book were developed from personal points of view, but with an awareness of the results of current research concerning competitive activities for girls and women. The book does not intend to present an analysis of basic skills in the sports covered; it is assumed such materials are available elsewhere for both coach and player. For this reason a carefully selected bibliography is suggested in each sports chapter. If there is a new concept, a refreshing thought or a thought-provoking idea within the contents, thanks should go to the students, colleagues and team-mates from whom we have gleaned our information and inspiration. The omissions, errors and contentious comments are the sole property of the authors.

HALLY B. W. POINDEXTER

CAROLE L. MUSHIER

Acknowledgments

The authors are indebted to many persons who provided inspiration, guidance and support throughout the preparation of the book. Our greatest appreciation is expressed to our mentors, students and colleagues who tested ideas and constructs and offered many helpful suggestions.

Special thanks are given to Nancy Hilliard Landon and Eva Jean Lee for their original illustrations, and to Aileen Lockhart, Martha E. Hawthorne, Margaret E. Wilson, Betty Lou Murphy, Judy Glazener, Jane Oswald and Margaret Zepeda for their review of selected chapters.

The finished product owes much to the efficient cooperation of Wallace Pennington, Karen Coady, Herbert Powell and John Hackmaster of W. B. Saunders Company. Their enthusiasm and support have made the venture a pleasurable experience.

H. B. W. P.
C. L. M.

Contents

1

The Role of Competition

Women in Competition

Athletic competition for high school, college and young adult women is now accepted as an important contemporary cultural phenomenon in American society. Total acceptability and social respectability for competitors in team sports are still incomplete.[1] It is important for the student of physical education and the teacher-coach to understand the philosophical points of view and the actual problems and prejudices attending competition by women in recent decades. A thorough historical treatment is not possible here; however, it is germane to review the immediate past in order to understand the present.

The active move toward a greater emphasis in competitive sports for girls and women had its real beginning in the last decade, specifically 1962. Prior to the sixties, most discussions and writings concerning competitive sports terminated in emotional treatises for and against with very few writings of the early sixties indicating a restive awareness that many girls and women were seeking respectable status for their competitive desires. By 1962 the Division for Girls' and Women's Sports (DGWS) began to encourage expanded competitive opportunities and in rapid progression four major events occurred that appreciably changed the competitive scene.

The Women's Advisory Board to the Olympic Development Committee was created in 1962 with the avowed purpose of improving the "participation of women in the Olympic Games, putting into action the philosophy and standards of the DGWS."[2]

---

[1] Harres, Bea: "Attitudes of students toward women's athletic competition." *Research Quarterly*, May 1968, pp. 283–84.

[2] Jernigan, Sara Staff: "Women and the Olympics." *Journal of Health, Physical Education and Recreation*, April 1962, p. 25.

In 1963, the revised DGWS *Policies for Competition in Girls' and Women's Sports* appeared. They were not merely a relaxed position of the 1957 "Policies" but were a basic realistic revision to face the changing cultural scene and the needs and interests of the highly-skilled girl. The revision included policies which strongly favored competition and permitted participation in leagues and season-long playing schedules. The statement that opposed the charging of admission was deleted and a junior high school program of interscholastic athletics was included. That year also marked the appearance of the first of the National Institutes on Girls' and Women's Sports. To date, five of these institutes have been held. They are singularly effective in improving communication between DGWS and women physical educators in the interpretation of competition in women's sports and in improving the competence of women in teaching, coaching and officiating sports.

In 1967 the Commission on Intercollegiate Athletics for Women (CIAW) was formed to facilitate the development of sound intercollegiate athletic programs for women. The Commission encouraged organization of colleges, universities and women physical educators to govern intercollegiate competition, sanctioned closed intercollegiate events, and sponsored DGWS National Championships. Three such championships were held in 1969 and seven in 1971–72.

The Association for Intercollegiate Athletics for Women (AIAW) was organized in 1971 to replace CIAW. Its purposes are to provide "a governing body and leadership for initiating and maintaining standards of excellence in women's intercollegiate athletic programs." Colleges and universities may become active participants and their faculty members will be eligible to serve as regional representatives, junior college representatives or officers.

RESEARCH RELATING TO WOMEN IN COMPETITION

There is little question that interest and momentum have increased and that the expansion of competitive sports opportunities for girls and women will continue to accelerate. With the expanding interest has come the need to understand more about the physiological and psychological responses of women in athletic competition. Research is far too inadequate to indicate with certainty what are the most appropriate competitive events and experiences. Studies investigating the woman athlete have dealt primarily with the relationship of participation to menstruation and pregnancy. Little study has been undertaken regarding work capacity or the appropriateness of specific activities for women. In general only those aspects of competitive activities that might be considered unique or detrimental to the female have been investigated.

It is now generally agreed that limitations are usually unnecessary for healthy, well-trained girls and women during the menstrual period[3-10] and the evidence suggests the continuation of usual patterns of exercise for the normal female during this period. Erdelyi,[7, 8] among others, has stated that performance is influenced more by psychological rather than by physiological factors during menstruation and that these psychological factors may hinder performance.

Results of studies dealing with disorders of pregnancy show no significant differences between athletes and nonathletes. Some evidence indicates advantages in favor of the athlete.[3, 7, 9, 11]

"The normal heart is invulnerable to the demands and stresses of physical exercise and athletic training. This statement is unqualified. It applies to men and women, to children and to adults."[12] It is true, however, that the ratio of heart weight to body weight is 85 to 90 per cent of the value for men. Coupled with the fact that women also have a poorer strength-weight ratio than men, it is obvious that women's and men's performances are not comparable.

If championship performance indicates peak proficiency in activity, Lehman[13] indicates that the range for men is 22–35 years. Recent performances among women, particularly swimmers, would indicate the lower limits of peak proficiency to be around 15 years.[14] Generally, peak performance is attained at an earlier age in activities requiring speed, strength and endurance and a later age in activities where experience is an important factor. Girls and women seem to adjust to heavy training, however, in much the same manner as the male and there is no evidence that the female is more unstable than the male at any given age.

Basic body structure and individual personality factors of men and

---

[3]Jokl, Ernest: "Some clinical data on women's athletics." *Journal of the Association for Physical and Mental Rehabilitation*, March–April 1956, p. 48.

[4]Hellebrandt, Frances and Meyer, Margaret: "Physiological data significant to participation by women in physical activities." *Research Quarterly*. March 1939, p. 20.

[5]Ingman, Ove: "Menstruation in Finnish top class sportswomen." *Sports Medicine*, Finnish Association of Sports Medicine, Helsinki, 1933, p.169–72.

[6]Harnik, M.: "Sport and menstruation." *First Asian Physical Education, Health, and Recreation Congress,* Bureau of Printing, Manila, 1955, p.30–33.

[7]Erdelyi, Gyula: "Women in athletics." *Proceedings of the Second National Conference on the Medical Aspects of Sport,* 1960.

[8]Erdelyi, Gyula: "Gynecological survey of female athletes." *Journal of Sports Medicine*, September 1962, pp.174–79.

[9]McCloy, C. H.: "On some factors regarding sex differences in relation to sports activities." *Studi di Medicina e Chirurgia Dello Sport*, 8:61–67, 1954.

[10]Harnik, M.: "Sport and menstruation." *Sport and Health*, February 1952, pp.149–51.

[11]Durant, Della: "The effect of vigorous sports participation on the duration of labor in childbearing." Unpublished M.S. Thesis, Pennsylvania State University, 1957.

[12]Jokl, Ernest: "The heart of the woman athlete." *AAU Study of Effect of Athletic Competition on Girls and Women*, 1956, p.9.

[13]Lehman, Harvey C.: *Age and Achievement*. Princeton University Press, 1953, p.256.

[14]Espenschade, A. S., and Eckert, H.: *Motor Development*. Columbus, Ohio, Charles E. Merrill Books, Inc., 1967, p.233.

women have much to do with both the selection of activities and one's success in participation. Different activities do not necessarily demand the same kinds of strength or body build; however, certain body structures seem more conducive to success in particular activities. There is no evidence to suggest that either certain types of athletics or competition in general will "muscularize" women participants.

Much research is presently being conducted in the psychological, sociological and physiological areas in relation to the female in athletics. This decade should provide some of the answers to the vital questions of what is appropriate, as well as what the potential for girls and women in competitive sports may be.

Purposes and Objectives

The justification for interscholastic and intercollegiate athletic programs is their contribution to total educational and physical education objectives. The frequently quoted statement of the National Education Association clearly identifies the place of athletics in an educational program:[15]

We believe in athletics as an important part of the school physical education program. We believe that the experience of playing athletic games should be a part of the education of all children and youth who attend school in the United States. . . . Participation in sound athletic programs, we believe, contributes to health and happiness, physical skill and emotional maturity, social competence, and moral values.

Competitive athletics in recreational settings need no formal justification other than the personal pleasure that accrues from participation. Varsity sports, interscholastic, intercollegiate or other extramural competitive athletics are a part of the total physical education program. Highly competitive programs serve the gifted, skilled athlete in ways in which she cannot generally be challenged in the general instructional and intramural programs. Perhaps of even greater importance in the education of a young woman is the fact that athletics can be the force that allows for and encourages excellence—excellence in understanding and performance:[16]

Some people are never challenged to do their best—the athlete is. Some people never know what it feels like to give everything within themselves to reach a goal—the athlete does. Some people can never deny themselves the trivial things in order to reach the more valuable

---

[15]Educational Policies Commission: *"School Athletics—Problems and Policies."* National Education Association, Washington, D.C., 1954.

[16]Neal, Patsy: *Basketball Techniques for Women.* New York, Ronald Press, 1966, p.4.

results—the athlete can. Some people never know what it is like to be an integrated individual with tension gone from the body and mind—the athlete knows.

Athletics are not a thing apart, but are a highly developed program with purposes and objectives compatible with excellence in education. The educational philosophy should place competition in the category of a cocurricular activity, according it the same benefits and obligations of any curricular offering.

Although not a thing apart, some athletic contributions are indeed unique. *Under proper guidance and leadership* athletics can be a powerful force in the development of social and moral, as well as physical qualities. The mere offering of an athletic program is no assurance that the potential values will accrue to one or all participants. Competition in and of itself is neither good nor bad—it is good only with proper leadership and guidance directed toward sound goals. The Division of Men's Athletics identifies four broad areas of major emphasis in educational athletic programs that pertain to women as well as men:[17]

1. Physical Fitness
2. Skill in Movement—performing at highest level possible for each individual—satisfaction—thrill of play
3. Social Development—emotional control—sportsmanship—working together—loyalty—self-confidence—feeling a part of something—acceptance—recognition
4. Recreation

Values

Positive values, difficult to define and uniquely individual, are the resultant outcomes of the achievement of educational objectives. Values can be achieved and changes in values can occur through sports participation and competition, but not by chance. To a great degree, the achievement of values depends upon the leadership and the plans which are made for their achievement. Good sportsmanship and emotional control are frequently mentioned as outcomes of athletic competition. If poor judgment and emphasis on winning supersede the educational objectives of competition, the process will become a detrimental educational experience. The coach who permits her players to make comments to officials or opponents (no matter what the circumstances), to foul intentionally because of some previous illegal contact by an opponent which was missed by the official, to foul in-

---

[17]Division of Men's Athletics: "Athletics in education." American Association for Health, Physical Education and Recreation, Washington, D.C., 1962.

tentionally to gain strategically in play, to berate fellow players on or off the field or court and to demonstrate other unacceptable behavior does a great injustice to the players, the game and to the entire value system in positive athletic competition. The coach should motivate her team members to achieve excellence in competition without allowing degradation of opponents or officials.

The teacher-coach who hopes to instill positive values in sports situations should consider the following principles of learning when planning for competitive experiences:

1. Commitment to value development is most meaningful when values are cooperatively defined by coach and team members.
2. The coach determines expectations. Her own value system must be conclusive, coherent and stable so that her team members can expect consistency and respond accordingly.
3. Once the desired values are defined for the team members, the coach must present them clearly, consistently and with emphasis.
4. Once she has presented what is desired, she must evaluate the responses.
5. Evaluation of behavior to be learned includes consideration of types and the manner of applying consequences. She should reinforce positive value responses and redirect negative value responses.

Student Goals

The teacher, coach and recreational specialist recognize the many educational objectives of an interscholastic or intercollegiate program. While students may participate for a number of personal reasons, some may be only distantly related to the accepted objectives of the adult leader. Some student goals are related to the social acceptance and the status of the activity in the student's particular environment or educational setting. Some students may participate because it is "the thing to do," while in another situation it may be "the thing not to do." How attitudes develop and spread is an area of concern to all social scientists. Suffice it to say here that the attitude of the student's peer group toward athletic competition is extremely important to most young people of high school age and, perhaps, of equal importance to college age women. Attitude development is of critical concern to the coach and athletic administrator.

In recent years many cocurricular activities have experienced a decline in attracting student interest. In some settings interest has lessened in intramural and varsity athletics both for men and women. Explanations are myriad, but most educators suggest that the scope of available activities has enlarged for young people and they are becoming increasingly aware and preoccupied with their role in the changing social and cultural scene. Others believe that early physical and social maturation brought about by the societal demands that require the young to assume adulthood much sooner than in previous generations may account for the change in student interest in cocurricular activities.

However, there is still a demand for competitive experiences in sport for youngsters and young adults. When asked why they participate in competitive athletics, the general responses and purposes given are:

1. Enjoyment of activity or of the specific activity.
2. Social opportunities and comradeship with friends.
3. Personal satisfaction (some socially desirable, some less desirable).
   a. Glory, status, recognition.
   b. Outlet for aggression not permitted the female in many other activities in society.
   c. Need and desire to master skills. The need to succeed; to complete something at a high level of effectiveness; ambition to accomplish.
   d. Desire for attention of adult (faculty member, coach, leader).

The coach who is committed to achieving the potential values of the program must remain alert to student motives for participating and, at the same time, be a strong enough leader to create positive attitudes and a socially desirable climate in competitive participation. Participation in competitive sports should remain voluntary.

Organizations Sponsoring Competition

Numerous organizations formulate rules and establish standards for the conduct of the various sports. Many of these organizations are concerned with establishing and directing play in a single sport at all levels of participation — local to national — and for both sexes. Other organizations direct all competitive play in specific geographic regions in a wide variety of sports. These groups are increasingly concerned with competition for girls and women.

The *Division for Girls' and Women's Sports* (DGWS) of the American Association for Health, Physical Education and Recreation is a nonprofit educational organization concerned with the conduct of all sports solely for girls and women. In promoting sports programs for girls and women, DGWS:

1. Formulates and publicizes principles and standards for desirable sports programs for the administrator, leader, official and player.

2. Publishes and interprets rules governing sports for girls and women.
3. Disseminates information on the conduct of girls' and women's sports.
4. Stimulates and evaluates research in the sports field.
5. Sponsors national tournaments in cooperation with the Committee on Intercollegiate Athletics for Women.

The *United States Field Hockey Association* and the *United States Women's Lacrosse Association* have similar emphases and educational motives to those of DGWS. Each of these associations, however, limits its concern to a single sport but can be considered the main source of assistance in forming clubs, giving demonstrations and clinics, promoting competition, training and rating officials and upgrading standards of play. These organizations work in close cooperation with DGWS.

The *American Softball Assocation* (ASA) and the *United States Volleyball Association* (USVBA) are also representative of organizations that promote interest in a single sport by assisting in program development, by developing standards, conducting training programs and certifying officials, as well as formulating and publishing rules. These organizations encourage and promote state, regional and national tournaments for both sexes.

The *Amateur Athletic Union* (AAU) sponsors age group competition in numerous sports. This body has jurisdiction over many competitive sports outside schools and colleges. AAU is a member of the International Amateur Federation which governs international competition in numerous sports.

The *National Collegiate Athletic Association* (NCAA) is a powerful organization that regulates and supervises men's college and university athletics throughout the United States. It encourages intramural as well as intercollegiate sports and stresses a uniform law of amateurism. The organization upholds the principle of institutional control and responsibility for competitive sports. To date, NCAA has not been actively involved in women's athletic programs.

The *National Association for Intercollegiate Athletics* (NAIA) serves purposes similar to NCAA for "colleges of limited enrollment."

The Association for Intercollegiate Athletics for Women (AIAW) provides a governing body and leadership in women's collegiate athletic programs. Many states and regions have established structures to guide women's intercollegiate competition. Although these groups are autonomous, they reflect the guidance and follow the administrative structure of AIAW.

The *National Federation of State High School Athletic Associations* (NFSH-SAA) serves many of the same purposes for high schools that NCAA accomplishes for colleges. The association determines eligibility rules, prescribes conditions of interstate competition and maintains consultant services. Very few women have been involved in the organizational structure of NFSHSAA in the past, but an increasing number are participating in state level organizations concerned with high school competition. State organizational structures vary; however, the control in each case usually rests with school principals and superintendents. A state executive secretary implements and enforces the established regulations. Most state athletic federations have rulings directly affecting girls' competitive sports.

The *United States Olympic Committee* is the representative body for the Olympic Games in the United States. The Committee is responsible for conducting all Olympic Games affairs in this country, including fund raising and selection of coaches, trainers and athletes to represent the nation. Since this committee certifies all entries to the Games, it exerts a powerful influence over all athletic organizations that provide athletes for our Olympic teams. Obviously, a close relationship is necessary between the Olympic Committee and AAU, NCAA and other amateur sports governing bodies. The role of women on the Olympic Committee is yet undetermined. At present there is representation from DGWS on the Women's Advisory Board to the U.S. Olympic Development Committee. Since 1963, National Institutes on Girls' Sports, sponsored jointly by DGWS and the Women's Board of the Olympic Development Committee, have focused on improving competition and developing skill in selected activities.

Bibliography

American Association for Health, Physical Education and Recreation: *Values in Sports.* AAHPER, Washington, D.C., 1963.

Association for Intercollegiate Athletics for Women: *AIAW Handbook of Policies and Interim Operating Procedures 1971–72.* American Association for Health, Physical Education and Recreation, Washington, D.C., 1971.

DeVries, Herbert A.: *Physiology of Exercise for Physical Education and Athletics.* Dubuque, Iowa, William C. Brown Company, 1966.

DGWS (Division for Girls' and Women's Sports): "First National Institute on Girls' Sports." AAHPER, Washington, D.C., 1964.

DGWS: "Guidelines for Intercollegiate Athletic Programs for Women." AAHPER, Washington, D.C., 1965.

DGWS: "Guidelines for Interscholastic Athletic Programs for High School Girls." AAHPER, Washington, D.C., 1965.

DGWS: "Guidelines for Interscholastic Athletic Programs for Junior High School Girls." AAHPER, Washington, D.C., 1966.

DGWS: "We believe." AAHPER, Washington, D.C., 1965.

Division of Men's Athletics: "Athletics in education." American Association for Health, Physical Education and Recreation, Washington, D.C., 1962.

Durant, Della: "The effect of vigorous sports participation on the duration of labor in childbearing." Unpublished M.S. Thesis, Pennsylvania State University, 1957.

Educational Policies Commission: *School Athletics—Problems and Policies.* National Education Association, Washington, D.C., 1954.

Edwards, Marigold: "Why should I strive?" *Journal of Health, Physical Education and Recreation,* January 1966, pp. 28–29, 60–62.

Erdelyi, Gyula J.: "Gynecological survey of female athletes." *Journal of Sports Medicine,* September 1962, pp.174–179.

Erdelyi, Gyula J.: "Women in athletics." *Proceedings of the Second National Conference on the Medical Aspects of Sport,* 1960.

Espenschade, A. S. and Eckert, H.: *Motor Development.* Columbus, Ohio, Charles E. Merrill Books, Inc., 1967.

Garlick, M. A. and Bernauer, E. M.: "Exercise during the menstrual cycle; variations in physiological baselines." *Research Quarterly,* October 1968, pp.533–542.

Gendel, Evalyn S.: "Physicians, females, physical exertion and sports." *Journal of the American Medical Association,* September 4, 1967, pp. 751–754.

Harnik, M.: "Sport and menstruation." *Sport and Health,* February 1952, pp. 149–151.

Harnik, M.: "Sport and menstruation." First Asian Physical Education, Health and Recreation Congress, Bureau of Printing, Manila, 1955.

Harres, Bea: "Attitudes of students toward women's athletic competition." *Research Quarterly,* May 1968, pp.278–284.

Harris, Dorothy V.: *DGWS Research Reports: Women in Sports.* American Association for Health, Physical Education and Recreation, Washington, D.C., 1971.

Hellebrandt, Frances A. and Meyer, Margaret H.: "Physiological data significant to participation by women in physical activities." *Research Quarterly,* March 1939, pp. 10–23.

Hirata, Kin-Itsu: "Physique and age of Tokyo Olympic champions." *Journal of Sports Medicine and Physical Fitness,* Vol. 6, 1966, pp.207–222.

Ingman, Ove: "Menstruation in Finnish top class sportswomen." *Sports Medicine,* Finnish Association of Sports Medicine, Helsinki, 1933.

Jernigan, Sara Staff: "Women and the Olympics." *Journal of Health, Physical Education and Recreation,* April 1962.

Johnson, Warren (ed.): *Science and Medicine of Exercise and Sports.* New York, Harper & Row, 1960.

Jokl, Ernest: "The heart of the woman athlete." *AAU Study of Effect of Athletic Competition on Girls and Women,* 1956.

Ley, Katherine and Jernigan, Sara Staff: "The roots and the tree." *Journal of Health, Physical Education and Recreation,* September 1962.

McCloy, C. H.: "On some factors regarding sex differences in relation to sports activities." *Studi di Medicina e Chirurgia Dello Sport,* 8:61–67, 1954.

Neal, Patsy: *Basketball Techniques for Women.* New York, The Ronald Press, 1966.

Neal, Patsy: "What more could one ask?" *Journal of Health, Physical Education and Recreation,* January 1966.

Scott, Harry A.: *Competitive Sports in Schools and Colleges.* New York, Harper & Brothers, 1951.

Shea, Edward and Wieman, Elton: *Administrative Policies for Intercollegiate Athletics.* Springfield, Charles C Thomas, 1967.

2

Organization and Administration

A well-grounded philosophical orientation to the role of competitive sports in schools, colleges and institutions is a prerequisite to the development of a sound administrative structure for athletics. The following statement of fundamental beliefs makes the transition from principles to practice an easy and educationally defensible progression:[1]

> We believe that sports programs for girls and women should be broad, varied, and planned for participants at differing levels of skill. There should be full awareness of the wide span of individual differences so that all types, ages and skill levels are considered in the planning of sports programs. In conducting the various phases of sports programs, principles must guide action. These principles should be based on the latest and soundest knowledge regarding
> 1. Growth and developmental factors
> 2. Motor Learning
> 3. Social and individual maturation and adjustment
> 4. The values of sports participation as recognized in our culture.

Administrative Structure

The success of an athletic program depends upon its leadership. Equipment, facilities and adequate financing are essential to the conduct of

---

[1] Division for Girls' and Women's Sports: "We Believe." American Association for Health, Physical Education and Recreation, Washington, D.C., 1965.

a sports program, but money cannot buy the type of leadership which wisely interprets the program, establishes rapport with administrators, parents and students and ultimately effects a desirable and challenging athletic program for girls or women. The qualities of leadership, like the identification of values or attitudes, escape clear definition. The leadership qualities displayed by a successful teacher or coach are probably attributable both to endowment and education. In the latter category these attributes are both "taught and caught." Peterson summarizes the "Art of Leadership."[2]

> The leader is a servant. As the Master of Man expressed it, "And whosoever would be chief among you, let him be your servant."
> The leader sees through the eyes of his followers.
> The leader says, "Let's go," and leads the way rather than, "Get going."
> The leader assumes his followers are working with him, not for him. He sees that they share in the rewards and glorifies the team spirit.
> The leader is a man builder. The more men he can build, the stronger the organization will be, including himself.
> The leader has faith in people. He believes in them, trusts them and thus draws out the best in them.
> The leader uses his heart as well as his head. After he has considered the facts with his head, he lets his heart take a look, too. He is a friend.
> The leader plans and sets things in motion. He is a man of action as well as a man of thought.
> The leader has a sense of humor. He is not a stuffed shirt. He has a humble spirit and can laugh at himself.
> The leader can be led. He is not interested in having his own way, but in finding the best way. He has an open mind.
> The leader keeps his eyes on high goals. He strives to make the efforts of his followers and himself contribute to the enrichment of personality, the achievement of more abundant living for all, and the improvement of all.

Traditionally men are directors of athletics in both schools and colleges. Their broad experience in athletics is the most obvious reason for the pattern. Though a woman may be assigned the direct responsibility for administering the girls' and women's program, most frequently, the man continues to control budget and, consequently, holds major authority. Common practice does not necessarily mean desirable practice. Situations and traditions vary, but it is logical to assume that a woman physical educator is more aware than a man can be of desirable standards and needs of girls and women in the athletic program. The issue is not really whether a man or a woman directs the program; the point of concern centers around the

---

[2]Peterson, Wilfred A.: "The Art of Leadership." Essay from *A New Treasury of Words to Live By*. William Nichols (ed.). New York, Simon and Schuster, Inc., 1959.

philosophy, understanding and competence of the *individual* who does direct the program.

Athletic problems are new to many women and lack of experience results in limited understanding and preparation in coping with some situations. Often it is desirable to have both a male and a female director, each with full responsibility for his or her individual program, but with the mutual appreciation and understanding which are necessary for cooperative sharing of funds, facilities and equipment. Where there are similar aims, objectives, activities, personnel and facilities, there is good reason to combine the interscholastic or intercollegiate, intramural and instructional programs into one integrated unit. If the departments are physically separated with men and women in separate facilities and operating under separate budgets, then it is logical to have an individual responsible for the administration of each program. The responsibility and authority for planning, organizing, coaching and supervising the girls' and women's athletic program should be delegated to the women physical education teachers with ultimate authority resting with the school or college administration. Women teachers or coaches must formulate policies for desirable athletic programs and recommend them to their respective institution's policy-approving body.

The actual administrative details of scheduling, planning for officials, purchasing and maintaining uniforms and equipment and maintaining facilities are tasks that do not appeal to all teachers or coaches. The person selected as the athletic administrator should bring interest and understanding of competitive sports and the talent of administrative ability together in a manner that warrants the confidence of the coaches. The coaches can be relieved of many time-consuming tasks, but they must make their reasonable needs and desires known to the administrator — always aware, however, of the pressures of time and the many demands which their colleagues also make on the total program budget. It must be remembered that, though important, the competitive program is but one aspect of a well-conceived total program of physical education.

Selection of Coaches

Coaches in the high school athletic program should be certified teachers regularly employed in the school system. Physical educators have the advantage of understanding the entire program of sports and the relationship of the athletic program to the total program. If teachers other than physical educators coach, they must work closely with the girls' physical education department. The sports leader and coach in a college or university also may be expected to meet professional standards and have a thorough understanding of: "(a) the place and purpose of sports in education, (b) the growth and development of children and youth, (c) the effects of exercise on the human organism, (d) first aid and accident prevention, (e) specific skills and (f) sound teaching methods."[3]

In essence, the criteria guiding selection of a coach for any situation are: that she be a good teacher, that she display patience and emotional control in her dealings with students and that she have the ability to establish rapport with both students and her colleagues. Her personal integrity and ethical character should, of course, be beyond question. She must know her participants and have their welfare as her *primary* concern; she must know the game and have a *desire to coach.* Her knowledge of the game is enhanced if she has been a competitor herself and has an official's rating in the sport. A coach who has prepared for and experienced officiating is not only well versed in the rules which govern play, but has an appreciation of the important and difficult tasks of the officials.

Financing

Finances for the athletic program should not depend upon income derived from gate receipts. Any gate receipts that are obtained should be assigned to a general fund that is completely separate from the athletic budget. The budget for the competitive sports program may be a separate budget or be a budget entry within the total physical education budget. An institution's acceptance of interscholastic or intercollegiate athletics as a phase of its educational curriculum should determine and be demonstrated in the line of control and delegation of powers. The financial support of the program should be budgeted and appropriated by the school board or college trustees in the same manner as practiced for other phases of the educational program. Any income derived from athletics should be returned to institutional funds to be used by school officials in any way deemed desirable. This does not preclude the use of federal, state and local monies, student fees, gate receipts or other sources of income. Since interscholastic and intercollegiate athletics are educational experiences, charging admission for spectators to view a competitive event may be incompatible with an institution's educational philosophy. In any case, financing the total athletic program or a specific activity should not depend upon fluctuating sources of income nor be related to a team's won-lost record.

Services needed for the operation of the athletic program, such as

---

[3] Division for Girls' and Women's Sports: *Philosophy and Standards for Girls' and Women's Sports.* AAHPER, Washington, D.C., 1969, p. 47.

medical services, transportation services and maintenance of buildings and grounds, are provided by the institution.

The instructional staff and other personnel required to conduct the athletic program must be selected in the same manner and on the same bases of predetermined qualifications as any other staff members. The same salary and plan of additional compensation, if any, should apply to members of the faculty responsible for competitive sports just as they apply to personnel of equal status in other departments.

Scheduling Contests

When the athletic program is financed in the same manner as other programs in the curriculum, it is possible to schedule contests with teams from schools or colleges of approximately the same size, educational requirements and financial circumstance. When the necessity of earning money is absent, schedules can be arranged to obtain the best educational results for the participants. This indicates that teams should be relatively evenly matched, with an equal opportunity to win. In order to achieve equitable competition, scheduling in a single sport need not be with the same institutions each year. (There is no necessity to arrange similar schedules in all sports.) There is merit in maintaining or developing some long-standing rivalry to enrich the tradition of competition and to add to the academic and social climate of the institution, but this practice should be secondary to the overall welfare of the participants.

League play and scheduled conference play opportunities are increasing. Leagues and conferences are typically developed around geographical areas and may not concern themselves with equitable competitive ability. Participation in leagues makes scheduling easier and it is often arranged in a central office with no involvement of the institution and coach. This more arbitrary scheduling, however, leaves little opportunity to select one's competitors and seek the best competition for a given team. Whether or not there will be participation in leagues and conferences should be a decision made solely by the institution.

It is most desirable to schedule like institutions, that is, colleges with colleges and universities, high schools with high schools of the same relative size, etc. When the budget is inadequate for travel, limited scheduling with outside organizations in the local area may be desirable. Church and industrial leagues can usually be found which have teams of similar philosophy, age and experience.

At no time should the schedule of a women's competitive team be dependent upon or required to conform to a league schedule established for boys or men. By the same token, the women's game should not be scheduled as a curtain raiser or half time spectacular for the more important men's event.

The responsibility of scheduling may fall to many different people:

1. The athletic director who schedules for both the men's and women's programs. In this case there must be close consultation with the coaches or the woman administrative assistant.
2. The woman director who must confer with the coaches and then coordinate her schedule with that of the men.
3. Coaches who do their own scheduling and coordinate their plans with the man or woman who is ultimately responsible. This is a most difficult plan to coordinate and can be very haphazard and beset by conflicts with the general school calendar and other athletic events unless a definite framework and policies are established.

Regular season competition should be conducted in a limited geographic area so that players return home at reasonable hours. Before seeking permission to engage in special events at the conclusion of the season, the team and coach must give this possibility serious consideration. These events require special plans, preparations, an additional budget and an examination of the real purposes for extending the season.

Players should be transported in comfortable and safe vehicles. Coaches and athletic administrators increasingly insist upon properly bonded public or institutional vehicles operated by experienced drivers. Private vehicles — coach, teacher or student owned and operated — should be avoided. If called upon in an emergency, private individuals transporting players must have adequate property damage and public liability insurance.

A balanced schedule of games helps maintain team morale and prevent staleness and overexertion. Neither all weak nor all strong competitors should be scheduled in sequence. A balance of home and away games — weekly and seasonal — should be achieved. Based on past seasonal experiences a coach can plan a possible balance of wins and losses (keeping the tally as privileged information) to prevent either a psychologically defeated or a euphoric state of the team. If games are scheduled properly, with no more than two a week with one away and one at home, and if a sensible practice schedule is maintained, there is little danger of physical inability. It is psychological inertia or staleness that results in dull play and a team's inability to "get up" for competition that presents a unique and worrisome problem for every coach.

Two other considerations are important in a total plan for scheduling:

(1) *Written contracts.* It is desirable to have some written agreement, signed by responsible adults, between teams. This may be a formal written contract or merely a postcard or letter that indicates date, time, place of competition, number of teams, planned social events, provision for inclement weather and provisions for officials. Aside from serving as a formal con-

tractual agreement, it is a practical reminder to the busy administrator or coach who has been known to "neglect to remember" vital statistics.

(2) *Provisions for officials.* The value of competent officials is known to every coach and competitor. Referees, umpires, scorers, timers and announcers all have an important role in team sports. They can make or break the game, and those who unobtrusively direct a safe and enjoyable game should be sought and utilized. There are several methods for providing officials. The home team may provide all officials. This is a convenient method if the two competitors alternate home contests every year or every other year and if the officials are satisfactory to the visiting team. In a second method each team provides one official. This is a good plan when schedules change from year to year or when each team wishes to provide one official. The plan should be discouraged when it carries with it the connotation of questioning the competence and honesty of officials.

In established leagues the officials are often designated and assigned by the league secretary. This plan takes all the responsibility and authority for selection away from both competing teams. Leagues utilizing this plan should survey the coaches for their recommendations for competent officials.

In all cases officials should hold a current DGWS rating in the specific sport. A state or local rating is recommended as the minimum acceptable qualification at high school games, and intercollegiate and adult events should be officiated by state, regionally or nationally rated officials. Such officials may not always be available, but this is the ideal toward which to work.

Prerequisites for Student Participation

The medical examination is the first and most important measure to be considered in proper health supervision of the athlete. In most schools and colleges it is routine procedure for the male athlete to have a medical examination prior to his acceptance in a varsity sports program, but the procedure is less common with girls and women. An examination should be given prior to participation and should be sufficiently thorough to evaluate the student's health status. It should include weight, nutrition, heart, blood pressure, lungs, abdomen, glands and general health of hair, skin and nails. It is most desirable to be able to give the examinations free of charge to students before the athletic season. If this provision cannot be made, the examination must be given by the family physician no earlier than six months prior to participation. The medical doctor should certify the health of all candidates for athletic teams. Continuous medical supervision of all students engaged in competitive athletics should be maintained and reevaluations made as the physician or coach deems necessary. After a confining illness or injury the student should be readmitted to athletic participation only upon recommendation of the medical doctor.

Cumulative records of the health examinations, dental records, description of injuries and illness of the athlete should be maintained. The record makes decisions concerning participation more meaningful and protects the institution against spurious claims of injury while in the competitive program.

Health and accident insurance protection should be provided by the institution for *all* members of the athletic team. Students may carry personal policies, but it is a common practice to have institutional coverage on the participant while traveling and during the season of participation. In some instances commercial companies underwrite the insurance program which is operated by state high school athletic associations. Colleges and universities frequently secure blanket accident expense policies such as the one available to member institutions of the National Association of Collegiate Directors of Athletics. The policy covers medical expense benefits to a player while participating as a team member in a scheduled practice session, in a competitive game or while traveling as a team member with the team. Accidental death benefits due to athletic injury are included in the blanket policy. These programs are expanding to include the female interscholastic and intercollegiate athlete. Personal liability insurance should be the concern of every coach and athletic director.

Parental permission slips may have little legal value, but they do serve as statements of parental acknowledgement that their daughter is participating in athletics. Colleges rarely use such permission slips since students, by their attendance at the institution, are considered to have parental permission to engage in activities sponsored by the college.

Academic Eligibility

Since the beginning of athletic competition in schools and colleges, scholastic eligibility has been a questionable prerequisite for competitive participation. Academic regulations, rightly or wrongly, are based on the assumptions that scholastic achievement is the primary purpose of schools and colleges and that varsity sports take time needed for study. Many administrators feel that unless definite standards of academic achievement are maintained as a form of restraint, some students and coaches would focus all time and effort on their sport and thus neglect scholastic endeavor. Since the program of athletics is accepted as a phase of general education, it is not logical to require a student to achieve certain marks in literature or math before she can participate in athletics. Any student should be allowed to participate in any school or college activity as long as she is a bona fide member of the student body and fulfilling its institutional requirements. Transfer students should become eligible for immediate participation. Students under temporary suspension or probation for disciplinary reasons should not be allowed to participate. Members of a team should be shown no special favors, nor should they be made to meet any requirements not exacted of other members of the student body.

At both high school and collegiate levels it is expected that students be amateurs (see next section). In colleges and universities only undergraduate, prebaccalaureate students should be permitted to participate. A five year plan of academic study is increasingly popular for the undergraduate and, realistically, she should be given the opportunity for participation during these years. Graduate students may be offered intramural and other extramural opportunities.

Many state and conference athletic organizations have very exacting eligibility requirements for boys and men regulated by NFSHSAA, NCAA and NAIA. Although local and state groups are developing eligibility policies for girls and women, few comparable regulations now exist. As a result of the omission of these special regulations, the standards expected of the boys and men are often applied to the girls and women. The typical regulation for boys involves passing scholastic work in three full credit subjects in the semester of participation and the semester prior to competition.

In colleges and universities women have not been compelled to follow the conference regulations of men, for their pattern of competition has been quite different. Women frequently have made their own academic eligibility requirements. The result often has been a set of requirements more stringent than the men's. There is wide variation, however, with some defining eligibility only as "currently a registered full time student." The most common requirement is a stipulated grade point average which indicates normal progress toward a degree. This is often interpreted as a C average after the freshman year. As competitive opportunities for girls and women expand, it is hoped that women administrators and coaches will avoid developing artificial barriers which limit the participation of students who may benefit most from the competitive sports program. No exact grade point requirement will be necessary if coaches and the public remain aware that the student has a primary responsibility to her educational studies and that the athletic program should enhance rather than exploit the student's ability in scholastic endeavor. If the academic focus is lost, and if the good of each participant is not of prime concern, then the "evils of competition" will surely be a natural consequence.

Amateurism

All students participating in school, college and recreational athletic programs should be amateurs. Ideally, the amateur athlete is one who participates in competitive sports for pleasure, not for gain beyond the physical, mental and social benefits derived from such activity. Realistically, the burden of proof of amateur status rests with the institutional authorities, although the motives for participation by an individual may be impossible to determine. A statement by the Association for Intercollegiate Athletics for Women of DGWS defines amateur status for those persons wishing to complete in DGWS Intercollegiate Championships as follows:[4]

Amateur status is maintained in a sport if a player has not received and does not receive money other than expenses as a participant in that sport. A participant may receive money from her own school to pay only for housing, meals, and transportation. A student who plays, coaches or officiates and who receives reimbursements in excess of her expenses for playing, coaching, or officiating may lose her amateur status for open competition.

A student who tries out for or is selected as a member of an international team is not ruled ineligible for further intercollegiate competition.

The coach faces dilemmas when operating within the framework of amateurism. For example, she encourages her player to further knowledge of the sport by obtaining the player's officiating rating. If the student then practices this skill as a member of a board of officials and receives fair compensation for this work as is indicated by approved fees, she may be penalized by losing her amateur status. The participant and the coach must be aware of the specific regulations regarding amateurism as established by the governing bodies in each sport. The Amateur Athletic Union, as the governing body for basketball, permits officials to receive only actual expenses in order to maintain amateur status. This ruling also applies to officiating in another sport other than basketball and is in keeping with the recent DGWS statement. The United States Volleyball Association has a regulation similar to that of AAU. The Amateur Softball Association, the United States Women's Lacrosse Association and the United States Field Hockey Association have taken the position that receiving a fee for officiating in any sport is not related to amateur standing in their specific sport.

Perhaps the real problem is that deceit and subterfuge are encouraged in order to maintain the letter of the law of amateur status. The deceit may be more harmful to the individual than the professionalism she is attempting to avoid. There are some doubts that the working definitions of amateurism are consistent and realistic in present day society. It is obvious that the question of amateurism must continue to be dealt with by all appropriate associations.

---

[4]*AIAW Handbook 1971–72.* p. 10

Conduct During the Contest

The game should be played for the benefit of the players — not the coach, officials, spectators or school. Toward this goal the following suggestions are offered.

Players should focus only on playing the game. There is no time for a thinking player to make comments to opponents, officials or spectators during the course of a game. Students should respect their opponents for the competition they are providing. Unsportsmanlike or disrespectful conduct can never be condoned, even in the most undesirable situations. Certainly this includes players' conduct toward officials. Facial expressions and gesticulations can be as undesirable as verbal expressions of displeasure.

Players and sympathetic spectators tend to react as the coach reacts. Less sympathetic spectators react to the *coach's reactions* and if the coach's response is questionable, the result is an overemotional situation in which the game is taken away from the players. It is *never* acceptable for the coach to yell at officials or opponents, or allow her emotions to be uncontrolled. The coach should be able to control spectator and player actions through the respect they have for her judgment and personal control.

The officials are basically responsible for conducting the game within the law and spirit of the rules. Their role is to make it possible for the players to compete safely and enjoyably. A good official blends into the entire conduct of the game, making her calls decisively but unobtrusively.

Spectator conduct is the concern of the school administration, student government, physical education department, the team and the coach. Many schools have established definite codes for spectator conduct and others have recognized the need for developing such a code. Spectators tend to react to the coaches and players, and a team's conduct can do much to bring about favorable spectator response.

Hosting Competition

Visiting teams are invited guests and as such should expect and receive certain social courtesies and physical comforts. They should be provided with their own dressing facilities — a clean, private place to dress, shower and retire between periods. This is more important to college and adult groups than to the high school girl who frequently travels a short distance in her game uniform. There must be a safe place for storing valuables in the dressing area or in a nearby office. On the field or courtside, teams should be furnished an area of their own with benches or chairs for coaches and team members. When the visitors arrive they should find a clean court or a freshly lined field ready for play. It goes without saying that proper marking, backboards, goal cages and the like are essential to the conduct of the game.

The host school may furnish oranges at half time, make provisions for ice, cups and additional towels as needed. If there is no water supply within reasonable distance of the field, water should be provided for both groups.

After the competition it is beneficial to have a planned social event with team members serving as hostesses. A Coke gathering for high school or college groups or dinner for the collegiate team affords an opportunity for socialization and exchange of ideas on academic and athletic programs. It is well for competitors to see their rivals in a different social setting.

Whether or not the home team is responsible for securing any or all of the officials, it may have the responsibility of promptly paying for their services. The officials are also guests and should be invited to participate in any social activities following the games.

A physician should be alerted and on call while contests are in progress and a person qualified in first aid procedures should be in attendance at the game. Frequently the college trainer is willing to attend such contests.

Away Games

Teams traveling from their campus should be accompanied by a faculty member from their institution. In the exceptional situation where the coach is not a member of the physical education department, a woman from the departmental faculty should supervise and chaperone the team. When preparing for departure, use the following items as a check list:

1. Arrange for transportation well in advance of the scheduled event.
2. Notify the team members of time and place of departure, length of trip and estimated time of return.
3. Take the necessary playing equipment, towels and first aid supplies.
4. Announce what constitutes appropriate dress for the team members. Short high school trips usually are made in playing uniforms, but for long distances and for college and adult groups appropriate street or campus clothing is suggested. Dress is often determined by the demand of the social events which are planned by the hostess institution.
5. Make provisions for meals and lodging on the road if necessary. It is advisable to notify a restaurant that a large group will appear at a given time. On one-day trips, a brief stop at the restaurant on the way to the contest to tell them of the planned return can save many minutes for hungry players. The coach must carry sufficient money to cover both food expenses and the unplanned emergencies that invariably arise.

When traveling, natural enthusiasm is to be expected as the group anticipates the match, but extreme emotional displays should be restrained. Game plans can be discussed with the captain and team.

Upon arrival at the hostess school, have students prepare for activity and report to the playing area in sufficient time for a proper warm-up. This settling-in period is very important in establishing both the physical and psychological readiness of the team. Warm-up must not be haphazard, but well organized and purposeful.

After the contest the team members should be encouraged to socialize with their opponents, whether or not a social event is planned. No one should be excused from this responsibility unless she is ill or injured. Whether a team has won or lost, it should respond to the hospitality and graciousness offered. Heated individual or team rivalry can be put in better perspective by a relaxed social setting.

Equipment and Facilities

A coach inherits existing facilities and, frequently, limited equipment. Much can be done to improve both, even with a limited budget, if small amounts are put into improvements over a period of several years. A playing field, for example, may require two budget years of grading and replenishing top soil before resodding is financially feasible. Basketball backboards may precede a relined and refinished floor by several years. The secret to adequate and improving facilities is constant attention and maintenance; these requirements do not demand a great expenditure of capital. When planning for new physical education and athletic facilities, the total physical education staff should be involved. Program needs must be defined and priorities established. Obviously this involves coaches and the athletic administrator.

The expenditure of budgeted funds for equipment should be made with the greatest care. Some institutions insist that competitive bids be submitted, with sample items furnished on all equipment. Other institutions permit the purchase of specified equipment through local vendors or national sales representatives. In any case, samples may be requested and costs of equipment and, in some cases, transportation charges must be determined. Value must be considered since it is common knowledge that it is not economical to purchase inferior goods simply because of the lower price tag. The most economical thing to do is to purchase the best quality of goods in a reasonable price range. Coaches have a right to their preferences in equipment — equipment they feel confident with — and sound preferences should be honored when possible. Both coaches and players have a psychological edge if the team is playing with sticks, bats and balls in which they have faith.

Uniforms and Dress

Uniforms are important to a team. First, they distinguish one team from another during competition; second, they are designed to permit the freedom of movement which is necessary and appropriate for a particular activity and third, uniforms develop and support team morale and unity. Uniforms should be washable and require little or no ironing. The tunic, and more recently the kilt, have typically been worn for hockey and lacrosse, and for basketball in some sections of the country. Shorts and shirts are usually worn for basketball, volleyball and softball. If softball competition permits sliding, shorts and knee socks or long pants (slacks or softball trousers) should be worn for protection. It is important that shorts or pants do not restrict leg movements. The newer stretch materials give the necessary freedom and are attractive on players of most sizes and shapes. Many new shirts are designed to be worn as overblouses, but if shirts are worn inside, the tails should be long enough so that they will not pull out during strenuous activity. Not only is this distracting to the player, it also gives an immediate appearance of untidiness. Uniforms should never make the wearer self-conscious. Many high school students dislike the traditional one-piece gymnasium costume and do not feel at their best in such attire. An effort should be made to find a more universally acceptable outfit. The decision to place numbers on shirts or to have the team wear pinnies is strictly a matter of individual team choice, available money and rule requirements. Attractive warm-ups are comfortable for travel when dressing facilities are not available at the game site. Their practical value is obvious in cold gymnasia and on windy, wet fields. The uniform need not be expensive; however, good quality material and workmanship cost less in the long run.

Footwear is extremely important and should be supplied by the school or college if the students do not have the proper equipment. Sneakers with cleats of hard rubber or plastic are necessary for hockey and lacrosse, some type of cleated shoe is required for softball and a good quality tennis-type sneaker or athletic shoe is necessary for basketball and volleyball. There is some question about the use of high-top sneakers, particularly for basketball. Studies have shown that they offer no greater protection than a good quality low sneaker and most girls and women find the low cut more attractive. In recent years male professional football and basketball players have been wearing low cut footwear.

Responsibilities of the Coach

The coach is ultimately responsible for the safety, welfare and conduct of her players. She is responsible for them and for their behavior. A coach must recognize this as she assumes the leadership responsibilities that accompany coaching. Preparations for the game are considered in some detail in Chapter 3; the following list serves as the coach's reminder at the game site.

1. Represent the institution as a faculty member, teacher and either hostess or guest.
2. Maintain control of the squad at all times. Prohibit unnecessary horseplay.
3. Supervise warm-up.
4. Observe members of the team for conditions which indicate referral to trainer, physician or counselor.
5. Remove any player from the game who appears to be injured, excessively fatigued or not in satisfactory physical or mental condition. In the case of injury or extreme fatigue, do not return the player to practice or competition without approval of the trainer or physician.
6. Direct the student manager and captain in conducting their responsibilities.

Responsibilities of the Captain and Student Manager

Too often the *captain* of a squad or team is merely a title which carries with it little or no responsibility. A captain should be more than the person who meets with officials to deliver instructions from her coach or the one who raises her hand to indicate that the team is ready to play. How much responsibility the captain should assume depends upon her leadership ability, the age and maturity of the team, the coach and the situation. The captain should have a good rapport with the coach and the squad and act as liaison between them. The captain should have complete understanding of and know the reasons for the plan of practice and of games, and she should lead the team in enthusiasm and seriousness of purpose. Specific responsibilities might include:

1. Conducting warm-up for practice sessions and games.
2. Directing changing patterns of play during the game while on the field or court.
3. Assisting the coach in analyzing the play of individuals and of the total team before, during and after practices and games.
4. Thanking the officials and opposing team and coach at the conclusion of the game.

The *student manager* or managers can be very valuable to the coach and team. Again, their duties may vary with the sport and level of competition. Some of their responsibilities might include:

1. Providing game equipment and first aid supplies at all practice sessions and games.

2. Keeping records of attendance at practices and recording results of achievement and performance requirements during practices (free throws, laps, hits, etc).
3. Recording the amount of time spent on each drill and situation for the coach's master schedule.
4. Putting equipment away at the end of practice and game sessions and referring equipment purchase and repair needs to the coach.
5. Submitting articles to the school or college newspapers.
6. Serving as scorer, timer or statistician at scrimmages or matches.
7. Preparing and serving oranges at half time of home matches.
8. Preparing and serving refreshments at the end of the match.
9. Conducting visitors (team, officials, coaches) to proper areas.

Some institutions encourage student participation on the athletic policy-making board or council, but it should not be within the sole jurisdiction of team members to establish policy or carry it out. Student leadership can be used at the playday and sportsday levels but it is a questtionable practice to involve the students in the scheduling of interscholastic or intercollegiate events and in the hiring of officials.

Awards

In keeping with the universal practice of honoring successful or outstanding performance, many schools and colleges grant awards to varsity girl and women athletes. Many times the award is the same for both sexes — a school or college letter for those qualifying. This award is symbolic of achievement and it seems unlikely that its value could ever be taken as the sole motivator for participation. Very few girls or women wear their letters and a more appropriate charm, certificate or pin is often indicated. There seems to be no conflict between the kinds of awards for major and minor sports, for women have long recognized that no sport is minor in the eyes of the participant nor in the benefits derived.

Requirements for achieving an award vary greatly, often depending on the philosophy of the department and the school or college itself. In the case in which a definite team is selected at the beginning of the season, it seems appropriate that all members should receive varsity awards. Some programs do give full and equal awards to all members on the selected squad while other programs require fulfillment of a quota system of total amount of participation. A system based on participation in games seems a realistic one for granting awards to members of a squad when players can be moved up and down between the varsity and junior varsity teams during the season.

Many teachers and coaches question the merit of granting varsity awards to club participants, that is, cheerleaders, performing dancers and noncompeting gymnastic groups. Certainly an award symbolic of participation and achievement in these areas is warranted, but it is doubtful that it should be the same as the "varsity team" award. A definite policy and definitive standards for all awards must be established before the season begins in order to avoid student misunderstanding and dissatisfaction. The student athletic council may offer valuable guides in determining policies for athletic awards.

It appears that some institutions diminish the value of awards intentionally by granting them for all types and amounts of participation so that no participant feels "left out." Would it not be sounder to allow participation to be its own reward and give additional merit awards only for "superior performance?" The task then, is to define superior performance.

Awards are usually given to the victorious teams in specific competitive tournaments. It is not common practice to award trophies when two or three teams compete in an informal, scheduled event. The tournament trophy or plaque represents the spoils of the victory and usually becomes the property of the institution represented by the winning team. It stands as visible evidence of the skill of the competitors and is frequently cherished by the team members. The nature of the tournament award may change—from team trophy to individual trophy or silver dishes—but the symbol of recognition will remain for years to come.

Athletic Scholarships and Grants-in-Aid

The college and university student has more opportunity for financial assistance than ever before. There are awards granted for general and specialized academic abilities, musical and artistic abilities and specialized athletic prowess. It seems a highly questionable practice to award grants-in-aid or scholarships to the female collegiate athlete:[5]

> The Division for Girls' and Women's Sports does not approve of awarding scholarships, financial awards, or of giving financial assistance designated for women participants in intercollegiate sports competition. This position is intended not to diminish, but to protect, the continued development of athletics for women. The purpose of this statement of belief is to discourage the buying or retaining of athletic talent by any college or university. Financial assistance includes any gift or gain presented prior to, or during, enrollment and/or attendance at the institution. This does not prohibit academic or economic-need scholarships but includes "talent scholarships awarded to those whose talent is athletic in nature. . . .
>
> This does not prohibit academic or economic-need scholarships awarded in open market competition with the general student population.

[5]DGWS: *Philosophy and Standards for Girls' and Women's Sports.* Rev. ed. 1972.

Expanding the above, the Association for Intercollegiate Athletics for Women recently issued the following statement concerning persons eligible for AIAW National Championship:[6]

Any student who receives an athletic scholarship, financial award(s), or other financial assistance specifically designated for athletics is ineligible to compete. An athletic scholarship is defined as a scholarship when one or more of the following conditions exist:
(a) It is primarily dependent upon athletic ability.
(b) It is dependent upon participation in the intercollegiate program.
(c) It is awarded as a result of undue influence by a member of the athletic department or physical education department, or by a coach who is aware of the applicant's ability. Athletes may receive academic scholarships or economic-need scholarships which are not defined as athletic scholarships provided none of the above conditions apply.

If scholarships are awarded to potential physical educators, sports ability may well be one criterion for selection as an award recipient, but there is no justification in awarding grants-in-aid on the *sole* basis of athletic ability. The training of professional athletes is not the focus of the college or university. The recruiting efforts and financial assistance given in some cases, and that planned for the future, should be spent in procuring the future educator—the teacher who will further the role of sports in education.

Bibliography

AIAW: *Handbook of Policies and Operating Procedures.* AAHPER, Washington, D.C., 1972–73.

American Assocation for Health, Physical Education and Recreation: *Administration of High School Athletics.* AAHPER, Washington, D.C., 1963.

AAHPER: *Spectator Sportsmanship.* AAHPER, Washington, D.C., 1961.

Barnes, Mildred: "Officiating and amateur status in girls' and women's sports." *Journal of Health, Physical Education and Recreation,* October 1968, pp. 24–27.

DGWS (Division for Girls' and Women's Sports): "Guidelines for Intercollegiate Athletic Programs for Women." AAHPER, Washington, D.C., 1965.

DGWS: "Guidelines for Interscholastic Athletic Programs for High School Girls." AAHPER, Washington, D.C., 1965.

DGWS: "Guidelines for Interscholastic Athletic Programs for Junior High School Girls." AAHPER, Washington, D.C., 1966.

DGWS: *Philosophy and Standards for Girls' and Women's Sports.* AAHPER, Washington, D.C., Rev. ed. 1972.

DGWS: *Procedures for Women's Intercollegiate Athletic Events.* AAHPER, Washington, D.C., Revised edition, 1968.

DGWS: "We believe." AAHPER, Washington, D.C., 1965.

George, Jack and Lehman, Harry A.: *School Athletic Administration.* New York, Harper and Row, 1966.

Peterson, Wilfred A.: "The Art of Leadership." In *A New Treasury of Words to Live By.* William Nichols (ed.). New York, Simon and Schuster, 1959.

Scott, Harry A.: *Competitive Sports in Schools and Colleges.* New York, Harper and Brothers, 1951.

Shea, Edward and Wieman, Elton: *Administrative Policies for Intercollegiate Athletics.* Springfield, Charles C Thomas, 1967.

[6]*AIAW Handbook 1972–73.* p. 12.

3

The Coach Prepares for Competition

A young woman who is asked to coach a competitive team has every right to be given a clear understanding of what coaching entails. Only when she understands the duties and expectations of a coach can she make the decision to devote her teaching abilities to a small group of skilled young women in an effort to develop their individual and team *excellence.*

Defining the term "coaching" is complicated by the fact that those persons affected by the ability and influence of a coach perceive the coach differently. The school administrator views the coach as the teacher who directs the competitive play and behavior of girls and women who represent the educational institution; the players see the coach as a highly skilled teacher who builds game skills, teaches competitive play and fosters an appreciation for both excellence in cooperation and excellence in competition.

Coaching is highly skilled teaching of a limited number of individuals. Coaching develops skills beyond the fundamentals and combines the abilities of individuals into a team effort with the focus on keen competition in the spirit of fair play, good sportsmanship and camaraderie. Competitive play permits a great depth and scope of experience for participants and coach. The experience and its demands are relatively complex and all persons concerned undergo a degree of intensity of effort and psychological stress.

The teacher cannot really learn to coach until she begins. Not all sports teachers have the interest, desire, personality or temperament to be coaches. Some teachers can coach individual and team sports, while others prefer and excel only in team sport development. The following topics are designed to assist the teacher contemplating coaching as she analyzes her interest and ability and considers the task of preparation for coaching.

1. Coaching is *teaching* — depth teaching of the advanced skills and strategies of a sport. The coach must develop a thorough understanding of the technical rules and develop not only the basic skills but also the *nuances* of the sport. She must look for the new, the different and the best way to accomplish for her players the purposes of the sport.

2. Coaching requires expert knowledge of a sport. A coach will find that personal experience as a player and a teacher is fundamental to coaching. Not only must she know the game; she must also continue to study the sport as it changes and alter her teaching techniques so she can impart the hidden skills and knowledge.

3. The coach must be willing to be a specialist. This is the era of the specialist in many fields, but the coach should be aware that the time devoted to the mastery of one or two activities limits the opportunities to expand her general knowledge in a broad specturm of sports. Often the teacher with a broad base of understanding of many sports is eager to "dig a small hole deeper" in one sport.

4. The coach must be willing to devote a large amount of time to a relatively small group of students. Some teachers who see the needs of so many are unwilling to give a seemingly disproportionate amount of time to the few. The coach recognizes that she enters into an intensive experience with a limited number of students over whom she can exert tremendous influence. The close relationship affords the coach insight into student relationships and social and academic behavior. This insight carries the burden of guidance and counseling responsibilities which she must equip herself to handle. This same intensity can be very satisfying to the teacher-coach who can evaluate the growth of individuals and of a team with individuality and personality.

5. A coach must be sensitive, firm, insightful, adaptable and flexible. Her temperament has a wide range of responses, yet her responses are *consistent*. She must be democratic in her organizational methods, yet firmly decisive in directing team behavior or play. With her concern for both the individual and team, there is never room for pettiness or biting sarcasm in dealing with students. She is the leader, and as such, must be tough-minded yet tenderhearted.

Refreshing Personal Knowledge

The preparation of the coach begins long before she is assigned to coach a specific team. In many cases her preparation began as a student where she was a member of the varsity squad. Actually the love of activity and sport, perhaps gained in early childhood, that encouraged her to try out for the team is even more fundamental to her preparation. In undergraduate preparation as a student in physical education, she is trained in participation and in theories and observation of coaching. From these basic experiences she develops the continuing interest and experience that directs her into coaching.

Every coach, no matter how experienced, should feel the need to refresh and review before beginning the season. This may consist of concentrated reading, attending workshops and clinics and obtaining DGWS-OSA official's ratings in special sports areas. Workshops and clinics are often held in local and regional areas sponsored by DGWS state committees, officiating boards, associations that conduct and further competition in certain sports and colleges that have an active interest in serving the professional community. Many theories of play and techniques of skills and strategy have changed over the years, just as the concept of competitive activities for women has changed. It is the coach's responsibility to be aware of changes. A suggested specific bibliography is included in each of the following sport chapters.

Selecting the Team

Skill Review Session.   The announcement that practice and try-outs will be held for girls and women interested in participating as a member of a team signals the beginning of the competitive season. The announcement is the first step in the screening process, for those volunteers responding are already motivated and eager to participate.

The first practice sessions should be designed to review individual skills and drills for basic play. These periods actually serve a dual purpose: first, they reacquaint the players with the game and its basic skills; and second, they give the coach an idea of the overall skill level and potential ability of the group. These practice sessions should be planned and organized to accommodate large numbers.

Conducting the first sessions often proves the most difficult task the coach encounters during the year. A beginning coach finds she has limited abilities and knack for picking the right players on the first meeting. She must look for both those players who bring a high level of skill and game ability and for those whom she feels have the greatest skill potential and coachability. As years pass, she may develop a sixth sense and an ability to select players by scanning their general ability and game sense. No matter how many years of experience a coach may have, there will be mistakes in player selection as long as players retain their individuality and coaches their human fallibility. No two players develop at the same pace physically, mentally, or emotionally. No two coaches have the same subjective criteria for selecting potential excellence.

The content of the sessions is largely determined by facilities, number of participants, available time and the coach's plans for participation. In addition to basic skill drills which each coach selects to review, she should refer to the following selected sports chapters for specific suggestions for the first practice sessions.

Evaluating Individual Skills.   Evaluating the skills of an individual is a difficult task particularly in a team sport where it is initially difficult to determine an individual's effectiveness as a member of a team. Certain individual skills can be observed apart from team play; for example, the volleyball serve or the basketball free throw. But many skills that are an integral part of play are observable only in a game setting. Some coaches and teachers advocate appraising individual skills through specific skill tests. Many tests are available through DGWS and AAHPER and references are made to others in basic sport skills books. These tests evaluate the level of skill an individual displays on a specific scale but tell little of how well this skill will be performed under pressures of a game situation.

Perhaps the more economical method of evaluating individual skills is a simple approximation of each candidate's skills on a coach-designed check sheet. The coach thus identifies the basic skills she feels are important. Later in scrimmage these individual skills may be checked and rechecked.

As the coach reviews her players she realizes that she begins the season with some players of above average skill, each with established skill patterns and individual style. To suggest major technique changes to these players can destroy their effectiveness. The key to style is efficient effectiveness. If a player has not developed this style, then form and major skill modifications may be in order. It is not the role of the coach to develop stereotyped form in her players, many of whom in fact have passed from the form stage into style.

Evaluating an Individual's Game Ability.   Once an individual's fundamental skills are evaluated it becomes the task of a coach to evaluate a player's ability to combine her skill with the necessary elements of game knowledge, game sense and competitive drive for effective team effort. An individual must be viewed in relation to her teammates and her teammates evaluated in relation to her. Thus, an individual must be seen in many different combinations to determine whether it is her game ability that is being seen or if a particular group of players is responsible for her play. A simple analogy might clarify the coach's approach. Her intent is to design a colorful, eye-appealing and artistic mosaic. She has more pieces than are absolutely necessary, so by trial and error placement she develops a pattern that has balance, beauty and meaning. The advantage of the "human mosaic" is that it need never be "fixed," but may change to increase its effectiveness.

Evaluating Leadership, Attitude and Competitive Drive.   Earlier mention has been made of the difficulty of defining terms of leadership and attitude and the consequent problems of identifying the *qualities* of such terms. Over a period of time a coach *can* identify certain types of behavior that generally indicate a player's ability as a competitor. These are listed below:

1. Ability to function under physical and emotional stress in a competitive situation.
2. Ability to play one's own style of game regardless of the tactics of the players of the other team. This also includes a player's ability to adapt or adjust her play as she deems necessary.
3. Ability to maintain her highest level of skill regardless of the skill and behavior of her opponents.
4. Ability to maintain emotional stability while others are losing theirs. Experience is a major factor in developing game stability, yet some players never attain real stability; other players need a strong leader to set the temper and maintain court composure. This person may be either the coach or captain but it is helpful if both present strong leadership, one from the bench, the other from the field or court. The coach influences thought and action by her facial expressions and general behavior. Generally, the more emotionally charged the situation, the calmer she must appear; yet some show of emotion, intensity, concern or calm elation may be beneficial depending upon the situation and the team personality. The captain and perhaps one other leader, not necessarily the strongest player, often give the cue for pace, style and pattern of play.

In addition to good basic skills and team play, there are other factors that must be considered in selecting an individual for competitive play. Perhaps the most important is the *competitive drive* of the individual. The coach can evaluate a player's game spirit by her observation and response to the following questions: (1) As a defender, does she refuse to give up, no matter what the score or the number of times her opponent has beaten her? (2) After making a mistake, can she be in the very next play without dwelling on the mistake? (3) Does she approach every game and every situation with a positive attitude toward winning and playing the best game possible, no matter what the adversities of the environment or superior opposition?

Seemingly, innate *game sense* is also an important factor. Players with this quality must be sought by the coach for they prove to be the playmakers and stalwart defense players. Even inexperienced players with game sense are often far more deadly in their positioning, offensive and defensive movement and anticipatory movements as beginners than their more experienced teammates without this quality. These players seem to "feel" the game rather than learning set patterns and modifying these patterns with difficulty. An example of such a player is the skilled basketball player with a knowledge of offense, defense and team work who transfers this knowledge as a beginner in lacrosse. Even though lacking a high degree of skill and stickwork, she is an effective player. The coach in evaluating this quality of game sense might ask the following questions: (1) Can a player sense when a standard pattern of play is not working and do the unexpected? (2) Can she play more than one position? (3) Is she coachable? That is, can she apply coaching to the game situation and profit from constructive criticism? (4) Can she sense her position in relation to her teammates and her opponents? (5) Can she change her mind when the situation changes?

Squad and Team Organization.   Before the final selection of players is made, the coach must decide whether she will organize a distinct team or teams, or a single squad. There are advantages and disadvantages for both patterns of selection.

Team Selection — Advantages

1. A unity of feeling and security develops within each team.
2. The players work with the same people immediately and a team unit can be formed quickly.
3. If there is a varsity and junior varsity, time is not wasted in organizing for drills and scrimmages at practice sessions since line-ups will not vary greatly.
4. If there are two people coaching, the group is naturally divided for coaching purposes and there is carry-over from day to day with the same coaching personnel.

Disadvantages

1. With the selection of players difficult at best, early mistakes cannot be changed — late developing players may be lost to the varsity for the season.
2. Players may let down since they have made the team for the season.

Squad Selection — Advantages

1. The teams are flexible and deserving players can be moved up or down easily as the season progresses.
2. Players "play up" to maintain their position.
3. The lower players continue to improve since there is a chance of moving up.
4. There is a squad unity that promotes greater interest and support in both varsity and junior varsity matches rather than the varsity being the only important game.

Disadvantages

1. Time must be spent before practices to organize the squad into groups for drills and scrimmage since there are no definite units.
2. It may be difficult for two coaches to work with this type of structure.
3. There is constant pressure on the coach and uncertainty among the players, for the coach is always selecting and moving players.

The squad or teams should be selected approximately three weeks before the first game. This will give the coach time to work with these groups and formulate a team. Any less time will create a rush to get ready and more than three weeks may dull the anticipation of the first game.

Whether definite teams or a squad are selected, it is important that the groups that will play as a team in the next match play together for a sufficient amount of time. There is a danger, particularly with squad organization, that in an attempt to find the strongest group, too many changes may occur and players never play as a settled group before the match.

In summary, the selection of one or more permanent teams is a difficult chore and the coach and team are committed to the selection for a season, but organization during the season is comparatively simple. The selection of a squad is easier initially but demands more time and effort on the part of the coach throughout the season. The flexibility offered by the squad arrangement generally produces the best competitive results.

The Coach's Expectations of Competitors and Team Members.   It is assumed that a position on a team or squad carries obligations as well as privileges to the player. Athletic competition is a selective decision for all players and unquestionably should remain so. However, once a commitment is made, the player should devote herself to her endeavor. The decision to play and be a member of a team carries the responsibility of maintaining herself and her skills at a competitive level. This often results in the necessity of sacrificing some social obligations for the team. The coach and other teammates should expect and receive promptness, attention to coaching and direction and general team concern.

By the same golden rule of team membership, a player has the right to expect similar behavior from her teammates and dedicated expertise from her coach. A coach establishes guidelines of behavior in concert with the team. She defines practice times, schedules and general expectations. Consistency of expectation and response on the part of players and coaches is imperative. The coach, without diminishing or depriving a person of her individual response, can mold a team-squad atmosphere.

Healthful Living: Social, Emotional and Physical Responsibilities of Team Members.   The competitive athlete should want to develop excellence in her performance, not only for the general team effort but also for the absolute knowledge that she is in the best possible condition to perform the skills demanded by the sport. Striving for excellence requires a body in agreement with a state of psychological readiness. Realistically, the pressures of home and social obligations and academic endeavors offer opportunities for excuses and delays in personal readiness for competition. Competitive athletes must make choices, but these choices must be based on adequate information. Girls and young women in normal health should be informed of the major factors in health maintenance and improvement during the competitive season.

REST.   Rest cannot be stored successfully for future use. It is imperative and is the major period when an organism rebuilds and strengthens itself. An individual's needs differ both physically and psychologically, but for the healthy young female of high school and college age more than nine hours of sleep in a 24 hour period is considered unnecessary. In a well-conditioned athlete longer periods may actually decondition and weaken her ability.

NUTRITION.   Optimum nutrition for an athlete should be a concomitant rather than a substitute for good physical training. Girls and young women rarely sit at training tables or eat carefully measured portions of protein, carbohydrates or experimental diets. In fact, the modification of a normal diet is relatively unnecessary unless an athlete is trying to reach a desirable weight at the onset of training. In the course of training for specific sports dietary variations may be beneficial, but basically the athlete's diet should be essentially the same as that for any normal person of similar age.

The benefit of diet supplement is frequently debated among athletes and coaches. Mayer and Bullen cite some of the difficulties in obtaining conclusive evidence:[1]

To evaluate the effects of such supplementation, one must be reasonably certain that pre-existing states of malnutrition or undernutrition do not exist. . . . If the pre-existing nutritional status is known to be adequate, then has supplementation been carried out with adequate control groups, so that the beneficial effects cannot be attributed to training or to other effects rather than to the supplementation?

The pattern of food intake has been studied in relation to industrial work performance, but little evidence regarding the possible benefits of varying meal patterns has been accumulated for athletic performance. Some evidence has indicated that five smaller meals rather than the traditional three large meals improve physical performance. There is some evi-

---

[1]Mayer, Jean and Bullen, Beverly: "Nutrition for the athlete." *Proceedings of the Second National Conference in the Medical Aspects of Sports,* American Medical Association, 1960.

dence that poor physical performance results with fewer than three meals.

It is difficult to say that beneficial performance effects can be attributed to a single food component or to any magical dietary blend of selected vitamins, proteins or carbohydrates. Most coaches agree that the steak dinner is not so much for protein as for its psychological effect — something special for a special person on a special occasion. Most investigators seem to indicate that the athlete should eat what she would normally eat, providing it is a well-balanced diet.

The following statements summarize the present knowledge which is meaningful and of practical use to the coach of girls and women.[2]

A well-balanced diet should provide an increased calorie intake as demanded by the increased amount of work done by the athlete.

Two factors should be considered when determining the pre-event meal: (1) possible discomfort from the mechanical effect of food on respiration and digestion when the meal is consumed too close to the event and (2) the effect of the composition of the meal on the length of time for digestion, on the amount of water in the body and on the level of blood glucose. A high fat meal is not digested as fast as a high carbohydrate meal. A high protein meal draws water in digestion that is necessary for perspiration and places a high oxygen demand on the body in the digestive process. A high carbohydrate meal gives a high level of readily available fuel for energy expenditure. Carbohydrates such as fruit juice raise the level of blood glucose immediately, followed by a sudden drop. Carbohydrates such as rice prolong the raised blood glucose effect.

It may be necessary to supplement the usual diet with salt if competition or practice will be held in extreme heat. Salt should be ingested well before (three hours) the event. An athlete should have a high water level before a contest but large amounts of water should be avoided immediately prior to competition. Limited water consumption during participation is recommended.

TOBACCO AND ALCOHOL.   There is no evidence to indicate that athletes who drink or smoke perform better than those who do not. There is, however, an increasing amount of evidence to the contrary. Even if there were no indications that alcohol and tobacco may limit the performance potential, the young, intelligent athlete should think of her future and weigh the accumulating evidence that associates smoking with certain cancerous conditions and cardiovascular difficulties. The excessive use of alcohol has both a physically and psychologically debilitating effect. There is no scientific evidence that gives justification to the use of alcohol or tobacco.

DRUGS.   Administered under proper medical supervision, drugs have proved helpful to many individuals with physical and psychological disabilities. These restorative drugs include anti-inflammatives, enzymes and muscle relaxants to aid muscle and tissue restoration. Other drugs theo-

---

[2.] *Ibid.*

retically used for the improvement of athlete performance include amphetamines, barbiturates and steroids. Steroids are hormone-derived and are taken for the long term effect of increasing muscle size and strength. There are serious doubts about the value of steroids, and many concerns about their safety. Drugs used for psychological release or expansion (LSD, marihuana and barbiturates) are both illegal and potentially harmful. The degree to which physical performance can be improved by drugs is questionable and there is always the danger that the drug may be physically hazardous or psychologically addictive. The improvement of performance by chemical means is clearly unethical. The use of such drugs cannot be condoned.

EMOTIONAL AND MENTAL STATE.   A major consideration in the health of young people is their emotional and mental state. In these days of rapid social change and attendant pressure, such considerations as grades, home problems and personal and social adjustments are of prime and constant concern to young athletes. There is no panacea for solutions to the myriad problems of the players, but the coach must be a patient listener and help establish direction for those who are in the difficult period of making social decisions. Young people often seek a clear definition of expectations and clear statements on the limits of their behavior. It is not unrealistic nor ultra-conservative to impose some group standards concerning minimum grades, dress while traveling and general campus behavior. A coach does need to realize that the social scene is constantly changing — nationally and locally. She must work in concert with her team members in developing guides and directing behavior during periods of uncertainty for individuals or for the entire team.

Practice Sessions

Practice sessions afford the time for players and coaches to develop individual talent and team skill and spirit. The competitive event is, in essence, the proving ground for the effectiveness of the practice sessions. The importance of planning for specific outcomes from these sessions cannot be overemphasized.

Conditioning.   Conditioning is both physical and mental. It results from permanent positive habits of health, diet, discipline and exercise and is maintained through continual work and mental discipline. The benefits that accrue to the individual are the inspiration and satisfaction that accompany a feeling of completeness and body-mind-spirit unity.

Physical and mental preparation varies with each individual. It is generally assumed that mental preparation is more complex than physical conditioning, for the individual's mental and emotional responses to internal and external influences are difficult to measure. Unlike physiological changes, mental and emotional changes can be viewed only by external behavior rather than by exact measuring devices.

No training program, however sound, can be effective unless the participant is convinced of its effectiveness. By the same token, the most effective program can result in mediocre results and performance if the individual's mental condition is not in harmony with her physical readiness.

The practice session begins with a period of *warm-ups*. Warming up is the process which elicits the acute physiological changes that prepare the individual for strenuous physical performance. It is generally agreed that warming up improves performance and prevents injury by two essential means:

1. Rehearsal of a skill or a complex of skills before competition fixes the nature of the task which is to be replicated later in the individual's neuromuscular coordinating system. It also heightens the kinesthetic senses. For example, execution of several jump shots in basketball brings into mental and kinesthetic focus the precise movements which will be employed in the game. Most athletes agree that establishing a performance pattern enhances performance when the game begins. Even if there were no physiological evidence to indicate the value of brief practice, time should be allowed for pregame skill execution for that majority of athletes who find a warm-up psychologically assuring. Individual variations in the need for a warm-up period indicate that the coach should arrive at the game site at least thirty minutes before the time of scheduled competition.
2. The rise in body temperature that accompanies a period of warm-up facilitates the biochemical reactions which supply energy for muscular contractions. Elevated body temperature also shortens the period of muscular relaxation and aids in reducing stiffness. As a result of these processes, strength and speed of movement and accuracy are improved; also warm-up increases tissue elasticity which seems to lessen the possibility for muscular injury.

It must be said that the value of warming-up exercises is questionable in improving performance in endurance events which require lower elements of skill, speed or strength.

The conditioning program should focus on the *areas of physiological change that enhance a player's ability*. These are discussed briefly below:

1. Increase in strength. Strength is the maximum amount of pulling force a muscle can exert. Strength is directly related to the cross-sectional area and quality of the muscle and can be developed through application of the principle of overload.
2. Increase of muscular endurance. Endurance is the ability of the muscle to work for a prolonged period of time. Endurance is best developed through many repetitions with a relatively light work load.
3. Increased cardiovascular and cardiorespiratory endurance. In-

creased efficiency is gained through increased demands (work load) on these systems.

4. Increased flexibility. Flexibility is developed through stretching and elongating activities in combination with a wide range of joint action. Such flexibility lessens the chance of unnecessary tearing of the tissues.

5. Better neuromuscular coordination. Coordination is the ability to use the correct muscles at the proper time (in response to stimulation) with the correct amount of force necessary to perform the desired movement effectively. Improved coordination can be accomplished by repetitions of a properly executed movement.

Physiological changes can be brought about by *various types of conditioning programs.* These include:

1. Circuit training. Six to ten different activities are performed in specific order and timed. The goal of the program is to reduce the time or increase the number of repetitions.

2. Interval training. The participant performs an all out effort followed by a rest period. The periods of exertion and rest are alternated, with the work periods increased and rest periods decreased. The program should begin with activities of short duration (10–15 seconds).

3. Fartlek. Fartlek is much like cross-country running. The participant combines periods of sprinting with periods of jogging and walking on all types of terrain. As conditioning improves, the period of running is longer than that of jogging, and more jogging than walking is done.

4. Steeplechase. This program is similar to fartlek with the inclusion of obstacles throughout the course.

5. Rhythmic continuous exercise. This program is similar to interval training with mild activity replacing the rest interval.

Conditioning Through the Activity Itself.   There is increasing evidence to indicate that the greatest gain and benefits from warm-up procedures come from activities that imitate as closely as possible the movements which are to be used in the event. Drills, practices, scrimmages and the competitive game itself provide the best conditioning for the activity. Physical development in this setting does not happen by chance or casual play; it must be planned for.

The exponents of this type of conditioning contend that conditioning and skill development can go on simultaneously and that the skill development will progress further in this type of program. Many girls react indifferently to conditioning programs that are separate and distinct from the activity itself. Some seasons are so short that separate conditioning programs are detrimental to skill development, yet conditioning is of prime importance to a competitive team.

Length of Season. The DGWS has developed clear statements concerning the desirable length of the competitive sports season. Coaches, consumed with the value of their selected sport and encouraging the development of excellence among the participants, have many valid arguments for extending the competitive season. Realistically, a breadth of opportunities should be offered the high school girl, though a college student or post-collegian may make a mature selection of one or two activities in which to strive toward excellence. Education must encourage an opportunity for excellence, but opportunities must not be limited to a select few students. A school does its students a disservice if it centers all its money and coaching talents on one or two team sports that attract and accommodate only a small percentage of the student body. An array of competitive opportunities must be offered and the seasons limited so sports participation takes its place in student life as a cocurricular offering and does not become *the* curriculum of the student. Reasonable limits on the sports season are suggested below:

High School:[3]

The maximum length of a sport season should be twelve weeks, with the first three weeks devoted to training and conditioning. The participant should take part in no more than five participation periods per week including games or contests. There should be no more than two games per week, which should not be played on consecutive days.

College:[4]

The length of the season and the number of games should be established and agreed upon by the participating schools. The length of the season will vary according to the locale and the sport but should not exceed twelve weeks including at least three weeks of preliminary conditioning and instruction.

Length of Practice Sessions. Research findings have not been very helpful in clearly defining the length of practice periods or the absolute amount of rest needed between practices for specific sports. There are

---

[3](DGWS) Division for Girls' and Women's Sports: "Guidelines for Interscholastic Athletic Programs for High School Girls." AAHPER, Washington, D.C., 1965.

[4]DGWS: "Guidelines for Intercollegiate Athletic Programs for Women." AAHPER, Washington, D.C., 1965.

some generally accepted and substantiated principles which should guide the coach in her practice sessions.

Spaced or distributed practice is superior to massed practice in many situations. *How* to distribute the practice for maximum efficiency is complicated by the nature of the task and the maturity of the learner.

The practice session work load is governed by work efficiency and the player's recuperative ability. In most practices the obvious objective is to achieve the greatest total amount of work without developing fatigue that cannot be dissipated with normal rest by the next day. Some practices are not sufficiently strenuous for the coach to be concerned about the fatigue element.

It is generally accepted that no more than five sessions per week, including games, should be planned. Each practice session should be approximately one and one half to two hours in length, depending on the purpose of the practice, the condition of the participants and the demands of the particular schedule of games. To expect girls on high school or college teams to practice longer than that may be unrealistic and inadvisable.

General Content of Practice Sessions.   The content of each practice session should be governed by the purposes of the specific session and the condition of the participants. Each session should be planned with a concern for the participant and how she best learns. The following principles merit consideration:

1. Practice should be satisfying and the learner should have a sense of accomplishment, if not success, at the end of the session.
2. For repetition to be effective, the learner must be rewarded or reinforced in some way or her drive will be reduced.
3. The participants should be motivated by the challenges of the session.
4. Throughout the session the participants should be aware of their individual importance as a part of an integral unit.
5. Some learning evidently can take place without the learner actually going through the physical motion. *Mental practice* is superior to no practice at all, while physical practice is more effective than mental practice alone. Thinking through the correct physical response, in combination with actual practice may be the most effective learning combination for most individuals.
6. Improvement in skill can take place during the interval between practice sessions. This phenomenon is known as *reminiscence* and is not clearly understood at this time. It may be related to *mental practice* and is believed to occur only when the task has been partially learned. Chance errors that occur in practice are thought to be less firmly established than the appropriate responses and hence forgotten sooner. It appears that intervals between practices aid in the elimination of errors. Learning takes time and

requires a period of rest as well as one of work; cramming is not an efficient way of learning.

7. Recent studies indicate that emphasis on controlled speed during the initial phase of learning may produce best results if speed and accuracy are to be involved in the finished performance. Otherwise, the learner develops patterns of coordination which might be quite different from those which are required at the normal speed of actual performance. Proceeding slowly but accurately may actually interfere with the development of the desirable performance, for working in slow motion may establish an incorrect neuromuscular pattern.

8. Practice scrimmage tempo should approximate the speed and tempo of an actual game. Changes in timing can upset performance.

9. No plan or kind of practice can replace the value of the actual competitive game experience, but no one can learn best on a diet of competition only.

10. The more highly conditioned the individual, the fewer breaks are needed in the practice session.

A general plan for an hour and a half or two hour practice session is suggested below:

Introductory Period: 15-20 Minutes

This is a period of general warm-up using a plan for conditioning that utilizes movements included in the game. Begin gradually with light work building up to a work load intensity of a game situation.

If there is to be a long talk during the practice session (and there probably should not be) it should come first. Short talks can be made during rest periods and opportunities for teachable moments should never be ignored, but lengthy discourses in the middle of a session require the players subsequently to build back up to the activity both physically and mentally.

Main Period: 60 Minutes

Drills — scrimmage.

Terminal Period: 15-20 Minutes

This is a period of tapering off from the hard physical work load and from intense emotional involvement. Recovery is enhanced by conditions which improve circulation and facilitate chemical reactions in the body. Mild activity and warmth provide these conditions.

A period of emotional recovery does not imply that the practice must end on a low key. It is highly desirable to leave the session on a pitch of psychological well-being. Often during the late moments of the main practice period a coach becomes aware of "the moment" when things have gelled and the team is aware of its togetherness. The feeling should be captured and the practice should lessen to leave the impression of this peak of accomplishment. Often indescribable, these moments make the next practice an anticipated pleasure.

Scouting

Scouting opponents in a competitive situation prior to the scheduled contest has not been a common practice in girl's and women's sports though it is quite the usual practice for senior high school and college men's athletics. It is difficult to justify the exchange of films, the road trips to see a team play several games or the lengthy telephone conversations with the coach of the team which last met the forthcoming competitors.

Coaches agree that one of the challenges of competition is how a team plays on a given day. Team members and the coach herself may find one of the greatest pleasures of competition in analyzing the opponent *during* competition and in developing the ability to adapt or adjust to the situation. If there is much pregame information on the opponent, the competitors may feel that their analysis while playing will be unnecessary and this will defeat one of the purposes of competition, as well as possibly defeat the team.

General patterns of play and general strengths and weaknesses of teams and individuals can of course be discerned by scouting, but these same items will be discovered within a short period of play by the alert coach and competitor. Just because a team plays a particular zone or player-to-player defense in basketball when scouted is no guarantee that it will use the same defense when playing another team. Perhaps the most valuable information to be gained by scouting in basketball is the favorite shooting position for various players. In field hockey and lacrosse, general patterns of play are fairly orthodox and, with no periods for time out, the competitors must be able to analyze players and the situations on their own.

The coach views her team against another during the game and has the opportunity to see the strengths and weaknesses of both. She is *teaching* when she shares this with her team; it is quite another thing to scout the opponents and then direct the play of her team on the basis of findings of another day and another game. Under these conditions it becomes a game for the coaches rather than a game for the players.

Bibliography

Cratty, Bryant J.: *Movement Behavior and Motor Learning.* Second Ed., Philadelphia, Lea & Febiger, 1967.

Davis, Elwood C. and Wallis, Earl: *Toward Better Teaching in Physical Education.* Englewood Cliffs, New Jersey, Prentice-Hall, 1961.

DeVries, Herbert: *Physiology of Exercise for Physical Education and Athletics.* Dubuque, Iowa, William C. Brown Company, 1966.

DGWS (Division for Girls' and Women's Sports): "Guidelines for Interscholastic Athletic Programs for High School Girls." AAHPER, Washington, D.C., 1965.

DGWS, "Guidelines for Interscholastic Athletic Programs for Junior High School Girls." AAHPER, Washington, D.C., 1966.

DGWS, "Guidelines for Intercollegiate Athletic Programs for Women." AAHPER, Washington, D.C., 1965.

Gagne, Robert M. and Fleishman, Edwin A.: *Psychology and Human Performance*. New York, Holt, Rinehart, and Winston, 1959.

Johnson, Warren (ed.): *Science and Medicine of Exercise and Sports*. New York, Harper and Row, 1960.

Lawther, John D.: *The Learning of Physical Skills*. Englewood Cliffs, New Jersey, Prentice-Hall, 1968.

Mayer, Jean and Bullen, Beverly: "Nutrition for the athlete." *Proceedings of the Second National Conference in the Medical Aspects of Sports*, American Medical Association, 1960.

Morehause, Laurence E. and Rasch, Philip J.: *Sports Medicine for Trainers*. Second Ed., Philadelphia, W. B. Saunders Co., 1963.

Oxendine, Joseph: *Psychology of Motor Learning*. New York, Appleton-Century-Crofts, 1968.

Robb, Margaret: *Dynamics of Skill Acquisition*. Englewood Cliffs, New Jersey, Prentice-Hall, 1972.

Singer, Robert N.: *Motor Learning and Human Performance*. New York, The Macmillan Company, 1968.

Singer, Robert N.: *Coaching, Athletics and Psychology*. New York, McGraw-Hill Book Company, 1972.

4

Basketball

The liberation of American women is mirrored in the evolutionary history of competitive basketball. Half a century of rule modification, misinterpretation and disagreement among professional groups reflected opposing views of the philosophy of basketball. The recent transition from the two court, six player game to the full court, five player game parallels increasing support for the psychological and physiological challenge for those who choose active competition.

Today the rules of collegiate women's basketball are governed by the Joint DGWS-AAU Basketball Rules Committee and are, in principle, the rules of international competition. It remains for the five player rules to be accepted for high school play in all geographical areas. As evidence is collected to assure high school officials and parents that no real physiological threat exists in the full court game, social acceptance will permit the five player game to capture the interest of younger athletes.

Individual Skills Necessary for Competitive Play

Competitive basketball requires both physical and mental commitment. The desire to play, combined with ball control, body control and a conditioned body are minimal requirements for team membership. One's desire to play and a competitive spirit may be the most important requisites for competitive play. Desire will control the discipline necessary for conditioning, and desire will direct the quality of effort one exerts to improve one's knowledge and skill.

Basic to specific game skills are agility, variable speed, flexibility, jumping ability and reach, body balance and control. Footwork and agility are imperative and can be improved with directed practice. Height is a decided asset when added to basic movement. The obvious ball handling skills include passing, catching, rebounding and shooting made effective by faking, cutting, pivoting and jumping. A balance of body control and ball handling skills, and excellence in one or more specialized skills are imperative for team membership. It remains for the coach and team to utilize individual excellence for the best combination resulting in successful play.

Selection of Players

The ball control skills mentioned previously are needed by all players. The responsibility of the positions of forward, guard and center suggests additional and specific skill qualities. The following qualifications are helpful in determining the best players for given positions. The duties are modified depending upon the type of offensive and defensive patterns played.

Forward Position

1. Speed and endurance are imperative, particularly in playing the fast break type of offense.
2. Aggressive and determined. She must carry the offense and be able to see and hit the "open player." Good teams usually have at least one player with this skill.
3. Alert to scoring opportunities. She must move quickly to an open spot for a shot; she must move for the ball or toward the basket for a lay-up.
4. Alert to defensive maneuvers to make the opponent commit errors.
5. Deceptive on all movements, offensive and defensive.
6. Hustles in all situations. She follows all shots and all rebound opportunites.
7. Skillful and relaxed shooter with a variety of shots when open or closely guarded. Skillful corner shooter. Forwards are responsible for the largest share of scoring as they are in the best position to score.
8. Ability to jump effectively. Height is important in controlling the boards but timing is more important.
9. Ability to display speed when there is a need to receive a pass or overtake an opponent.
10. Thinks and reacts quickly to either offensive or defensive situations.
11. Excellent passer in close situations.
12. Excellent at the free throw line.

Center Position.   The qualifications of the center player are those of an excellent forward plus enough additional height and aggressiveness to direct jump balls and take rebounds. She is expected to rebound at both baskets and consequently must develop stamina to cover the court. In addition, she must:

1. Demonstrate consistent height in jumps.
2. Use finger tips for controlled tap of the ball.
3. Time jumps accurately on toss up and for rebound.
4. Jump vertically to avoid interference with opponent and recover position for either offensive or defensive play.
5. As a post player, be able to shoot in a confined area. Must have a good jump shot or hook shot inside the free throw line. Must have the ability to shoot after receiving a pass with her back toward the basket.
6. Position properly for rebounds; *move aggressively* for the rebound.
7. Break from the ball as it is tapped after the toss up.
8. Tip in for scores.

Guard Position.   Height is an asset to a guard but an aggressive, strong player may more than compensate for her small size. Guards must be "scrappers" who carry the burden of defense and offense as the ball is moved down the court. One major responsibility is getting the ball and then relaying it to the person in the best scoring position. She must:

1. Be shifty and agile, able to move in all directions while retaining balance and body control.
2. Display aggressiveness and determination in gaining and maintaining possession of the ball.
3. Have excellent timing on her jumps, particularly if she is not as tall as her opponents.
4. Know and utilize the techniques of guarding. For example, how to keep an opponent out after she shoots and how to press a player who has completed her dribble.
5. Serve as the playmaker of the team. Be able to spot and pass to the open player.
6. Have the ability to read fakes. While focusing at the opponent's waist level, her peripheral vision should allow her to see the ball and the remainder of her opponent's body.
7. Be a good outside shooter.

Advanced Skills for Competitive Play

The fundamental skills of the game, well-rehearsed and performed in errorless fashion under competitive stress, are responsible for more victories than complicated systems of offensive and defensive play developed on the shaky foundation of poor skill execution. The conscientious player and coach will utilize numerous references to review techniques of basic skills.

The skills discussed below deserve consideration by players beyond the beginning competitive level.

Passing and Receiving.   These are the most important fundamentals. At the onset coaches must stress the execution of quick, crisp passes as opposed to soft, lobbing passes. Obviously the techniques of catching must be adapted to receive these passes. It is expected that all players have sound passing skills, including the chest, bounce, underhand, baseball, overhead, shoulder and hook passes. More difficult passes include:

1. Slap pass: used to deflect rather than throw the ball in a close play when a fast return is needed.
2. Flip pass: used for close passing in a pivot offense. Frequently used in the "give and go" situation.
3. Backhand pass: used in the give and go game and by a dribbler cutting to the basket. If she is cut off in front, she flips the ball around her body and passes to a teammate.

Dribbling.   Dribbling is an important technique when used to move the ball to avoid being tied by an opponent, to advance the ball, to draw defensive players away from the basket and to drive toward the basket. When overused the skill is more harmful than beneficial, as evidenced by coaches who admonish players, "Never dribble when it is possible to pass."

Pivoting.   Effective smooth pivots reverse the position of the player and are used against a charging defense, to block out defensive players and to free players on the inside screening attack.

Faking.   An intentional action used to mislead an opponent and draw her off balance or out of position constitutes a fake. Fakes can be offensive or defensive and can be executed with eyes, head, shoulders, feet, voice, ball or any combination of these.

Defensive Guarding Skills.   Ultimately it is each individual's responsibility to keep the opponent from shooting, passing, positioning to receive a pass and from dribbling into an advantageous position. The following fundamentals should be reviewed:

1. A boxer's stance with one foot slightly forward insures balance. The slight forward stride aids in quick change of direction. The position of the hands depends upon court position and skill of the opponent from that position. One hand is up and forward in an attempt to block or deflect shots; the other arm is extended to the side and low to defend against passes or a dribble. Some coaches prefer that both hands remain low when the player is "out" to maintain balance or take advantage of the opportunity to intercept the ball.

Figure 4–1.   Basic guarding stance with varying hand positions.

2. Feet "shuffle." The lead foot moves in a short step with the trailing foot pulling to correspond to the original position; legs must not cross.
3. When guarding a player with the ball, be prepared for a shot, pass or dribble.
   a. The distance the defender stands from her opponent depends upon the attacking player's skill. A poor shooter may be loosely guarded outside to avoid having her drive. An agile, accurate shooter must be guarded closely and straight away. The defense stays just far enough to recover if the player attempts to drive.
   b. A defender must keep her feet in contact with the floor to avoid being pulled off balance by a fake.
   c. The player defending the post player attempts to keep the post from getting the ball. Overplay the post slightly on the ball side in hopes of deflecting an incoming pass. Beyond the free throw line stay between the post and the goal.
4. When guarding a player without the ball, step back to prevent the offensive player from cutting around. Try to follow the ball position but always keep the player in view.

More advanced guarding techniques include blocking shots and working against screens.

To become proficient at *blocking shots* the player must determine the kind of shots her opponent uses most successfully. Very early in the game the guard should know if her opponent jump shoots, set shoots or hooks; the hand preference for these shots and the fakes that precede the shots. Does she jump shoot straight away or fade away? As the guard anticipates a jump shot she moves a step closer and overplays her opponent on the shooting hand side. She jumps simultaneously with the shooter and turns her body slightly to extend her reach. Her hand is out and over the ball to block the shot or get a jump ball. On a fade away shot the defense jumps forward and to the side to avoid contact.

The principles of blocking a set or hook shot are similar. If the player set shoots with one hand, overplay to the shooting side. On two-hand set shots the guard must delay as long as possible, for the offense has good control of the ball and may stop the shot and drive around if the defender crowds or leaves the ground before the shot is taken. The two-hand shooter must be guarded straight away. When blocking the hook shot, if the shooter can shoot moving in one direction only, the guard steps toward the shooting hand as the move begins; she then takes another step as the shooter makes her turn and reaches up to block the shot. If the post player can go in either direction with either hand, the defense must stay between the post and the goal, watching the middle of the post's back to read the direction of the shooting movement. She then quickly shuffles to the shooting side to block. It is very helpful if another defensive player sags to close one path to the basket and thus give the defending player an edge in anticipating the post player's action.

On *screen plays* the options of the defense are: (1) step closer to the offensive player and squeeze around the screen; (2) go behind the screen by stepping back from the offensive player and going between a teammate and her offensive player; (3) switch defensive responsibilities with a teammate.

Possession Skills.   It is obvious that the technique of gaining possession of the ball must be mastered by each individual. Opportunities to gain the ball can result in free ball, jump ball and rebounding situations.

Free balls result from poor passes, deflected balls and broken plays. The skilled player is aggressive in her pursuit and possession of the ball.

Jump ball situations occur many times during the game and deserve strategic consideration. However, the ability of the jumper is basic to effective play. In anticipation of the toss the jumper's knees are bent, weight forward toward the toes. As she jumps her arm is straight and extended to the ball; she keeps her eyes on the ball throughout the jump. The cushions of the three middle fingers place the ball, arching it slightly. Timing the jump to the ball toss is the most important element and is perfected only through practice.

Rebounding becomes increasingly important as a larger number of shots are taken from the outcourt. Statistics indicate that control of the backboards is a major factor in winning or losing. Control of the defensive board can result in clearing the ball more quickly, thus making the fast break possible. The player and coach striving to improve rebounding statistics should consider:

1. Height is an obvious advantage but a smaller player can compensate by blocking out her opponent and properly timing her jump.
2. Defensively, the guard has the advantage of the inside position. Once the shot is up, the defensive player watches her opponent as she moves to the ball. The defender shifts so she blocks the offensive player's path toward the ball. When the ball is caught, the player jackknifes away from her opponent with the ball firmly held and arms spread for protection. Legs are spread as she lands in balanced position.
3. Offensive rebounding enables a team to get "easy scores." An offensive player must get around her defense to an inside position unless she has a great height advantage. Getting inside is best accomplished by a player who anticipates a shot by her teammate and who gets a step on her guard. A shooter may step inside following a quickly executed fake. Once the ball is controlled it may be tipped back to the basket or passed out to a teammate.

Individual Offensive Skills.   It is imperative that each player be an effective shooter in the five player game. Each player should develop a set shot, drive-in (lay-up) and a jump shot. Good outside shooting and an effective jump shot give the smaller player a chance to compete.

Styles of shooting are well described in many books on technique. It remains for the coach and individual player to develop the player's best style of play in relation to her height, speed and most effective shots. Several advanced techniques are worthy of review:

1. *Jump shot.* The jump shot enables a player to shoot very quickly while on the move. This shot has done more to change the style and pace of play than any other single development. The shot is executed much like a one-hand shot except the player jumps high in the air and does not release the ball until she has reached her maximum jump height. The take-off is from both feet, the jump is straight up or slightly backward if the forward momentum has been fast (fade-away shot). The ball is carried upward into shooting position during the jump. There is a brief instant of relaxation at the height of the jump before the ball is released. A fade-away shot is most effective against a defensive player who guards very closely. After the shot the shooter often must take several steps back from rebounding position to regain her balance.
2. The *tip shot (tip-in).* This is most effective when the ball is free in

Figure 4–2.   Offensive rebound followed by tip-in.

Fig. 4–3   Fig. 4–4

Figures 4–3 to 4–6 show the sequence of receiving a pass and moving into a jump shot.

Figure 4–5.

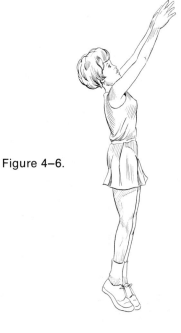

Figure 4–6.

the air, when rebounding on a high pass and when close to the offensive basket. It is an excellent move from an offensive rebound position when time and the position of opponents make it expedient to tip the ball back to the basket rather than to bring it down to shoot or pass out. The ball is tapped with wide spread fingers at the height of the jump. The jump should be high with the arm slightly flexed as the finger tips contact the ball ahead of the body. The shot is the result of pressure by the tips of the fingers, a slight wrist flip and arm extension rather than a batting or slapping action.

3. *Lay-up shots.* The lay-up brings the ball close to the basket so it can be placed against the backboard and carom into the hoop. Logically the player should lay the ball up with the hand which is protected from the guard—the right hand as she approaches on the right side, the left hand on the left side. An advanced player lets the ball roll from her finger tips with the palm of her hand under the ball. (Less advanced players will push the ball toward the boards with the hand behind the ball.) She lands, prepared to rebound if necessary, with her body turned toward the court. The cross over lay-up is used when the offensive player is deep along the baseline and goes under the goal before releasing the ball. She shoots the ball backward over her head, imparting spin to bank it from the board. She may also use the hook shot motion, with her body turning as she releases the ball.

Combining Individuals for Team Play

The most difficult yet vital job of the coach is that of selecting players who combine their talents into the most effective team. Basic to player selection is the predetermination of the coach either to have players fit an established pattern of play or to alter the team style to fit individual talent. In either case it is wise to remember that players well grounded in fundamentals can adjust to many styles of play under proper instruction while withstanding the stress of competition.

A team must have scoring power, ball handling ability, rebound strength, defensive ability, speed, some height and competitive drive. Experience and judgment must be weighed against the potential and the initiative of youth. The following guides are helpful in detecting talent and latent ability:

1. Individual factors of attitude, self-discipline, emotional control, competitive desire and sportsmanship.
2. Individual physical attributes such as height, speed, agility and reaction time.
3. Individual fundamental basketball ability such as footwork, response to passes, shooting, jumping, passing and dribbling.

The coach must have a method of evaluating both tangible and intangible evidence. Assessment of intangible evidence may involve the use of anecdotal records of the behavior of each individual during all aspects of practices and scrimmages. Consider:

1. Promptness and regularity in reporting to practice.
2. Extent a player works on her weaknesses during informal practice periods.
3. Extent and manner in which she works with teammates.
4. Reaction of the other team members toward her.
5. Reaction to coaching, to discipline, to criticism and to adverse conditions.
6. Reaction to stress and pressure of competition.

A player's individual physical attributes and game skills are subject to more tangible evidence. Measures such as the height of a vertical jump or the time on a thirty yard dash can be meaningful when viewed in perspective of the statistical records of practices and scrimmages.

Shooting, rebounding, turnover, tie ball, stolen ball and foul records are discussed on page 98. These defensive and offensive play records tend to verify the selections the coach makes from game to game.

If the coach is confronted with a large number of candidates, she may choose to group them in three categories:

1. Those who appear very impressive and stand out during early practices.
2. Those who do not impress because of their apparent lack of talent.
3. Those who do their job relatively effectively but not spectacularly.

These groupings can result from observations of passing, shooting, weave patterns and informal scrimmages. Many players make self-evaluations and eliminate themselves; the coach eliminates those in group two early in tryouts. The elimination process continues until the squad is reduced to desirable size. When possible the squad should remain large enough to insure team scrimmage situations. Often a coach resists cutting and tries to keep a large group for the good of individual players. This philosophy should be examined in light of the team goals, for large numbers may limit the time a coach can devote to a player striving for excellence.

The process of selection and alteration of players goes on throughout the season. After each practice an evaluation and rating should take place. The coach should discuss the performance with each individual, identifying areas where she should exert mental and physical effort for improvement.

Practice Sessions

Players and coaches agree that a preseason conditioning program is beneficial for physical and mental readiness. Some evidence is accumulating stating that players beginning practice in poor physical condition are more subject to injury than those conditioned. High school, college and recreational athletic assocations generally establish calendars to insure a reasonable but not excessive practice and playing season. It is advisable for players to begin their personal conditioning program four to six weeks prior to the date of official practice. The program should begin only after a thorough medical examination.

The *preseason program* should be designed to improve strength, agility and cardiorespiratory endurance. Additional focus should be directed toward bringing the player to a desirable playing weight, improving her jumping ability and enhancing her peripheral vision. Suggestions of activities and methods to assist in achieving these goals include:

1. Strength and agility. Strive for general body strength and control with emphasis on arm and leg strength.
   a. General conditioning exercises and running.
   b. Agility drills stressing directional change and footwork used in basketball.
   c. Jump rope activities; climbing of stairs and stadium risers.
   d. Weight training for specific muscle group development. Use Universal Gym or hand apparatus in an interval training program.
   e. Interval training involves a stringent work period of a designated time followed by a recovery period; then work, recovery and so forth for a number of repetitions in keeping with the condition of the player. Interval training patterns may be used for weight training, specific exercise bouts, skill drills and running. The pace of the exercise can be intensified, the number of repetitions increased and the recovery period shortened as the condition of the player improves.
   f. Circuit training program designed to incoporate many of the strength building activities. It lends itself to an individual, partner or team conditioning program. A sequence of exercises is performed with the individual competing against herself as she moves from station to station performing the assigned tasks. The time or number of repetitions required may be established initially; thereafter the circuit can be intensified by increased work load or number of repetitions, increased time with constant load or increased load during decreased time.
2. Endurance (muscular and cardiorespiratory).
   a. Distance running.
   b. Fartlek—speed play with periods of running, jogging and striding interspersed.
   c. Interval training principles applied to running bouts.
   d. Circuit training program.

Some coaches arrange for players to work together three or four times a week under supervision. Others find that limited facilities, inadequate supervisory staff and institutional regulations relegate the prospective player to individual or partner plans for conditioning.

The preseason program should be alloted approximately two hours four times a week with emphasis on the individual player's specific needs. A typical partner workout during the preseason period follows:*

1. Fifteen minutes—circuit (each partner working for six minutes). The circuit is developed as follows: One partner times the other for one minute on each exercise. The maximum number of repetitions is recorded. A work load is arbitrarily established of one half the repetitions and the total time allowed is six minutes, including time to change stations. As a player executes the circuit each day, she attempts to increase the number of laps or circuit repetition in the six minute period. Once she achieves her target of three or four laps she may assume a greater work load or shorter time limit.
   a. Jump rope—45 repetitions using the two foot takeoff.
   b. Vertical jump—jump vertically from a two foot takeoff 15 times. Jump as high as possible extending an arm to touch a jump board.
   c. Agility run—three lines are placed parallel and 25 feet apart (50 feet overall). The performer runs from the first to the third at top speed; she turns and assumes a guarding stance; slides to line #2, returns to line #3 and turns and runs to line #1 (Fig. 4–7). This is one complete repetition. Complete three repetitions.

*For other suggestions see Sandoval, Earline Young: "Circuit training for basketball." *Basketball Guide,* DGWS., AAHPER, 1971–72.

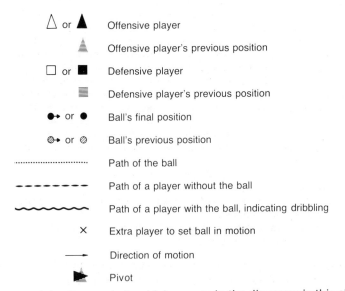

△ or ▲   Offensive player

≜   Offensive player's previous position

□ or ■   Defensive player

≡   Defensive player's previous position

●→ or ●   Ball's final position

⊘→ or ⊘   Ball's previous position

·······················   Path of the ball

– – – – – – –   Path of a player without the ball

〜〜〜〜   Path of a player with the ball, indicating dribbling

×   Extra player to set ball in motion

———   Direction of motion

▟   Pivot

This chart explains the symbols which appear in the diagrams in this chapter.

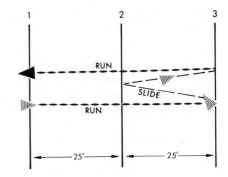

Figure 4–7.   Agility run.

   d. Sit-ups—flexed leg sit-up with partner holding the legs. Ten repetitions.

   e. Dribble drill—follows the pattern of the agility drill over a 50 foot course; dribble while running, sliding. Players should alternate hands on each repetition. Two repetitions.

   f. Bench jump—a bench approximately 18 inches tall and two feet long. The participant stands with one side next to the bench and executes a two foot takeoff across the bench. Ten repetitions.

2. Thirty minutes—running (Fartlek, interval training, etc.).
3. Thirty minutes—weight training and rest period.
4. Forty-five minutes—This period may be added several days a week to change the pace of training. Partners play racquetball or badminton or volleyball if other players are available. An occasional two-on-two, three-on-three using one basketball goal should be encouraged.

Conduct of Practice Sessions.   Organized practices afford the time to further physical and mental conditioning, and to develop fundamental skills, strategy, confidence and teamwork. There should be few secrets from the team in terms of objectives and methods. The suggestions below aid in the conduct and administration of practices:

1. Day by day planning assures coverage of fundamentals and strategy.
2. Time must be budgeted; consequently, start on time and follow an established schedule.
3. Practice schedules and materials to be covered should be made available to players and assistants.
4. Post plans and strategic details so players can visualize the purposes and outcomes of the sessions.
5. Strive for some variety in practice sessions by revolving the sequence of drills and general practice format.

Practices are generally grouped into (1) preseason (before the first game) and (2) normal season sessions. Sessions averaging two hours are desirable with reasonable variations to take advantage of teachable moments. At least three weeks of organized practice should precede the first game.

Each day as players report to practice they should immediately begin warming up by shooting. As soon as all gather, the group conditioning program begins. The preseason practices require more frequent rest periods and drills that are designed to change pace.

Division of Practice Time

1. Warm-up shooting—15 minutes.
2. Conditioning (general and specific)—15 minutes. As physical condition peaks during the season, sufficient maintenance may come through skill drills and scrimmages.
3. Skill drills—30–45 minutes. Early in the season the majority of time is devoted to fundamental skills of passing, shooting, guarding, dribbling, etc. Gradually the emphasis shifts to skill drills that incorporate strategy.
4. Situational drills—30–45 minutes. Strategic plays or scrimmage.
5. Free throws—15 minutes. Free throws should be practiced under conditions of fatigue. This less strenuous period also serves to taper off, and seems to prevent emotional let down after a vigorous practice.

Drills.   Drills are designed to stress game fundamentals and duplicate play situations occurring in a game. They should be executed in the setting and at the speed of competitive play. Drills focusing on skill fundamentals are most often used in the early sessions, with situational drills used throughout the season. Long drills tend to become monotonous. When possible use a variety of drills rather than an isolated drill to develop sequential skills as they are used in a game.

The drills suggested are a sampling of fundamental skill drills, combination skill drills, offensive-defensive patterns and situational drills.*

1. Drills for execution of fundamental skills. The skills stressed should be so thoroughly rehearsed that execution becomes a habit, freeing players to think about strategic application.
   A. Passing
      (1) Shuttle passing. Players are in two lines facing each other at a distance of ten to 25 feet. Different types of passes may be used. The ball is passed back and forth until it reaches the last player. Modify the drill by having the passer follow the pass.
      (2) Double circle passing. Players form two large circles, one within the other. Circles move in opposite directions as players running in the outside circle begin by passing the

---

*Numerous drills are suggested in the references found in the bibliography. The drills included are representative, not exhaustive.

ball or balls to players in the inside circle. Passing continues from circle to circle.

(3) Figure eight passing, breaking. Three columns are formed at one end of the floor. Player #2 passes to #3 who crosses to the other side of the court. Player #2 goes behind #3 after passing the ball; #3 then passes to #1 crossing to the other side of the court. The player who passes the ball goes behind the player to whom she passed. Outside players progress down the court in a straight line (Fig. 4–8). Do not let players pinch toward the middle; use the entire width of the court. Play continues to the end of the court. Variations include shooting at the end of the court and moving the ball against defensive players.

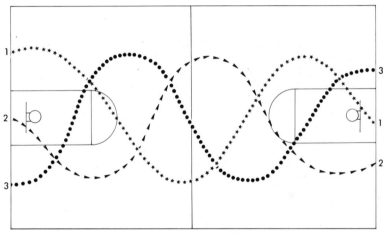

Figure 4–8.   Figure eight drill.

(4) Star drill. The drill requires the player to meet the pass, pass quickly and accurately and move to a new position. The drill is continuous.

    (a) Four players form a square standing ten feet apart with a fifth player in the middle (Fig. 4–9).

    (b) Middle player has the ball; she passes to any player and then takes her place.

    (c) Receiver passes to either player on her right or left and takes her place.

    (d) Second receiver passes across the square to the opposite corner player and takes her place.

    (e) The third receiver passes to the player on her right or left and takes her place.

    (f) The drill continues with the ball moving across (corner to corner), to the side, across, side, etc.
For variation differ the passes, add pivot or fake before the pass.

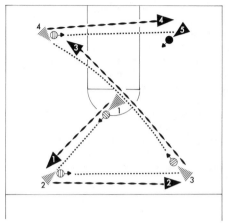

Figure 4-9.   Star drill (one variation).

B. Dribble drills. A number of patterns can be established to focus on cutting, changing hands while controlling the ball and controlling body speed.

   (1) Obstacle dribble. A row of six chairs approximately ten feet apart is set from one baseline to the other. First player moves to the first chair passing it on the right, dribbling with the right hand protecting the ball from the obstacle with her body. She changes hands to keep the ball maximum distance from the next chair which she passes to the left. The second player begins as the first clears the third chair. Players return dribbling down the sideline.

   (2) Progression dribble. Figure 4-10 illustrates groups of players stationed around the court. Several balls may be used. A player dribbles to the next group, passes the ball and goes to the end of the line of the new group.

   (3) Dribble-pass. A player from line #1 dribbles past the center line and makes a long pass to a player from line #2 who is breaking from the side for the basket (Fig. 4-11). The drill stresses timing and ball control as used in the fast break.

C. Individual Shooting Drills. These drills are introduced early in the season so players can self-test during each practice session.

   (1) Basketball golf. Nine spots are taped on the floor from which players shoot. Each player shoots from each spot until she makes a basket. After completing the course the total number of "strokes" is recorded. The player with the fewest shots is declared winner. Daily records may be posted to encourage individual improvement.

   (2) Twenty-one. This drill is designed for practice of long and short shots. Speed is not a factor; accuracy is stressed. A long shot counts two points and a short shot one point. The game is terminated at 21 points.

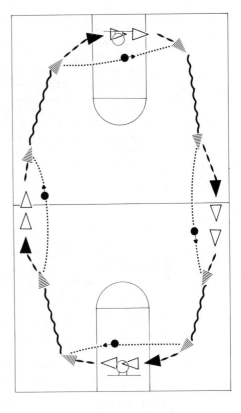

Figure 4–10.   Progression dribble drill.

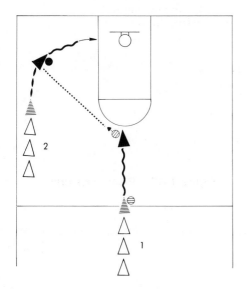

Figure 4–11.   Dribble, pass drill.

(3) Freeze out. Any type of shot may be used in this drill. All players shoot the same type of shot. As an individual misses she drops out. Shooting continues until only one player remains.

(4) Pressure shooting. Any type of floor shot may be used. Players shoot against time. Several groups are formed; on signal, shooting begins with each player taking her turn. As a shot is made the group shouts its score. Shooting continues until 50 or 100 baskets are made.

(5) Free throw shooting drills. Five players are at each basket. Each player shoots twice so the maximum score is ten points. Groups compete.

2. Combination skill drills.

A. Two ball split vision drill. The drill is designed to improve peripheral vision. Four to six players form a line parallel to and facing the center line. One player with a ball is approximately eight feet in front and facing the line of players. One player in the line has a second ball. As the player out front passes to a player in the line, the other ball is passed to her. Pressure passing and catching continues for 20 or 30 seconds before changing the out front player.

B. Dribble-pass-rebound. The same pattern is used as that in the Dribble-Pass drill (p. 63). After receiving the pass, player #2 shoots as in a fast break and player #1 follows to rebound. Variations include a pivot-pass by #2 to #1 who uses #2 as a screen. Player #1 shoots.

C. Pivot-pass. The drill is designed to give players practice in pivoting, catching the ball on the run and shooting. Form two columns of players, one on each side of the court. A player is under the basket to begin the drill by passing to #1. Player #1 receives the ball at the free throw line, pivots, passes to #2 who is driving for the basket. Player #2 shoots; #3 takes #1's place as player #1 takes the rebound. Player #1 passes to #3 who has moved to the free throw line to continue the pattern (Fig. 4–12).

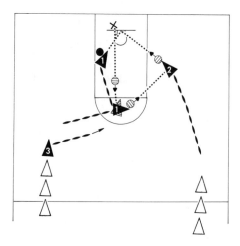

Figure 4–12.   Pivot, pass drill.

D. Dribble, pivot, screen. Two guards are placed near the basket. A #1 player dribbles to the guard, executes a full pivot to a #2 player following her. Player #1 screens as #2 shoots (Fig. 4–13). All follow for the rebound. The pass goes back to a #1 player to begin the sequence again. Change guards occasionally.

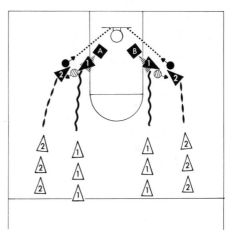

Figure 4–13. Dribble, pivot, screen drill.

E. Front half pivot. A player from #1 column dribbles to the end of the court and stops quickly with her right foot advanced. She pivots toward the basket and passes quickly to #2 player, who is following to the inside. Player #2 drives and shoots (Fig. 4–14). Run this drill from both sides of the court.

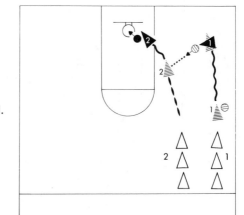

Figure 4–14. Front half pivot drill.

F. Passing, guarding. One guard is placed deep in the key mid-way between two offensive players. Players from columns #1 and #2 attempt to work the ball past the guard with short passes for a close shot (Fig. 4–15).

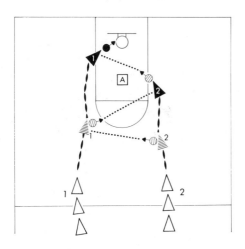

Figure 4–15.   Two on one; passing-guarding drill.

3. Offensive-defensive drills.
  A. Single line pass, pivot, lay-up and rebound. This drill incorporates many fundamentals. Players are positioned as in Figure 4–16. Player #1 passes to #2; #2 passes to #3 who pivots and bounce passes to #4 cutting for the right hand lay-up. Player #2 rebounds. Player #1 takes #3's place; #2 takes #1's place and #3 goes to the end of the line. Player #4 takes #2's position. The new pass sequences is #2 to #4 to #1 to #5. Players continue to shift in this manner until all players have been in each position. Work the drill from both sides of the floor.

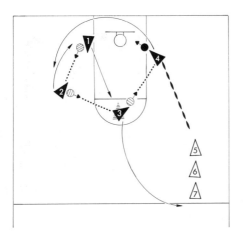

Figure 4–16.   Pass, pivot, lay-up and rebound drill.

B. Position set shooting. The drill stresses shooting accuracy from a player's normal offensive position. Each player is placed in the spot where her shot is most effective. Place a defensive player on each shooter. Let defensive and offensive players change roles every few minutes.

C. Jump shooting drill. All players are in normal offensive positions. Players drive for one or two dribbles to the left, stop and jump shoot. Repeat several times and then run to the right. Place a sagging defensive player on each offensive player. Let the pivot work for a short time in each line.

D. Rebounding drill. Defensive players (#1's) and offensive players (#2's) are positioned near the free throw and end lines. Player #3 shoots the ball and the first defensive player on each side steps across the line with her outside foot in an attempt to screen the offensive player (Fig. 4–17).

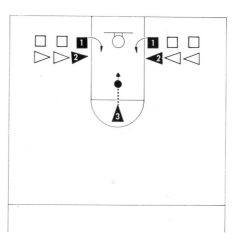

Figure 4–17.   Rebounding drill.

E. Distance rebounding. A defensive and offensive player are on either side of the shooter. Player #3 shoots, #1 and #2 vie for the rebound (Fig. 4–18). Rebounders move the instant the ball leaves the shooter's hand to simulate a game situation.

F. Rebounding, tip-in. Defensive players (squares) are positioned as in Figure 4–19. Three lines of players are formed; #1 player from line #1 shoots and goes in with players from lines #2 and #3 for the rebound. Defensive players attempt to form a triangle to screen out the offense. If successful in rebounding the offensive players attempt to tip the ball into the basket.

Other rebounding drills should be developed which stress rotation of players on the rebound so all areas are covered. For example, Figure 4–20 illustrates player #3 passing to #1 who shoots. Player #2 crosses to the right side to fill the area; #3 follows her own pass to the center area and #1 shoots and covers from the left.

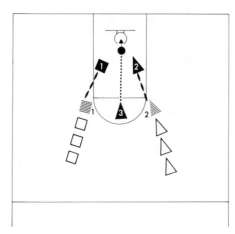

Figure 4–18. Distance rebounding drill.

Figure 4–19. Rebounding, tip-in drill.

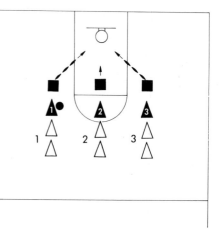

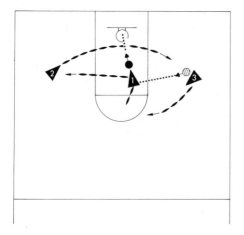

Figure 4–20. Offensive rebounding, rotation drill.

Scrimmages. There is no better way to learn to play basketball than to play under controlled, competitive conditions. Scrimmages and practice games are intended to replicate a game situation with some of the stress, strategic play and "unexpected" from the opponent (even though she may be a teammate). Scrimmages are a vital part of the practice routine and should be carefully planned. A few guidelines to consider follow:

1. Make known the general objectives of the scrimmage and emphasize them when possible (e.g., increased ball control).
2. Emphasize specific objectives prior to and throughout play. Objectives may be of two types — individual and team (e.g., individual defensive rebounding, team execution of a fast break pattern and a zone pressure defense).
3. Chart the scrimmage as if it were a competitive game. A manager or student can be trained so the coach can observe overall play. Information should be reviewed with players immediately after the scrimmage.
4. Coach and observe both offensive and defensive play. Many tend to coach offense to the neglect of defense. A balance must be sought.
5. Stop play at appropriate times to change patterns, adjust attack or defense or work with individuals. Do not disrupt play so often that continuity is lost.
6. Avoid constant coaching. Many players are stifled if they are constantly reprimanded and they may never settle to their game.
7. Scrimmages should be officiated. "One plays as she practices," and poor techniques develop when officiating is inadequate or absent.

Intrasquad scrimmages should be designed so that members of the starting team can play together frequently. Playing offensive strength against defensive is desirable but not always possible. Team strategy must not always suffer by trying to balance team strength, but neither should the less skilled team be so overwhelmed that they are demoralized. While planning for the future and plotting for the present, the coach must remember there is an age, strength and skill gap between the varsity and junior varsity.

Strategy

Strategy is simply determination of how one chooses to play in varying situations. Several general guides direct offensive and defensive play.

1. Play the opponent's style of game only if it is also your team's best game. If the coach judges that the best results will be gained by staying with the established pattern, she must go with this strategy. Invariably, a team will do its best when playing the style

of game to which it is accustomed. A competitive game is not the place to change well-rehearsed patterns.

2. Make your opponents play your style of game. Try to set the patterns of play by forcing tempo and style. Players and coaches often become confused when their normal pattern is blocked.

3. Be prepared for any eventuality. Scouting a team may not be possible and their personnel and style may change during the season. The best preparation for meeting the unknown is ball control, rebound strength and fundamental defense skills with consistent shooting.

OFFENSIVE STRATEGY

Offensive styles and options are limitless but there are certain essentials found in all successful offenses, regardless of the patterns. The ability to shoot, to pass, to dribble, to drive and to execute basic screens is essential. When incorporated into a team offense they afford: (1) movement of the ball; (2) movement of players; (3) obtaining the good shot; (4) obtaining the second shot; (5) maintaining floor balance, and (6) maintaining one-on-one situations.

It is obvious that the offense must move the ball if the defense is to be penetrated, whether it is a player-to-player, zone or combination defense. The team that passes the ball slowly allows the defense time to shift, sag or otherwise move to counteract the offense. The team that keeps the ball moving keeps the defense off balance.

Sound offensive patterns allow for movement of players in conjunction with movement of the ball. Constant movement, fakes and cuts are necessary. When players pose no offensive threat, the defense can use sinking or double teaming strategy and congest potentially vulnerable areas.

The offense must work for the good percentage shot, one that the shooter has the ability to make and one that the rebounders are positioned to recover if missed.

Good offensive play will keep players in open positions to eliminate congestion in and near the basket and prevent one defensive player from guarding two offensive players.

The coach should consider the following points in selecting the team's basic offense:

1. Player personnel available.
2. Type of defense to be faced throughout the season. Even though an opponent's style is well known, be prepared for any eventuality with a simple alternate offensive pattern.
3. Confidence the coach displays in the offense. The coach must believe in the offense, have knowledge to teach it and analyze mistakes in its execution.

4. Simplicity or complexity of the pattern in keeping with age, skill and maturity of players.
5. Additional patterns for out-of-bounds, jump balls and back court play.

It is unrealistic to attempt to describe all possible patterns of offensive play. Numerous books are devoted to the exposition of winning patterns. Each coach will find those most suitable to her personnel and preference. The suggestions presented are basic to the fast break and deliberate attacks, and offer points of departure for all teams.

Fast Break. The fast break is the strategy by which an offensive team beats the defense to the basket for a score. Its execution develops in three phases; (1) ball possession; (2) clearing pass and (3) player movement.

1. Ball possession. A fast break is initiated only after clear possession of the ball. The best opportunity occurs from defensive rebounding but may result from ball interception, loose ball recovery or out-of-bounds play.
2. Clearing action. After possession the fast break is initiated by a controlled clearing pass or a dribble. Dribble *only* to secure possession, to allow better timing or spacing or to make a defensive player commit herself to cover the dribbler and open breaking lanes for teammates. The outlet pass should be quick and sharp. Occasionally rapid relay passes are useful in initiating the break.
3. Player movement. Players without the ball quickly react and move to the outlet area. This is the secret of the controlled fast break. Players spread as wide as necessary to fill the three lanes. Players running down court must be ahead of opponents or they must change pace to let the defensive opponent pass them so that the ball can be handled behind. One defensive player through gives 3 on 1; two defensive players through gives 3 on 2; three through, 3 on 3. If more defensive players pass, the break should be abandoned and a deliberate attack set. Do not let the break become helter-skelter. *It must be held up and possession of the ball retained when good scoring opportunity or control is not certain.*

The two basic types of fast break are the three lane and the crisscross. The simplest is the three lane pattern in which a player with the ball breaks down the center with cutters in the outside lanes breaking toward the goal. Play progresses as follows:

1. Ball is rebounded and cleared to the side. Many teams throw to *spots* to initiate the fast break. This plan requires extensive practice and is easily defended if the opponents pick it up. Young teams should not attempt it.
2. As the ball is rebounded a player on the same side breaks to the sideline; the opposite guard moves to the middle and a third

player goes to the open lane. The center player should receive the pass well down court (Fig. 4–21).

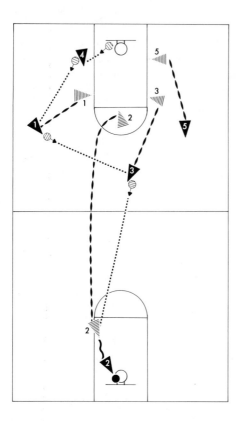

Figure 4–21. Fast break—three lane pattern.

3. The player rebounding generally stays back for safety and, with the fifth player, becomes a trailer. Trailers are responsible for defensive balance and being alert for offensive options as out-court players in the second wave of the fast break attack. Trailers must not follow too closely behind the front line. They move down court about fifteen feet in from the sideline.
4. The center lane player stops at the free throw line unless she has a clear path to the basket for a lay-up. From the free throw line she can exercise the options of shooting or passing to a teammate. She tries to draw a defensive player if her opponents are playing tandem so she can pass; she usually has an easy shot if the two opponents are playing side by side.
5. When the defense gets three players back covering the lanes, trailer options can be exercised.
   a. The center widens to either left or right with one or two dribbles, turns inside and the trailer on the opposite side of the widening move shuttles through for the pass and scoring opportunity (Fig. 4–22).

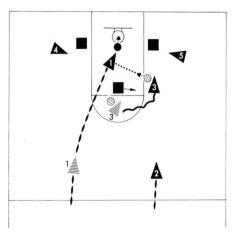

Figure 4–22. Fast break–trailer option.

b. The ball is passed to a wing player if the trailer does not have a scoring opportunity. The wing puts pressure on the baseline with a driving dribble to the corner. She abruptly stops, turns inside and initiates the backward pass if trailer options are open. The front line of the fast break continues to the board; the middle player may button hook into a single pivot if trailer options do not develop.

When utilizing crisscross patterns, players cut across lanes hoping to deceive defensive players; however, the purpose of getting the ball to the center lane player with outside lane players cutting into the scoring area remains unchanged. If pattern play is disrupted, players should capitalize on free-lance options.

Deliberate Offense. Most scoring efforts involve only two or three players in execution. Realizing this, offensive patterns involving two or three persons form the basis of all offense. These fundamentals prepare the offense to attack a variety of defenses, including player-to-player, switching player-to-player, combination defense, varying zone defenses and pressure defenses.

In working against player-to-player the problem the offense faces is simply getting around one or perhaps two players to get a shot. Screen, dribble and cut against the player-to-player defense. The simple offenses noted include both two and three player patterns.

A *screen* is set when an offensive player positions herself between another offensive player with the ball and her guard. The screen allows the offensive player to make an unguarded shot or drive toward the goal behind the protection of the screening player. The player with the ball, going off the screen, has the responsibility to make the screen effective. She fakes her defensive player and cuts as close to the screen as possible so the defense cannot get through (Fig. 4–23). To complete the pick and roll pattern the screener turns toward the cut using a back pivot with a long step. She then

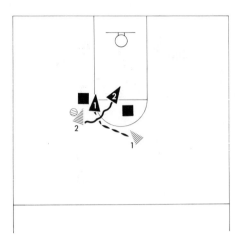

Figure 4–23.   Basic screen play.

moves toward the basket looking for a pass if the defense switches. If she receives a pass and is stopped by a deep defensive player she may pass to an unguarded pivot (Fig. 4–24).

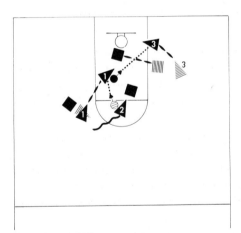

Figure 4–24.   Screen and roll.

Screens can also be set away from the ball to free an offensive player on the side opposite the ball. The offensive player then fakes her guard toward the baseline, cuts around the screen and receives a pass as she goes toward the boards. A pivot player can also break from the post position and set a screen for a forward. If the screen and roll pattern is stopped by an ineffective screen, the offensive player with the ball moves out and another screen is set.

GIVE AND GO PATTERN.   An offensive player passes to a teammate, then runs a path designed to look like a screen. At just the right moment she plants her lead foot and cuts toward the basket. She extends her lead hand as a target and catches the ball near the basket (Fig. 4–25).

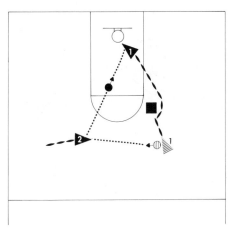

Figure 4–25. Give and go pattern.

Go-behind. An offensive player passes to a teammate, follows the pass and runs to the outside of the teammate. She brushes her guard on the teammate and drives for a return pass.

Cat and mouse. This pattern is run in the same manner as the go-behind but the cutter stops in back of her teammate for a return pass. She may shoot over the screen if there is no pressure, or drive to the opposite side if the defense attempts to move past the screen.

Screen and step back. It is run like other screens but the screener steps back for a return pass when the guard sags to stop the cutter.

Split the post. This is a simplified pattern with several options. The pivot player moves to a high post position and the two closest offensive players form the three player pattern. The ball is passed to the post by a forward who immediately fakes away from the intended cut and then scissors around the post attempting to screen her guard on the post player. The pivot may pass the ball back to the cutter if her guard was screened. The cut of the first forward is followed by a fake and a cut by a second forward who moves around the other side of the post. If her guard is held by the screen she may receive the pass. If the pivot player's guard switches on either cutter, the pivot player may shoot or drive for goal. If none of these options develops, a pass may be cleared to a player whose guard has sagged to defend against a cutter (Fig. 4–26).

The literature is replete with offensive plays that can be run from patterns of three-two; two-three; one-three-one; single pivot post; double pivot post and figure eight. Remembering that any offense must be fitted to personnel, no attempt is made to recommend any single system nor to present extensive plays. Simple play patterns described below sample the varied systems and are suitable for high school and college teams.

Three-two. Three players are in, two out. Players #1 and #2 maneuver with the ball with #1 passing to #3 who cuts to the center after

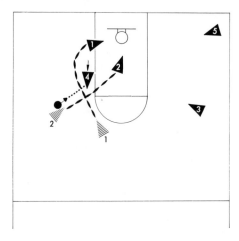

Figure 4–26.   Split the post offensive pattern.

#5 screens #3's guard. Player #3 can shoot from the free throw line or drive (Fig. 4–27).

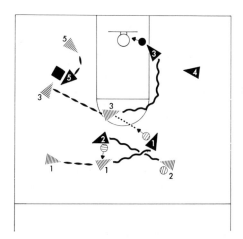

Figure 4–27.   Three-two offense; basic option.

Figure 4–28 shows the same pattern with #3 stopping at the free throw line, pivoting and setting a screen for #4 to shoot over. This can be run from either side with #5 adjusting.

Figure 4–29 shows the same beginning pattern of #1 passing to #3 breaking into center around a screen by #5. Player #1 cuts around #4 and can receive a pass from #3 for a close in shot. Player #3 has the option of passing to #4 if she is free.

The pattern shown in Figure 4–30 begins with #1 passing to #3; #3 then passes to #5 who has executed a reverse pivot after screening for #3. Player #5 cuts back under the basket. This play is used when the defensive players of #3 and #5 are switching.

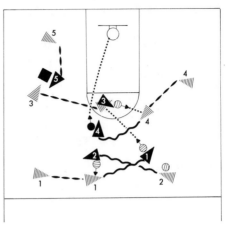

Figure 4–28. Three-two offense; pivot and screen.

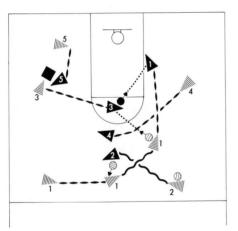

Figure 4–29. Three-two offense; option 1.

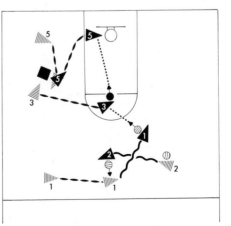

Figure 4–30. Three-two offense; option 2.

Figure 4–31 shows player #1 passing to #4 and then screening for #4. Player #4 passes to #3 who cuts toward the center after a screen by #5. Player #3 passes to #1 who rolls from her screen position. She may shoot. The same pattern can be used with #3 passing to #4 who shoots from the front of the key.

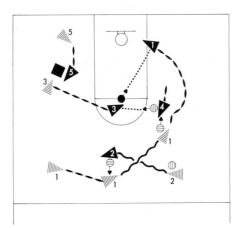

Figure 4–31.   Three-two offense; option 3.

Two-three.   Two players are in, three are out in this pattern that involves screening and good ball handling to free a player for a good shot or a drive to the basket. The three front players must be adept pass fakers with driving ability.

Player #2 passes to #1 who dribbles across court giving the ball to #3. Player #1 screens for #3 and #2 screens for #4 who cuts to the free throw line receiving a pass from #3 (Fig. 4–32).

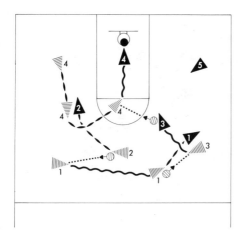

Figure 4–32.   Two-three offense.

An option to the above play has #3 dribbling by the screen for a lay-up rather than passing to #4.

SINGLE PIVOT POST OFFENSE.   This pattern is built around the basic concept of the split the post pattern previously described. The idea is to get the ball to the pivot player and have the passer cut in for a return pass and shot. Player #4 takes #2's position in case of an interception (Fig. 4–33).

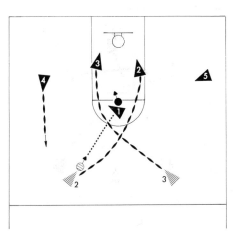

Figure 4–33. Single pivot post offense.

In the following pattern (Fig. 4–34), player #2 passes to #1 and then drives down the center to the right of player #1. Player #3 also drives to the right of #1 but stops quickly and cuts in front of #1 whom she uses for a screen as she executes a quick set or jump shot.

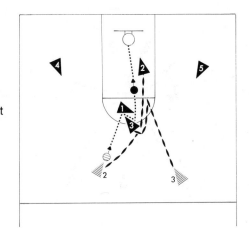

Figure 4–34. Single pivot post offense; option.

DOUBLE PIVOT POST OFFENSE.   This is a variation of the single pivot. The two tallest girls are on either side of the lane. The closer they are to the basket the greater their threat as shooters. Their main functions in the double pivot pattern are as ball handlers and screeners. The real advantage of this type of offense is the excellent rebounding position gained. Figure 4–35 illustrates a basic pattern. Player #1 passes to #5 who moves in the

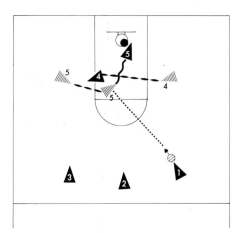

Figure 4–35. Double pivot post offense; basic pattern.

key by the screen set by #4. Figure 4–36 shows player #3 passing to #5. Player #3 breaks across the center. Player #1 also cuts down the center; #5 fakes to either or both and hands off to #4 who moves across the lane immediately after the pass. Players must clear the lane after the fakes.

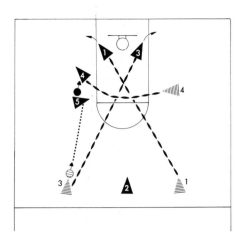

Figure 4–36. Double pivot post offense; option.

WEAVE OFFENSE.   The figure eight pattern is an excellent offense to combat player-to-player defense but ineffective against a zone. Ball handling skills and timing of the break are essential if the weave is to accomplish the major purpose of keeping the opponents moving until a screen can be set and a player freed to break for a lay-up. The basic pattern begins with three players in front, two in the corners and the ball in the middle so it can be run left or right (Fig. 4–37). The simplest option finds one of the three players running the weave to cut for the goal.

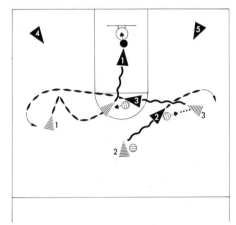

Figure 4–37.   Weave offense; basic pattern.

The weave can be run on the side of the court with only three players. Figure 4–38 illustrates the pattern. Player #3 passes to #1 and screens. Player #1 has the option of driving to the basket or passing to #4 who has taken #3's position. After #1 passes to #4 she screens and #4 passes to #3 who has taken #1's position. Play on the other side of the court can be initiated by a pass to #5; only players #2, #5 and #4 are involved.

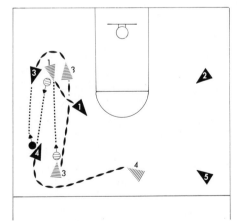

Figure 4–38.   Weave offense; side court pattern.

Figure 4–39 illustrates the use of the corners in running the weave. Player #1 passes to #3 who moves to meet #1. Player #1 cuts down the center of the court. Player #3 may return pass to #1 or pass to #2. If #1 does not receive a pass, she screens for #5 who breaks for the basket or takes #3's original position. If #5 breaks for the basket, #2 should be alert to pass to her. After passing to #2, player #3 looks for a return pass and, in case she does not receive it, she screens for #4, who breaks for the basket or takes #2's original position. Player #5 is alert to pass to #4 if she cuts to the basket.

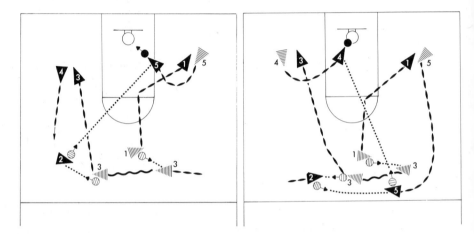

Figure 4–39. Weave offense; corner options.

Figure 4–39A. Alternate pattern.

ONE-THREE-ONE.   This offense has gained popularity for it can be used against player-to-player and zone defenses. The pattern enables the tall player to stay close to the basket in good rebounding position; spreads the defense so the offense can drive and it tends to keep defensive rebounders in poor position. The offensive spread, relying heavily on out-court screens and jumps shots, eliminates some of the effectiveness of the zone. To those who believe it is possible to screen and drive against the zone, the one-three-one presents the basic pattern.

Offense Against a Zone Defense.   The purpose of the zone is to concentrate defense players close to the basket to reduce the easy shots. Dribbling, driving around a guard and passing to teammates cutting around screens are not as effective against zone patterns. Consider the following in combating a zone defense:

1. A team should use an offensive pattern not too different from its basic offense to conserve learning time and to maintain the same tempo and style of play.

2. Effective outside shooting is the best weapon against the zone for it forces the defense to spread or switch to player-to-player.
3. Fast break as often as possible before the defense is set.
4. Quick, sharp and accurate passes are vital to combating a zone. When the zone is set the success of the offense lies in its ability to move the ball faster than the defensive players can shift. Figure 4–40 illustrates the effect. Player #1 passes to #4 who passes immediately to #2. Player #2 passes to #5 who has come across the key to a corner position. Player #2 breaks for the basket and receives a return pass from #5.

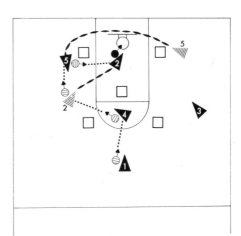

Figure 4–40.   Offense against the zone; passing more rapidly than the zone can shift.

5. Quick shots, particularly the jump shot, must be used. Most offensive systems attempt to move a player into an open spot for quick pass reception and a shot. Once inside the zone the player must get the shot away quickly. At the same time, a player must know *when* to take the quick shot and when to wait for the sure shot or for teammates to get in rebound position.
6. Offensive players away from the ball (weak side) should constantly maneuver to split the defense by moving between two defensive players. They move into open spaces to receive a pass, spread the defense and keep pressure off teammates handling the ball.
7. Overloading a zone is basically aligning players so that the offense outnumbers the defense. Attempt to get an alignment of three on two or four on three and then move the ball quickly until a player is momentarily unguarded and can get a shot. If the defense moves players into the overloaded area, an offensive player on the weak side should be open briefly. The pattern is shown in, Figure 4–41. Player #1 passes to #3 who may pass to either #2 or #5 depending on the defensive shift. The ball is moved quickly. If the ball goes to #2, player #1 circles to the weak side to receive a pass from #2. Figure 4–42 illustrates one way the play may be moved to the opposite side of the floor. Player #1 may dribble to the left or pass to player #2 who has started to move to the left.

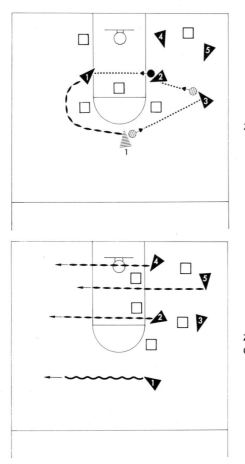

Figure 4–41.   Offense against the zone; overloading a zone.

Figure 4–42.   Offense against the zone; shifting play to opposite side of court.

Offense Against Pressure Defenses.   A team can expect to meet various styles of zone and player-to-player pressure defenses—full court, three quarter court and half court. To combat player-to-player presses the following points warrant review:

1. The greatest weapon against the full court press is to start the attack as soon as possible and not allow the defense to get organized.
2. Keep the offense spread and move passes and players toward the sidelines to keep out of congested areas.
3. Work the ball to the offensive court as quickly as possible by using short passes, screens and drives around the defense.
4. Remain calm and make certain the passes and ball handling are good.
5. Never take one's own guard to the ball as it gives the defensive players an opportunity to double team the ball handler.
6. Players must keep moving to meet the offensive passes and to prevent a defensive player from intercepting a pass.

7. Dribble only if a pass is not possible.
8. Protect the ball when it is possessed. Avoid pivoting toward a guard.

To combat a zone press:

1. Quick passes will prevent the defense from setting up correctly. The ball must get to the offensive court before the defense is set; once in the offensive court the opposing team must go to its regular zone or player-to-player pattern.
2. If the zone is set, be deliberate, for most zones do not play the ball handler closely but stay back to intercept the dribbler or the low pass.
3. A good long pass can break the press but a poor pass may lose the ball.
4. The middle of the court is the weak area in the zone suggesting that one offensive player should cut across the center line at center circle or up center of the court. This may pull the zone in to this player and leave another player open.

Special Offensive Situations.   Each team should have several rehearsed plays for bringing the ball in bounds, for jump balls and for free throw situations.

OUT-OF-BOUNDS PLAY.   During a game a team will have situations which allow them to bring the ball in bounds from both sidelines and from the endline by the opponent's goal. A standard pattern for an inexperienced team in all situations is to use two receivers who drive toward the basket as the ball handler signals and then cut back sharply toward the ball to free themselves to receive the ball. Three other "basic plays" are diagrammed below.

Figure 4–43 illustrates a pattern which is effective against player-to-player defense in a team's offensive court. Player #4 screens #2's guard; #2 pivots and drives for the basket. Player #1 passes successfully to #2.

Figure 4–43.   Out-of-bounds play.

Player #4 cuts toward #1 who has the ball out of bounds. Player #4 screens for #1 who passes to #2 who is moving toward her to receive the ball. Player #1 then cuts for the basket and a return pass from #2. (Fig. 4–44).

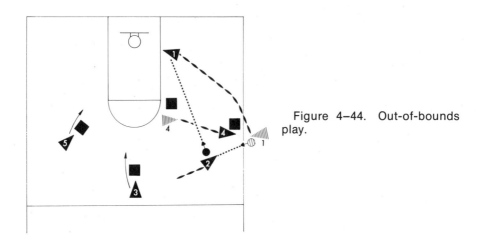

Figure 4–44. Out-of-bounds play.

Figure 4–45 is a diagram of a play suitable for sideline or end of the court inbounding. Player #1 has the ball out of bounds; #2 screens #3's opponent; #3 screens #4's opponent. Player #4 cuts for the center of the court to receive a pass. The play can be run the other way with #2 going for the pass when at the sideline or when there is room to maneuver at the baseline.

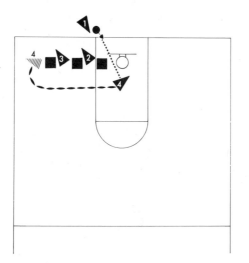

Figure 4–45. Inbounding; play for endline or sideline.

JUMP BALL SITUATIONS.   The key to control of the tip is the height of
the jump and the timing and touch in contacting the ball. In *center jump
situations* where one team has the advantage, the center may tap the ball to
an aggressive player in the offensive court who takes possession and moves
the ball quickly. Figure 4–46 illustrates a play designed for a quick basket
but one that is not dangerous if the ball is lost. Player #3 tips the ball to #4
who flip passes to #1 who has cut for the basket after being freed by a
screen from player #2. Player #2 drops back to guard the defensive basket
immediately after the screen.

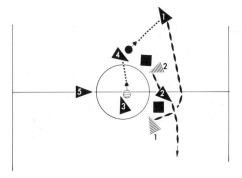

Figure 4–46. Center jump situation; play designed for quick score
when there is clear jump advantage.

If there is not a clear jump advantage, the ball may be tapped between
two players who rotate in an attempt to cut in front of a defensive player.
The direction of the rotation, clockwise or counterclockwise, should
be signaled by the jumper. Tip toward the offensive basket so more time
is available to adjust if opponents gain possession.

If it appears the tip will go to the opponents, one player goes deep to
forestall a fast break while the other defensive players rotate toward the
defensive area in an attempt to steal the tap (Fig. 4–47).

When jumping in the *offensive circle*, if control is certain, the ball is
tipped to the pivot or one of the two side players. Both side players move

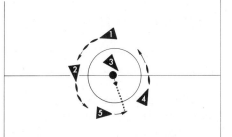

Figure 4–47. Center jump situation; rotational movement.

toward the pivot on the tap. If the pivot player receives the ball, she may have a shot or she can pass to either side player who has pulled out.

If the control of the tip is uncertain in the offensive circle, a center jump alignment can be used. If the opponents have a clear advantage, it is advisable to defense a fast break.

When jumping in the *defensive circle* it is safer to have a good defensive alignment with two players back and the others ready to move to the offensive players as the ball is tapped. If the advantage is clearly with the defensive team a diagonal (diamond) pattern may be used with four players equally spaced around the circle.

FOUL LINE PLAY. The defending players have a clear rebounding advantage because they occupy close positions in both lanes. In addition, a fast break team has a psychological advantage controlling the defensive boards, for the conservative offense pulls away to defend against the break.

The offensive team places its tallest players near the backboard. They attempt to tip the ball back for an easy score. Failing a tip-in, the rebounding player taps or passes the ball to a teammate, player #4, to begin an offensive play as illustrated (Fig. 4–48).

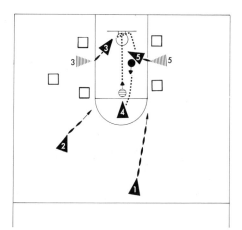

Figure 4–48. Offensive foul line play.

DEFENSIVE STRATEGY

The basic defensive systems are player-to-player and zone patterns. There are numerous combination systems.

Player-to-Player Defense. Player-to-player defense should be a basic pattern to all teams. In strict player-to-player play each defensive player is responsible for play on a single opponent. The defense closest to the player with the ball pressures the attack in hopes of forcing a bad pass, dribble or inaccurate shot. The defensive players away from the ball *sag* to intercept the ball or a loose player evading her defensive player.

Figure 4–49 diagrams an effective sagging defense. Player #1 evades her defensive player A; B, who is sagging, stops the drive of #1; A drops back in the lane to look for the offensive player freed by the switch made by B. Other defensive players are alert for passes to their offensive players, but within scoring range the player with the ball must be stopped by the closest defensive players.

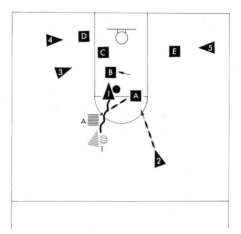

Figure 4–49.   Player-to-player sagging defense.

SWITCHING PLAYER-TO-PLAYER.   This is designed to stop the screening offense. When a defensive player is screened, the closest defensive player calls a switch if the defensive player cannot slide through the screen (between the offensive screen and her defensive teammate). The defensive player calling the switch then guards the offensive player of the screened defense. The player screened switches to the offensive player left by the switching defense.

DEFENDING AGAINST AN EFFECTIVE PIVOT PLAYER.   In a player-to-player defensive pattern, this move requires a special technique. Pivot players receiving the ball close to the free throw line or basket usually score or draw a foul. The defensive player must keep the pivot from receiving the ball by positioning herself between the pivot player and the ball so she may intercept a pass. If the pivot player has a height advantage and is given a high pass, the defensive player must time her jump carefully to avoid fouling. If the offensive player gains possession, the only hope is to block the shot if her height advantage is not too great. (See p. 51.) If the defensive player fails to maintain balance or overcommits herself and the post has the ball, the offensive player has a clear path to the goal.

PLAYER-TO-PLAYER PRESSING DEFENSE.   This pattern pits the skill of each defensive player against her opponent. Each defensive player moves to her opponent as soon as the offensive team gets the ball (loose ball, rebound, throw-in, etc.). On a throw-in the player guarding the out of bounds player overplays to one side, forcing the throw in to the other side. The offense is vulnerable on the throw-in. Players away from the ball play loosely in an attempt to cut off passing lanes or force players to the ball so they can double team the player with the ball. The defense tries to force the offense to pass to the congested middle of the court. Defensive players harass the dribbler and force her to pickup or go to the sideline for a trap.

Zone Defense. The zone defense is designed to concentrate five defensive players relatively close to the basket to limit the sure shots by the offense. The zone gives up occasional outside points. It focuses on the ball and identifies specific areas to be covered. In execution it involves player-to-player techniques with principles of zone responsibility. Effectiveness depends upon teamwork but zone patterns are easily learned by players with sound individual defensive techniques. The advantages of the zone when compared to player-to-player are:

1. It limits driving, cutting and screening patterns of the offense.
2. The number of fouls committed are usually fewer.
3. It affords good defensive rebounding positions.
4. It lends itself to initiating a fast break offense.
5. It forces the offense to rely on outside shooting by keeping the defense massed between the ball and the basket.
6. It is effective in changing the tempo of the game and is less tiring to individuals when alternated with player-to-player patterns.

Each zone pattern has particular strengths and weaknesses in rebounding position, defending the pivot player, guarding shooting areas and setting for the fast break. The selection of zone patterns depends upon defensive personnel and the opposition one expects to meet. The following examples illustrate basic formations and the zone shift in relation to ball movement.

The 2-1-2 zone defense is designed to protect against strong post offense (Fig. 4–50). As the ball moves to the corner player E near the ball assumes responsibility. Player C moves to protect against a pass to the post player or a cutting player. Player A moves toward the free throw line to prevent a pass to a high post or cutting player.

Three large players are placed under the basket and two smaller players move as chasers in the 2-3 zone defense pattern (Fig. 4–51).

In the 3-2 zone the personnel are reversed from 2-3 pattern with the strength at the top of the key (Fig. 4–52). Movement keeps players out of the dangerous shooting area.

The diamond defense, 1-3-1 zone, is popular because of its adaptability and versatility in running the fast break. It is used to stop the big pivot

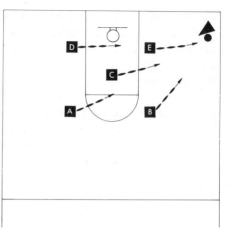

Figure 4–50. 2-1-2 zone defense.

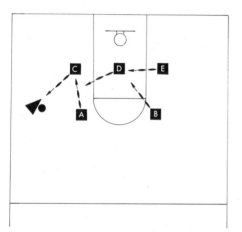

Figure 4–51. 2-3 zone defense.

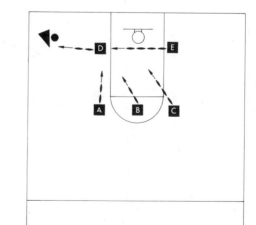

Figure 4–52. 3-2 zone defense.

player as there are three players between the ball and the basket at all times. This zone allows defensive players pursuing the player with the ball to take more chances as two players are behind to cover mistakes. The zone is weak in the corners so player E must be quick in covering corners. Player A has a major responsibility in moving play to one side of the floor by herding the offensive player with the ball. This prevents E from being out of position if she can anticipate play on one side of the floor. Player C should be the best rebounder; she must be agile, as she has a large area and distance to cover in directing the defense (Fig. 4–53).

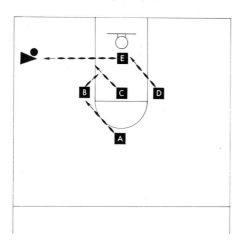

Figure 4–53. 1-3-1 (diamond) zone defense.

The 1-2-2 zone defense is called a box and one pattern (Fig. 4–54). As the ball is moved the player closest to the ball becomes the point and the other players then form a box behind her. The box reforms each time the point changes.

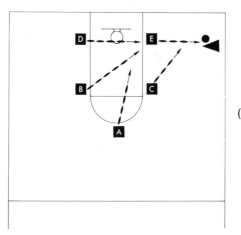

Figure 4–54. 1-2-2 zone defense (box and one).

Figure 4–55 shows the 1-2-2 variation. The point, player A, becomes a chaser, pursuing the ball wherever it goes in an attempt to rush the ball handler. The four remaining players maintain the box unit shift behind the chaser.

Figure 4–55. 1-2-2 zone defense; variation of box and a chaser.

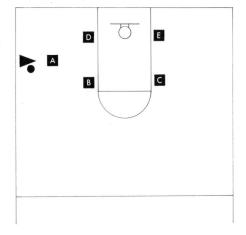

Zone Pressure Defenses.   The press is designed to defense the back court in an attempt to steal the ball or prevent a pass. The offense is allowed to bring the ball in uncontested. Executing a *1-3-1 press* the double team concept is followed with the point and wing on the side with the ball. The middle player 3 protects against the pass down the sideline with the wing and deep player overplaying the area where the pass might go. The deep player overplays on the ball side of the court as shown in Figure 4–56.

Figure 4–56. 1-3-1 zone pressure defense.

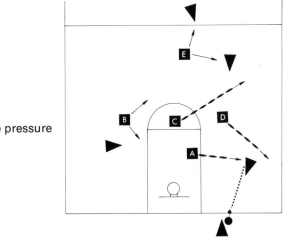

The 2-2-1 zone press allows the ball to be brought inbounds only in front of the first two defensive players. The front line defensive player on the ball side of the court forces play toward the center. The other front defensive player moves to the middle to stop a return pass to the inbounding player or to intercept passes to cutting players. The second line defensive player on the side of the court with the ball protects against a pass along the sideline. The other second line player moves to the center to intercept cross court passes. The safety player moves along the ball side of the court to protect against or to intercept the long pass (Fig. 4–57).

If the offensive team gets through the press, the defense must quickly shift to its forecourt defense pattern.

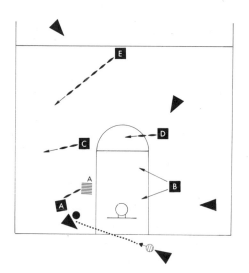

Figure 4–57. 2-2-1 zone press.

Defense Against the Fast Break. Principles of the fast break should be clearly understood from the explanation of offensive tactics. The following guides serve as a defensive summary.

1. The best defense is strong rebounding.
2. If the other team gets the rebound, harass the player with the ball to deter a clearing pass.
3. If a team spot passes, be alert to interceptions at these points. A few unsuccessful passes will force a play change.
4. If a single player is defending, she should stay in the middle of the lane and feint as offensive players approach. Eventually she must move to the ball to slow play even though she leaves an opponent open. Only the player with the ball can score.
5. With two defense players it is wise to drop back in tandem position beneath the goal. The front defensive player, A, attempts to stop the ball; the deep defense, B, moves from the middle of the lane to defend against the player receiving the pass. Player A drops to the middle of the lane to stop a cross court pass as shown in Figure 4–58.

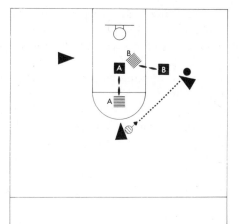

Figure 4–58. Defense against the fast break.

6. If a pass is made to the middle, player A comes out to guard and B returns to tandem position as shown in Figure 4–59. Other defensive help should be available after these exchanges.

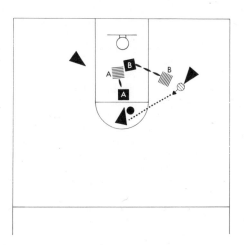

Figure 4–59. Defense against the fast break.

Coaching the Game

Pregame Warm-up.   The pregame warm-up should give players an opportunity to use individual court and free throw shooting skills they will need in the game. There is little need to rehearse strategy with a well-prepared team. A few snappy drills of lay-ups, jump shots and cutting generate player momentum and psychologically set the stage.

An astute coach observes the opponents during the warm-up period. Even with the benefit of films and scouting reports, there is need to verify how they handle the ball, who the key rebounder is, who shoots left-handed and what moves the pivot makes. The most pertinent information should be passed to the players prior to the game.

Scouting.   Scouting opponents prior to competition serves to prepare a team to compete on an equal basis. It is becoming more common in women's competitive play. A certain amount of information is valuable and should be passed along to team members; too much detailed information about the opponents can be confusing to one's own team. The coach and players must be aware that team personnel and patterns change and there is no assurance teams will look the same throughout the season.

Many coaches believe two kinds of information are needed about opponents: (1) individual player characteristics and (2) general offensive and defensive play patterns. Reports are more organized if they focus on special points and are complemented by charts. The following suggest one coach's preference:

1. Pregame
   a. Names and numbers of starters; height, physique, left-handed shooters.
   b. Shooting areas and spots.
   c. Pivot player's moves; her aggressiveness; does she use both hands?
2. Start of game
   a. Where is the ball tapped; does a play work from the jump?
   b. How does the offense start? (A team often runs patterns early in the game as players are fresh and are feeling out opponent).
   c. What kinds of shots are taken? Are there favorite spots from which certain players always shoot?
3. Offense during the game
   a. Is there a consistent pattern? Are shots a result of screens, picks, cuts?
   b. Note scoring plays.
   c. Note player characteristics. Does she screen for a shot, drive the baseline, go all the way? Do forwards play only one side of the floor? Post positions? Good rebounders? Do they follow shots?
   d. Do forwards come back on defense; do they prepare for fast break? Do they dribble before a shot? Do they set before each shot or can they move into shots?
4. Defense during the game
   a. Best defensive players.
   b. Patterns of defense.
   c. When do they set up? Do they fall back immediately?
   d. Can individual players be faked? Are they aggressive rebounders?
   e. Presses: what kind, when used, weak defenders?
5. Situations
   a. Out of bounds player line-up. Favorite play.
   b. Free throws: does player lay back? do they tip out? do they fast break?

Strategy of Play.   Once begun the game is mutually in the hands of coach and players. It is generally wise to begin with a conservative game plan, for many mistakes are made by stressed players early in the game. Players must immediately assess the offensive and defensive patterns of the opposition and begin adjustments.

The coach should control time-outs and substitutions. *Time-outs* should be called to:

1. Make changes in strategy.
2. Correct offensive and defensive mistakes.
3. Stop opponent's rallies.
4. Combat surprise strategy of opponent.
5. Allow players to rest. This time out should rarely be needed by a well-conditioned team.

Time-outs should be called sparingly against a poorly conditioned opponent.

Substitutions. Any player carried by the team should be able to help and should be given the opportunity. A few guides are helpful in making substitutions.

1. Substitute early in the game and let all players who will be needed enter during the first half. A player gets the feeling of the game and is then ready to reenter any time.
2. Tired or injured players are of limited value; do not wait too long to substitute.
3. Remove a player making repeated mistakes who is off her game or cannot get the tempo going.
4. Substitute when necessary to cope with offensive and defensive changes by opponents.
5. Substitute to maintain discipline and morale.
6. Substitute to obtain special skills of speed, more height for rebounding or a player whose guarding style can match an offensive player.

Half Time. Half time provides the opportunity to make intelligent changes in order to strengthen play. A coach's checklist to evaluate the team's status includes the following:

1. Adjustment to officiating.
2. Control of game tempo.
3. When ahead in the score:
   a. Use safe and certain shots.
   b. Stress possession and ball control.
   c. Avoid long "hope" shots.
   d. Use set scoring plays.
   e. Do not force play or take chances late in the game.
4. When behind in the score:
   a. Early in the game emphasize fast break and consider pressure defenses.
   b. Late in the game consider free lance offense; take chances; full court defensive press.

Each player is reminded of her fouls and her first half play as recorded by the game statistics. The coach makes a general evaluation of offense and defense of both teams. Players should have at least three minutes to warm up before the second half. If the game plan was successful during the first half, it is generally wise to continue the plan for the second half. If one's own team is ahead, be alert to changes in the opponent's play in the second half.

End of Game. The final minutes of the game are a true test of coaching ability. To retain a lead the team must constantly threaten and increase the advantage if possible. The team that stops its attempts to score finds it difficult to regain an aggressive edge necessary to win close games.

When a team is trailing in the closing minutes, defensive tactics that result in ball possession must be used. Take more chances, use more pressure defenses and take advantage of the team that feels comfortable with its lead. Once in possession of the ball the amount of time taken to set up a shot is determined by the amount of time remaining and the score deficit. If a team is only a point behind and one and a half minutes remain, it is wise to put pressure on the opponent by scoring at the first opportunity. If the score is tied with very little time remaining, the coach must decide whether to go for the field goal immediately or possess the ball and get a final shot. The opponent's defense may set the course of action. A defense laying back will allow possession but a pressure defense may have a lapse and the offense can work a high percentage shot. When the lead is taken, go to a pressure defense to use time in advancing the ball, but avoid being drawn into a foul.

Charting and Statistical Evaluation. Some concrete evidence is needed to help the coach assess the effectiveness of the team and each player. Mention was made earlier to the value of charting opponents and one's own team in all scrimmages and games. It is apparent that many valuable individual qualities, such as drive and the ability to withstand stress, will not be recorded in such an evaluation. The form suggested is largely self-explanatory and is charted as follows:

1. Information is gathered on both teams. Each player's name and number are recorded.
2. A player's number is marked on the court layout at the point from which she shot. A successful shot is encircled.
3. Columns are labeled so that tallies can be made for field goals (attempts and those made); free throws (attempts and those made); offensive rebounds; defensive rebounds; turnovers; stolen balls; assists and fouls.
4. Columns are added so percentages can be calculated for use at halftime.
5. A new chart is used each half.
6. Limited space is given for coach's observations and for percentages on field goals, free throws and rebounds. The game statistics are then incorporated into the team's season record.

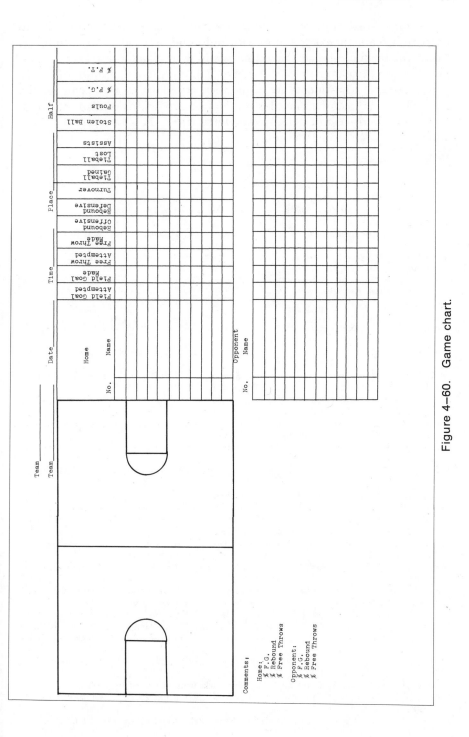

Figure 4-60.   Game chart.

A final word must be said to the beginning coach. It is unrealistic to prepare a team for competition with only one defense and one offense. Coach the team to play several offenses and several defenses. True, a team must rely on the pattern it performs best but it must make simple offensive and defensive adjustments to counteract situations as they arise in the game. These adjustments are dependent upon individual skill of the opponents, the offensive and defensive patterns the team is running, the score and the time remaining in the game.

Bibliography

Baisi, Neal: *Coaching the Zone and Man-to-Man Pressing Defenses.* Englewood Cliffs, New Jersey, Prentice-Hall, Inc., 1961.

Bee, Clair and Norton, Ken: *Basketball Fundamentals and Techniques.* New York, Ronald Press Co., 1959.

Bee, Clair and Norton, Ken: *Individual and Team Basketball Drills.* New York, Ronald Press Co., 1959.

Brown, Lyle: *Offensive and Defensive Drills for Winning Basketball.* Englewood Cliffs, New Jersey, Prentice-Hall, Inc., 1965.

Bunn, John: *The Basketball Coach: Guides to Success.* Englewood Cliffs, New Jersey, Prentice-Hall, Inc., 1961.

Cooper, John M. and Siedentop, Daryl: *The Theory and Science of Basketball.* Philadelphia, Lea and Febiger, 1969.

Cousey, Bob and Power, Frank Jr.: *Basketball Concepts and Techniques.* Rockleigh, New Jersey, Allyn and Bacon, 1970.

DGWS (Division for Girls' and Women's Sports): *Basketball Guide.* Published Annually. AAHPER, 1201 16th Street N.W., Washington, D.C.

Ebert, Frances H. and Cheatum, Billye Ann: *Basketball—Five Player.* Philadelphia, W. B. Saunders Co., 1972.

Healey, William: *High School Basketball—Coaching, Managing, Administering.* Danville, Illinois, Interstate Printers and Publishers, Inc., 1962.

Herndon, Myrtis E. and Thompson, Carol (eds.): *Selected Basketball Articles.* DGWS, AAHPER, Washington, D.C., 1971.

LaGrand, Louis: *Coach's Complete Guide to Winning Basketball.* West Nyack, New York, Parker Publishing Co., 1967.

Lindeburg, Franklin A.: *How to Play and Teach Basketball.* New York, Association Press, 1967.

McArdle, William D., Magel, John R. and Kyvallos, Lucille C.: "Aerobic capacity, heart rate and estimated energy cost during women's competitive basketball." *The Research Quarterly,* AAHPER, Vol. 42, No. 2, May 1971, pp.178–186.

McGuire, Frank: *Team Basketball: Offense and Defense.* Englewood Cliffs, New Jersey, Prentice-Hall, Inc., 1966.

Miller, Kenneth D. and Horky, Rita Jean: *Modern Basketball for Women.* Columbus, Ohio, Charles E. Merrill Publishing Co., 1970.

Mundell, Chuck: *Triple Threat Basketball.* West Nyack, New York, Parker Publishing Co., 1968.

Neal, Patsy: *Basketball Techniques for Women.* New York, Ronald Press Co., 1966.

Newell, Pete and Bennington, John: *Basketball Methods.* New York, Ronald Press Co., 1962.

Ramsey, J. D., Ayoub, M. M., Dudek, R. A. and Edgar, H. S.: "Heart rate recovery during a college basketball game." *The Research Quarterly,* Vol. 41, No. 4, December 1970, AAHPER, pp.528–535.

Rupp, Adolph: *Championship Basketball, for Player, Coach and Fan.* 2nd Ed. Englewood Cliffs, New Jersey, Prentice-Hall, Inc., 1957.

Teague, Bertha Frank: *Basketball for Girls.* New York, Ronald Press Co., 1962.

Wilkes, Glenn: *Basketball Coach's Complete Handbook.* Englewood Cliffs, New Jersey, Prentice-Hall, Inc., 1962.

Wooden, John R.: *Practical Modern Basketball.* New York, Ronald Press Co., 1966.

5

Field Hockey

Field hockey was one of the first competitive team sports for women in the United States. It is played in high schools and colleges throughout the country. Through the efforts of the United States Field Hockey Association, there is a large number of women participating in club and association play. Approximately 20 countries play international hockey and participate in exchange tours and the International Field Hockey Conference.

Individual Skills Necessary for Competitive Play

The individual possessing good basic skills in the dribble, drive, pass, dodge and tackle is ready for beginning competitive play. Specific skills in shooting, bully, roll in and a number of dodges and tackles are essential in performing the duties of different positions, but these can be developed along with play.

As in all running sports, speed and agility are extremely important assets for the competitive player. Basic knowledge of the strategy of the game and a willingness to learn and be coached are also important as well as those items of competitive drive discussed in Chapter Three.

The more advanced competitive player should show a smoothness of play, executing her skills effectively and with finesse. A variety of accurate passes, dodges and tackles combined with acceleration, change of pace, body control, footwork and effective positioning in addition to good endurance are hallmarks of the advanced player.

Selection of Players

In addition to the basic skills already mentioned, there are certain somewhat unique requirements for specific positions. The following delineation of these requirements includes particular stickwork often used in one position and physical and mental qualities:

1. Forwards
    Left Wing
       a. Receives passes from right exceptionally well.
       b. Excellent right drive and pass.
       c. Good centering hit and shot.
       d. Good speed for medium runs.
       e. Variety of centering.
    Left Inner
       a. Good dodges.
       b. Makes spaces.
       c. Good variety of shots with quick backswing.
       d. Good rush at goalkeeper.
       e. Tackles back.
       f. Aggressive—desire to score.
       g. Quick spurt.
       h. Does not crowd center.
       i. Hard to mark.
    Center Forward
       a. Excellent bully.
       b. Good long and short pass to right and left.
       c. Tackles back.
       d. Makes spaces.
       e. Exceptionally good at rushing the goalkeeper.
       f. Aggressive—desire to score.
       g. Quick spurt.
       h. Good variety of shots with quick backswing.
       i. Does not crowd inners.
       j. Hard to mark.
       k. Good dodges to both sides.
       l. Uses good judgment in letting passes go through the center position.
    Right Inner
       a. Good dodges.
       b. Makes spaces.
       c. Tackles back.
       d. Good rush at goalkeeper.
       e. Aggressive—desire to score.
       f. Quick spurt.
       g. Hard to mark.
    Right Wing
       a. Good centering hit and shot.
       b. Good speed for medium runs.
       c. Variety of centering.

2. Halfbacks
   General for all halfbacks
   a. Anticipation for interception.
   b. Stamina — perseverance.
   c. Set up shots for goal.
   d. Shoot when possible.
   e. Solid, sympathetic passes that forwards can handle.
   f. Speed.
   Left Halfback
   a. Good right drive and pass.
   b. Good circular tackle.
   c. Marks and covers equally well.
   Center Halfback
   a. Good long and short passes to both sides.
   b. In most cases, marks center forward only.
   Right Halfback
   a. Good left hand lunge.
   b. Marks and covers equally well.
3. Fullbacks
   a. Steady and reliable.
   b. Good hard clear.
   c. Marks and covers equally well, coordinated with other full-back.
   d. Tackles well timed and executed.
   e. Marks closely.
   f. Does not fool with ball but moves it quickly.
4. Goalkeeper
   a. Excellent timing, fast reaction and movement time.
   b. Agile.
   c. Quick and decisive.
   d. Good clears to both sides.
   e. Determined, steady and cool under pressure.
   f. Courageous.

Combining Individuals for Team Play

Chapter Three considers the evaluation of competitive spirit and combinations of players in a team unit. It also lists general methods for selecting individuals and squads.

Initially, the coach will want to differentiate between offense and defense players in field hockey. This in itself may prove difficult, for a player's own selection of position may not be the one in which she will be most effective as an individual or most valuable as a team member. A player may select center forward thinking that this central offensive position has greater status than other positions; yet she might prove to be a superb left wing and a mediocre center forward. The first challenge therefore is to have all players recognize the need for *all* positions on the field, no one position being more important than another. Once this is accomplished, the players themselves will have a more realistic approach to their own and the coach's selection of their positions.

The qualities listed in the section on selection of players on page 102 may be used as a guide for placement of players in general categories of attack and defense and specific positions. Within these categories, the players should then be ranked using one of the following methods:

1. Rank players according to position.
2. Rank players as offensive and defensive players without regard for position.

At this point, suitable combinations of players must be found by analyzing the game play of all possible line-ups. Each of the possible offensive and defensive combinations must play against the same opposing combinations in order to make comparisons as individuals and as units. This can be a long but fair process if there are a number of possible line-ups.

In observing the different combinations, the coach will look for the following as representing the best combinations:

Offense

1. An awareness of teammates; their abilities, capabilities and positioning.
2. Unselfish play for the best effort of the team.
3. A total aggressive, sustained scoring threat.
4. Ability to adjust to the play of others.
5. A smooth cohesive unit.

Defense

1. Good individual defensive skills with smooth effective teamwork in covering, particularly when the ball shifts from one side to the other or when a teammate is behind her opponent.
2. Quickly adjusting to offensive play, moving the ball quickly on to the attack.

Practice Sessions

Practice sessions are a very necessary part of development, team morale and game play. *Indoor practices* in field hockey are not very analogous to the game situation as a smooth floor cannot approximate a grassy field.

Practices should challenge the endurance of the players. Therefore, the intensity of practices should increase each week, beginning with frequent rest periods and change of pace drills during the first week.

As in all sports, the basic skills are the foundation of the game and cannot be overly stressed. Drills incorporating a number of skills in a challenging and gamelike manner can achieve a good foundation. Dribbling, passing and receiving the ball are most important. A team well-skilled in these three techniques has the potential for success. Many other skills are nothing more than specific control of the basic three; for example, shooting is accurate passing; dodging is controlled dribbling.

Players cannot learn everything at once. An outline of skills and concepts to be learned should be planned for the season. A few key factors for everyone to concentrate on during different practices will be more valuable than a great many items that cannot realistically be accomplished at one time. Key words to direct the team during play can be helpful such as:

"Feet toward goal" — meaning every player should have her feet pointing toward the opponent's goal whenever possible to insure best positioning. There are obvious exceptions that will occur; for example, a defense player chasing her opponent. Even then the basic concept holds, for this player should attempt to get her feet around at the earliest possible moment for most effective play.

"Tackle back" — pertaining particularly to forwards whenever they lose the ball to their opponents. This is a hard habit for forwards to acquire, but it will often destroy an attacking move of the opponents and will permit the defense to position itself for the next play.

Scrimmaging is an important part of practice sessions, but it should not become so important that it always becomes the entire practice session. The scrimmage points out strengths and weaknesses of individuals and of the entire team, provides motivation for further skill development and understanding of strategy and provides practice in the game situation.

Division of Time

Warm up: 10–15 minutes.   This is best accomplished through individual and small group work on skills typical to the game, building up to top speed. A general pattern can be established so time is not wasted.

1. Hitting and fielding the ball in twos and threes beginning at a trot and working up to top speed.
2. Quick stop and hit in twos.
3. Attack and defense combining dodging and tackling.

Skill Drills and Scrimmage: 60–80 minutes. In the beginning of the season, most of the practice time should be devoted to basic skill drills. As the season progresses, one or two skills should be selected for special attention each day. There are unlimited areas of concern in each basic skill.

Tapering Off: 10 minutes. A cooling down period is often forgotten at the end of a practice session. A light intensity activity for five to ten minutes permits a gradual letdown from vigorous physical and mental work. Warm-up activities or individual and small group work on specific areas of difficulty can help prevent muscle soreness and a psychological letdown.

Specific Conditioning. Field hockey demands a high level of endurance. The player must be able to play two 25 to 35 minute halves in top form. There are two commonly accepted methods of achieving this endurance: (1) through a formal physical conditioning program or (2) through demanding skill drills and scrimmage designed to promote the necessary conditioning. The theories behind each of these methods are described in Chapter Three. No matter which method is used, it must cause the participant to be able to play the entire game in top form.

Some specific suggestions for each method follow:

Physical Conditioning Program[1]

1. Jump over the hockey stick on ground 100 times (over and back count once)
2. Crawl stroke (bend forward from the waist) 10 counts, then stretch upward. (Repeat four times.)
3. Run 25 yards; reverse quickly, run back 25 yards, and reverse quickly. Repeat entire action 4 times.
4. Leg stretches and bounces. Squat with hands on ground. Count 1—extend right leg behind, count 2—bring right leg back and extend left.
5. Dribble 100 yards (endline to endline on a hockey field) and back.
6. Walk 25 yards on outside borders of feet.
7. A variation of toe touch exercise. At starting position: arms stretched overhead, feet 12 inches apart in side stride. Count 1—twist left and touch both hands to ground outside left heel; count 2—touch both hands in front of left toe; count 3—touch both hands inside left heel; count 4—stretch arms overhead. Repeat all to the right. Do whole exercise 5 times. Repeat entire circuit. Time each circuit and record.

Conditioning Through Skill Development Drills.   The following skill drills lend themselves to conditioning, provided there are small numbers in each group and they are performed at top speed:

1. Footwork drills.
2. Dodging and tackling drills.
3. Passing drills.
4. Shooting drills.

Drills.   There are many skill development and situational drills used in the basic instruction of field hockey that are applicable when developing

---

[1]Wright, Lilyan: "Circuit Training Program for Field Hockey." Paper distributed at New Jersey DGWS Coaching Clinic, October 1966.

a competitive team. Care must be taken, however, that these drills do not become stereotyped and monotonous for the participant who is in the intermediate and advanced stages of play. Basic drills can be modified and particular drills devised to meet the needs of the individual situation. It is extremely important that drills be challenging and meaningful to the participant and that they be executed at the speed that will be required in the actual game situation.

The following section includes: (1) some suggestions that will assist the coach in devising her drills, (2) some specific skill development drills and situational drills and (3) sources for further drills.

Skill development drills should include all the possible situations in which the skill may be used in competitive play. Three specific abilities follow as examples:

Receiving the ball—from all angles—with an opponent marking closely—with an opponent marking loosely—from a push pass—from a hard drive—with one of the following as the next move: pass, dodge, shot, dribble.

Hitting the ball—a sharp direct pass—a long through pass—a deflection pass—a long, hard shot for goal—a corner hit.

Carrying the ball—a loose dribble—a tight, controlled dribble—various dodges with one or more opponents near.

Many drills combine several skills, e.g., field-dribble—dodge-pass—receive-shoot.

SPECIFIC SKILL DEVELOPMENT DRILLS

1. *Footwork*—can be used as basic warm-up for practice sessions.
   a. 25 two foot hops back and forth over a hockey stick placed on the ground.
   b. Taking small prancing steps back and forth over hockey sticks as quickly as possible.
2. *Quick stop and hit*—a ball between every two players approximately ten yards apart. Working first from a stationary position and then moving within a ten yard circle, players hit back and forth attempting to control the ball as they hit back as quickly as possible with a *short* backswing.
3. *Drive and pass*—each player with a ball dribbles forward one at a time at top speed and drives at an object (can, pinnie, etc.). Ball must be hit before a designated line is passed; the object is moved periodically so that all possible angles are required on the player's drive.
4. *Receiving the ball and passing*—ball is hit or rolled to the player who must run to meet it, control it and immediately pass to a predetermined target. All of this must be accomplished within a five yard area. The angle of the pass to the player should change so that the ball approaches from all angles.
5. *Shooting*—inside forwards (inners and center forwards) are positioned in lines just outside the striking circle. One forward at a time moves forward to receive first a rolled ball and later a centering hit from the left or right to various spots within the circle.

If the ball is received near the edge of the circle, it is controlled first and then followed by a quick hit at a goal. If it is received closer to goal, a sweep stroke is used.

6. *Rushing the goal* — five forwards take normal positions in the circle. The ball is hit from the edge of the circle toward the goal by a sixth player. On the backswing the three inside forwards rush the goal attempting to reach the ball as it hits the goalkeeper's pads. The wings position for a clear to the side. The forwards attempt to score on the second shot.

7. *One-on-one* — starting just outside the circle, an offense player with the ball attempts to dodge her opponent and shoot at goal. This is similar to the one-on-one used in basketball or lacrosse.

8. *Two-on-one* — starting just outside the circle, two offense players, one with the ball, attempt to deceive one defense player and get a shot at goal. The defense player should be encouraged to try different strategies to confuse the offense.

GAME SITUATION DRILLS

1. *Corners* — corners can be practiced with or without defense, long or short, sending the ball to the nearest inner or center forward. The most gamelike is having a defense against the forwards. With offense halfbacks behind the attack, play can continue until a goal is scored, the ball goes over the endline, the defense clears beyond the 25 yard line or a foul occurs.

2. *Roll-in* — a roll-in can be practiced with two through seven players.
   a. Halfback and wing.
   b. Add opposing halfback.
   c. Add offensive inner.
   d. Add defensive wing.
   e. Add offensive fullback.
   f. Add defensive inner.

3. *Half field game* — this is useful when specific situations are to be repeated. It permits two groups working on the same or different items of play to be on the field at one time.

SOURCES FOR FURTHER DRILLS

DGWS Field Hockey/Lacrosse Guides
    Cadel, Marjorie: "Building a hockey team." 1958–60.
    Laurie, Kathleen: "Achieving better stickwork." 1962–64.
    Miller, Betty: "Individual and group practice drills for ball control." 1970–72.
    Poisson, Angela: "Clues for strengthening team play." 1964–66.
    West, Barbara: "Indoor practices for field hockey." 1964–66.
Selected Field Hockey/Lacrosse Articles
    Arnold, Eileen: "Stickwork games." 1955.
    Volpe, Anne. "Coaching forwards." 1955.
Books and Pamphlets
    Mackey, Helen T.: *Field Hockey, An International Team Sport.* Englewood Cliffs, N.J., Prentice-Hall, Inc., 1963.

Powell, Agneta M.: *Hockey Stickwork Games and Rotations.* Agneta M. Powell, 1960.

Taylor, Eileen: *Coaching Hockey in Schools.* Oxford, England, Marjorie Pollard Publications Ltd.

West, Barbara: *Practices for Hockey Players.* Oxford, England, Marjorie Pollard Publications Ltd.

Scrimmage. The learning situation for the actual playing of the game is the scrimmage. The coach must make it a learning experience for each player on the field. Some players may find it difficult to play at top form in practice. These players must be challenged and all players must work toward some definite objectives. The following suggestions will aid the coach in conducting the scrimmage:

1. One general objective for all players on the field (e. g., feet toward attacking goal) allows for general comments to all players on the field.
2. Further general objectives should be set for attack and defense (e.g., attack—tackle back; defense—marking to within two to three feet of opponent at all times except when covering).
3. Each individual on the field should have one or two specific objectives applicable to her. These may even be seasonal objectives.
4. Constant talking to the field at large by the coach may cause her instructions to lose effectiveness. The coach should choose her times and the key words that identify a situation.
5. Stopping play for instruction or questioning is a good technique but should not be done so often as to disrupt the flow and pattern of play or to neglect one end of the field.
6. Each player must be treated as an individual. Some players react well to constant coaching and others do not.
7. Since the attack must initiate play, there is a tendency to coach attack play first. Great care must be taken to achieve a balance of coaching, both attack and defense.

The general objectives will change from time to time in order to achieve all the aspects of play and enable team members to change their pattern of play and adjust to the different types of play they will meet in competition.

The coach should be free to work with both ends of the field during play. If the coach officiates the scrimmage, she cannot observe the total action nor speak to individuals or small groups without stopping play. A manager or assistant should be trained to officiate scrimmages.

The organization of teams for scrimmage can take varying forms. The strongest team line-up can play against the weaker team line-up or the stronger offensive line-up can play against the strongest defensive line-up (strength vs. strength). There is much merit in both forms, but each accomplishes a different purpose. Each team must have sufficient opportunity to play a team that will aid in the development of its continuity of play.

Each team also must be challenged offensively and defensively. The combination of both types of line-ups for scrimmage can accomplish both objectives. At no time should the weakest group feel that they are of secondary importance or merely pawns of the stronger line-up.

Strategy

OFFENSIVE STRATEGY

The offense or attack in field hockey begins when a team member secures possession of the ball. This player may be a fullback or the center forward, but she is the first player to begin the attack. The entire team now is offensive or attacking and should play with this thought in mind.

There are a number of ways of initiating the attack and taking the ball down the field into scoring position:

1. Hard hit into a space.
2. Diagonal pass to a moving player.
3. Combination of passes—long or short.
4. Solo run with dodging.

It is probable that a team would use all these methods during a game at one time or another depending on the position of the ball and the opposing team. It is a basic principle to *pass to a space if a player is closely marked and directly to the player if she is marked loosely.* This would then be one of the factors determining the method to be used.

The solo run or dash of a player the length of the field or even 30 to 40 yards may prove successful as a surprise maneuver but it will not be effective if used too often. It destroys the team attitude of the offense and the opposing defense will soon stop this type of play easily. The combination of through and direct passes, depending on the situation, is the most sensible form of attack with other methods used as surprise tactics.

When a team crosses its opponent's 25 yard line, it is approaching the scoring area and must not let the play break down. Too many teams, beginners through international competitors, have difficulty in maintaining a scoring threat or in scoring at all. Some feel that a part of the problem lies in the uneven, rough fields found in most areas of this country. For truly skilled, neat offensive play the ground must be smooth with short grass, but this is not totally responsible for loss of scoring power. The real problem is the lack of a truly coordinated attack within the scoring area. To have a coordinated attack, the following should occur:

1. Forwards
   a. Have feet pointed toward goal.

b. Be able to shoot on the run with a quick backswing.

c. Watch the goalkeeper and aim shots accordingly.

d. The three inside forwards rush the goal on the backswing for the shot, arriving as the ball hits the goalkeeper's pads. The inners moving toward their respective goal posts, center forward on the ball.

e. Keep repositioning and moving to cause the defense to move and thus create spaces in order to have a clear line to the ball and the goal.

f. Tackle back quickly without hesitation.

2. Halfbacks

a. Be a real part of the offense approximately five to ten yards behind the forward line, *not* 25 yards behind.

b. Feed the ball to forwards where they can handle it and get off an immediate shot.

c. Anticipate through passes by the opposing defense, intercept and feed quickly.

d. Reposition as the ball moves in order to cover the spaces adequately.

e. Shoot quickly when the opportunity presents itself.

3. Fullbacks

a. The "up" fullback should be truly up, covering the space between the center halfback and the side halfback on the side of the ball.

b. Quickly and accurately feed the ball to offense before being tackled.

Figure 5–1 shows the relative position of a team in the scoring area that is ready to sustain its attack.

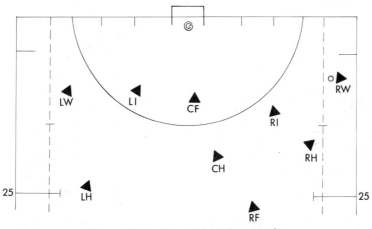

Figure 5–1. Sustaining the attack.

Team Play. Field hockey offensive strategy has suffered from the same problem that is common in other sports—the playing of a textbook strategy with little or no flexibility. Only in the past few years have the top groups in this country displayed real initiative, flexibility, creativity and effective offensive play.

One of the elements of this type of effective play is the ability of the team members to adjust to one another, the ball and their opponents no matter what the situation. The forwards should feel as though they are a unit working together rather than five players in specific positions with definite position areas never to be violated by another forward. Since possession of the ball is of paramount importance, the player with the best and quickest opportunity for possession should make the attempt. For example, if the left inner can reach a long hit ball in the right alley before anyone else on her team, she should go for it and the rest of the forwards will adjust their positioning accordingly. This type of play should be carried throughout the entire offensive strategy. Changing positions on the field is done only with purpose, however, and is not a haphazard, unorganized, unnecessary process.

This approach can also be applied to such situations as corners. On a corner, the ball should be hit sharply and firmly along the ground. Ideally, it should not bounce and should continue traveling to the edge of the circle with good speed. If the wing has not perfected this corner hit, then have the most skilled player take the hit. The forward receiving the ball on the edge of the circle, particularly in the penalty corner, should have the best stop and a quick, hard hit. Again, the forwards should position accordingly to permit the best player to receive the hit.

Corners. Perhaps the biggest fallacy in field hockey is the statement, "Every corner is a goal!" In analyzing the scoring of goals, it is found that very few are scored from the initial shot after the corner hit. There are a number of reasons why this is true:

1. The angle of the shot when the ball is hit to the inner is very small.
2. If the ball is hit to the center forward to increase the angle, the extra time it takes to arrive there permits the defense to be on the ball before the hit.
3. A poor corner hit ruins the chance for an immediate goal shot.
4. A one second hesitation on the part of the receiving forward puts the defense on the ball.
5. The defense are all gathered and concentrating on spoiling the corner attempt.

Some suggestions toward a more effective corner shot attempt are:

1. A well hit ball to the edge of the circle.
2. Receiving forward waits for the ball at the edge of the circle and does not move in unless it is a poor hit.

3. Receiver controls the ball with her left foot forward and left shoulder pointing toward the goal.
4. The control and hit are one continuous action — stop, and hit.
5. There should be a good *second* shot attempt with the other two inside forwards rushing on the control of the ball, with sticks low, toward the two goal posts. If the receiving forward shoots quickly, there is no danger of these rushing forwards being off side and they will be in excellent position to have the second shot attempt on the rebound from the goalkeeper's pads. Their constant rush will cause the goalkeeper to hurry, possibly forcing her to make a mistake.

Shooting.   Shooting is very important. Good shots are not just hard hit balls in the general vicinity of the goal cage. Shooting in field hockey, as in other sports, is a skill that must be practiced for many hours before it will be effective. First, the forward must know where the goalkeeper is, where she is going and what the strategy of goalkeeping is. Second, she must have a variety of shots at her command and know when to use them. Among these shots should be:

1. A *hard drive* from the edge of the striking circle from a stationary position, e. g., a corner. This same skill should be mastered while moving at top speed after a player has carried the ball into the circle herself.
2. A *flick stroke*, controlled and directed high into the corners from five to seven yards in front of the cage after having dodged an opponent or received a pass from a teammate.
3. A *push stroke* serves as a very quick shot when in the circle and when receiving a pass from a teammate or a deflection from the goalkeeper or a defense player.
4. A *sweep stroke* used to redirect a centering pass into the goal.
5. A *reverse stick hit* so the ball can be shot even if it is on the left side of the body. A reverse stick scoop shot will put the ball in the air.
6. A *simple deflection* of a pass toward the goal.

Whenever possible, the shooting forward should have her feet pointed toward the goal.

Formations.   There are various positions that a forward line can take when the ball is behind its defending 25 yard line. Different formations can be used by the same team in a game depending on the situation. The following are four of the most commonly used formations with suggestions for their use:

1. The "W" formation with both wings and center forward up and inners back. This is a very demanding situation for the inners who must pick up any short passes and direct them to the center forward or wings and still be up in time to shoot at the opposing goal. This formation would be used when the defense is able to get good long clears off and the inners have good speed and endurance (Fig. 5–2).

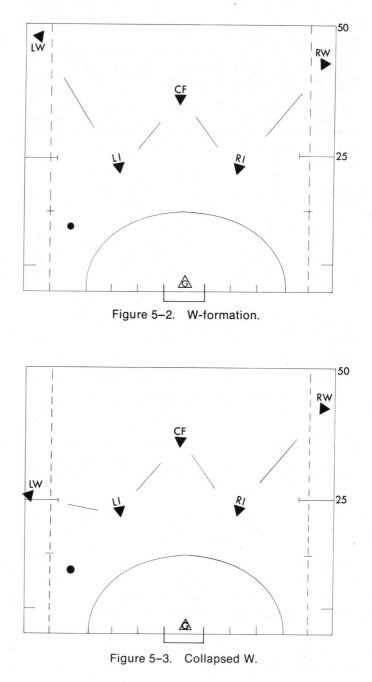

Figure 5–2.   W-formation.

Figure 5–3.   Collapsed W.

2. Collapsed "W" – same formation as the "W" except the wing on the same side as the ball drops back to help a somewhat pressed defense (Fig. 5–3).

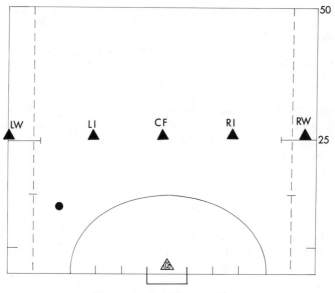

Figure 5–4.   Straight line.

3. Straight line—all five forwards are back. This defensive position sacrifices getting a jump on the opposing defense but must be used when the defense is being pressed badly and is having difficulty in clearing. It might also be used when the opposing halfbacks are shooting frequently (Fig. 5–4).

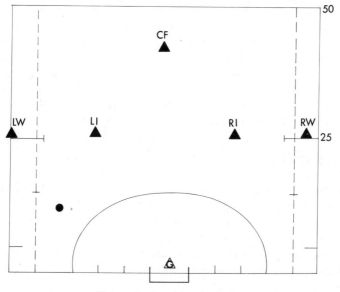

Figure 5–5.   4 back, 1 up.

4. Four back, one up—wings and inners are back and center forward only is up. This is a compromise between the "W" or squashed "W" and the straight line formation. It permits four forwards to pick up the short clears of a pressed defense and yet have one forward who can be set up for a quick dash down the field (Fig. 5–5).

Roll-in.   Positioning and strategy for a roll-in varies with the position of the ball. When the ball is deep in the defending area, it is usually wise to put the ball long down the side line. In this case, the closest inner might drop back but only as an emergency outlet. When the ball is in midfield or the attacking end of the field, more intricate patterns can be used. The wing can position for a long or short roll-in, the inner dropping back for a diagonal roll-in to the inner position or cut over for a short roll-in close to the alley. In the attacking end of the field, the fullback can move up close to the alley to receive the roll-in and direct a pass to a free forward. If the ball is over the 25 yard line, the wing may take the roll-in and the halfback becomes a possible receiver.

Free Hits.   Positioning on offensive free hits also varies according to the position of the ball. It is extremely important that free hits be taken quickly before the opposing team is set, but not before the hitter's team is ready. When the free hit is taken in the defensive end of the field, particularly on the edge of the circle or a 16 yard hit, if time is allowed for the opposing team to get set there is little advantage in the hit. If the opponents are set, it is difficult to power the ball past them. Looking in one direction and hitting in another is advantageous if the hit can be directed to a teammate. The forwards must move to create space and cause the opponents to shift. It may be dangerous to pass to another defense player if the hit is being taken deep in the defending area. When taking a free hit in the offensive end of the field, the opposing team is definitely on the defensive. A deep defense allows for more chances to connect with a pass, particularly if the forwards come back to meet the pass. The key to a successful offensive action is that the pass be one that the forwards can handle and that the forwards move positively to create spaces and get the ball.

DEFENSIVE STRATEGY

The defensive players in field hockey are called defense because they try to prohibit the opposing team from scoring, not because they play in a defensive manner. All members of the team without the ball are the defense. No matter what the situation, the defense must be planning how it can be offensive in its tactics and strategy. A team that thinks defensively will find itself consistently on the defense.

Patterns of defense play vary somewhat from country to country and team to team, depending upon the current thinking and abilities of the personnel. There are no strategic absolutes as far as the rules are concerned so teams are free to experiment and develop patterns depending upon their own strengths and weaknesses. Every situation and every opponent may call for some variation.

The following section explains some of the "whys" of positioning, tactics and strategy of the defense players in specific situations.

Center Bully.   One of the first considerations when positioning players is which fullback should be up on the center bully. The answer depends on the offensive pattern of the opposing team. Many teams will play the right fullback up since many center forwards will direct the bully to their left. If the right fullback does not come well up, however, it will give the opposing left inner time to field the ball and direct it to the relatively free opposing right inner. Other teams, feeling that the center halfback's non-stick side is unprotected, will play the left fullback up to cut off the more difficult pass to the opposing right inner. Fullbacks should watch the center forward and her pattern on the bully. If she is highly skilled, she will be able to direct the ball to either side and will usually check to see which fullback is up. In this case, it is probably best to let the center halfback cut off the pass to the left inner and play the left fullback up. Some center forwards consistently send the ball to the stronger side of her forward line and in that case the fullback on that side would play up.

Marking.   Marking refers to a defense player being close enough to prohibit her attack player from receiving the ball, and should she receive it, being able to tackle her immediately. When marking, it is essential to be on the goal side *and ball side* of the opponent. The defender's stick should be down and her feet facing her attacking goal whenever possible. She must decide: "How close must I be when marking?" Each player must judge her opponent's speed, agility and stickwork and play her accordingly. An offensive player, faster or more highly skilled than her defensive opponent, should not be allowed a five yard free area in which to work. This establishes defensive position and the defense player will find herself behind the play. The defense player must anticipate what her opponent can and will do as early as possible.

Covering.   Covering refers to covering a space rather than marking a player. Covering requires specific positioning according to the position of the ball, other defense and offense players on the same team and opposing offense players. The primary responsibilities of a covering player are to anticipate a through pass, intercept the ball and pick up a free player who has passed her defense. The common questions, "When should I take the free player?" and "Should the fullback ever take the wing?" must be answered. First, whenever a player can reach a free ball before anyone else, she should go for it and the others on her team will adjust. A team must have possession of the ball in order to eventually score. The covering player should not take the oncoming free player if the free player's defense is chasing and can catch her before she enters the circle. The covering fullback leaves an extremely vulnerable area open if she tackles too soon. Unless there is an excellent chance of obtaining the ball or the other fullback is covering, a free wing should not be tackled until she reaches the edge of the circle. Often a move in the direction of the free player will cause her to pass.

Positioning in Circle.   The positioning of the defense in its own circle should be that of marking. This is a small area and covering players would find themselves in the way of other defense, particularly the goalkeeper. Also, it is dangerous to give any attacking forward the freedom to play the ball, as occurs when the defense is covering. The following are most important when marking in the circle:

1. All defense must be able to see the ball and their opponent.
2. The defense should keep both feet facing their attacking goal.
3. The stick should be kept low as it will have to be used immediately when the occasion arises.
4. When clearing, it should not be a panic hit but one that is constructive.
5. The defense should make it difficult for their opponents to rush the goal, remembering that it is a foul to keep an opponent from the play with body contact.

Free Hits.   The team members on defense against a free hit must establish their positions quickly. When the hit is being taken in their defensive end of the field, the forwards should fall back quickly and very closely mark their opposing forwards on the ball side. This allows the defense to cover the spaces while their opponents are marked. The forwards are defending against the direct pass and the defense against the through pass. When the hit is being taken in the offensive end of the field, the forwards on defense should quickly ring the hitter, no more than five yards away, with their sticks down. The player taking the hit will find it difficult to locate a spot to put the ball through and the defense may be able to intercept any pass that does get by the ring.

Corners.   As corners and penalty corners occur rather frequently in a game, it is important that the defensive team be coordinated in its attempt to counteract this play. A forward is hoping that there will be enough time to field the ball at the edge of the circle and get a hard, well-directed shot off for goal. Even if the corner hit is well taken, it is very difficult for this to occur if the opposing defense player *sprints on the hit* to a stick-to-stick position with her opponent. Very often a deflection occurs by the forward fielding the ball which gives another forward the opportunity to score. Therefore, all forwards must be marked as soon as possible. Close marking of the forwards must continue even to the goal line as very few goals are scored on the long hits. Most are scored after the ball has deflected off the goalkeeper's pads. Defense lining up behind the goal line must make sure that their rush forward will take them slightly to the goal side of their opponent.

Roll-in. Defensing against the opponent's roll-in is a matter of positioning and anticipating the offensive moves. The side halfback must mark the wing on the goal side. The opposing wing marks the offensive wing on the ball side. It is important that the offensive wing be made to feel crowded before making her move for the roll-in. Left wings can be marked even more closely than right wings, since the right halfback has the stick side advantage over her opponent. The defensive wing should attempt to cut off any roll-in. The offensive inner should be marked primarily by the defensive inner. This defensive inner will also attempt to cut off any roll-ins to the offensive fullback.

"Unorthodox" Strategies. The following "unorthodox" defense strategies are not in common practice. They are presented to show that there are many ways to play the game, and perhaps the best solution is yet to be found.

The concept that *the up fullback should remain up* even if the ball changes sides of the field is being used more frequently when the ball is in the attacking end of the field. There are many times when the up fullback can simply shift from side to side as the ball shifts rather than having the two fullbacks changing positions. This is also useful when one fullback is definitely faster than the other and can get back more quickly. There is a point in play, as the ball moves toward the defense end of the field, when the fullbacks would change because a pass across the field would leave the up fullback out of the play.

The *rotating system of defense*, patterned after men's soccer, may seem radical to many, and it is doubtful if it has ever been tried in women's field hockey. Basically, the rotating system of defense is used only when a defense player has been passed by her opposing offensive player who has the ball or is about to receive the ball. Until this point, the players have been marking and covering as usual. Figure 5–6 shows how the defense would

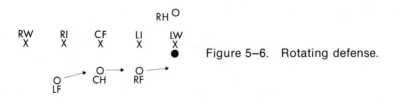

Figure 5–6.   Rotating defense.

rotate so as to tackle the free forward immediately rather than waiting until she reached the edge of the circle. It is similar to the interchange in lacrosse or a shifting zone defense in basketball.

Left wing has passed her right halfback. Right halfback attempts to reposition back into the defense as soon as possible and pick up the free player. If the ball is shifted to the weak side, the defense would shift as well. This obviously demands a great deal of coordination on the part of the defense.

Coaching the Game

Pregame Warm-up.   As indicated in Chapter Three, the greatest benefit from warming-up procedures occurs when they imitate, as closely as possible, the movements which are to be used in the game. With this in mind, players should not stand and hit the ball to each other. While this does loosen the muscles and get the eye on the ball, it does not require the timing and balance demanded at game speed. Therefore, players, whether in a prearranged manner or on their own, should warm up building up to game speed. The goalkeeper should not be neglected in this warm-up. She must familiarize herself with the goal cages and ground area within the circles. Several players should take long shots at her from the edge of the circle.

Pregame Instructions.   The pregame instructions should be positive, general statements of a motivating nature, specific reminders and encouragements. The repeating of key words used in practice (e.g., feet toward goal, tackle back) are reinforcing. A few quiet words of a reassuring nature to those who are inexperienced in competition can be a settling influence. Begin to gear their total concentration on their role in the game before it starts.

During the Game.   Once the game is underway, there is little the coach can do other than observe play very keenly, relate some observations to those players sitting out and control her desire to coach the players on the field. The captain takes charge of the team once it is on the field and will be the one to make any comments, if necessary, to anyone on the team. It is against the rules and unbecoming for the coach to shout and coach her players during play.

Half Time Procedures.   At half time, ten minutes are allotted for rest. During this time the players catch their breath and get ready for the next half. At this time substitutes, if any, enter the game, first half strengths and weaknesses are indicated and plans for the second half formulated. In most cases the substitutions are made by the coach. Depending on her level of skill and maturity, this can be done in consultation with the captain. It must be realized that the coach and players on the side line have an unobstructed view of the total game while players on the field must, of necessity, concentrate on their own aspect of play and may not see the total situation. With this in mind, and again depending upon the team's level of skill, understanding and maturity, the half time coaching can be handled in a number of ways:

1. Coach does all the talking, indicating problems and solutions.
2. Coach talks first indicating the problems, then asks for solutions from the team.
3. Coach asks the team what the problems are and what can be done to solve them.

The particular situation will determine which method is best. Number three may be the best method. This might appear to be a weak approach but it will be the most meaningful to the players. This method might not be suggested for the coach who has not established her knowledge and ability with her team. This method does presuppose good rapport between the coach and the team and within the team itself. The discussion should not become a personal attack on members of the team but a constructive discussion. There will be times when all three methods would be employed. Regardless of the method used, the coach must know her players and how they react to criticism and praise. Some players need direct, specific comments in order to improve their play. Others may become so overly concerned by direct comments and criticism that they will not be able to function effectively.

When general coaching is involved at the beginning, half time or end of the game, the entire squad should take part in the learning situation, not just those playing at the time.

End of Game Comments.   A detailed analysis of the game should be saved for the next team practice when the proper amount of time can be spent on specifics. A "well done" at the end of the game or even a "well tried" if the game has not gone well or other appropriate comments will suffice. Participants are very aware of the sincerity of comments such as these at the end of the game. There is no purpose in telling someone that she has played well if this is not the case. There is, however, always *some* positive thing that can be said about a person's play.

Charting and Statistical Evaluation of a Game.   Charting a field hockey game has not been a standard practice. Many coaches have devised their own methods and others simply write down comments as the game progresses. Some suggestions for possible charting are:

1. Number of shots taken by both teams.
2. Number of corners taken by both teams.
3. Number of times ball is lost by
   a. Poor pass.
   b. Tackle.
   c. Poor skill.

Advanced Skills for Competitive Play

Most of the following skills, with the possible exception of the reverse stick hits, are taught in the typical field hockey class. The reason for their inclusion in this section is that most beginners do not master these skills and both the player preparing for competition and the seasoned competitor must continue their learning to develop total effectiveness as players.

Bully.   In the past few years the bully has lost some of its importance, since the 16 yard hit has replaced the 25 yard line bully. However, the bully is still used by center forwards at the beginning of each half and after each goal, after the defense wins a penalty bully, in case of a double foul and in the penalty bully. The bully has been a skill that never has been practiced enough by defense players, particularly goalkeepers and fullbacks, as is usually shown when one of these players must take a penalty bully. Now the trend is to push this skill even further in the background, since its use seems limited. If this continues to occur, players will be handicapped when the situation demands that they participate in a bully. For this reason the following suggestions for the defense taking the penalty bully are offered.

The basic body position for the bully is feet six to eight inches apart, weight on the balls of the feet with the head over the ball. As both players will attempt to get their heads over the ball, some adjustment will be necessary, with the player in position first having the right to the position. The right hand should be in a strong position down the stick as far as is necessary to achieve the needed strength. The knees are bent slightly. This basic position is very important and is mentioned in most basic analyses of this skill, but it is not seen very often in actual performance.

The mechanics of the bully include:

1. Keep the blade of the stick close to the ball at all times. Do not lift the stick more than one to two inches higher than the ball to hit the opponent's stick.
2. The rate of the bully on the first two hits should be at a medium pace with a quick third hit. This change of pace is essential for winning the bully.
3. Move the feet immediately after the third hit of sticks to the best position to execute the desired bully.

The defense player is limited as to the types of bullies she can attempt with her goal just five yards away. Basically, she must counteract the intention of her opponent while attempting to clear the ball out of the circle. Toward this end she may:

1. Pull and pass left—the player must move her feet quickly as she draws the ball slightly toward her. She must avoid committing obstruction as she pushes or hits her left. Depending on the amount of time available, the clear can be an actual hit or a long push pass, the push pass being a continuation of the pull.
2. Execute a lift over or defensive bully—this bully would be used when a deadlock of two sticks on the ball occurs from an equal bully. With both players exerting pressure on the ball from opposite sides, one player can lift the ball up and over her opponent's stick. At no time would the players begin slashing at the ball in an attempt to win the bully. As a defensive measure, holding the stick on the ball no matter what the opponent does can be a good defensive procedure, but must be followed by a constructive move to clear the ball.

Drive to Right. Many players find it difficult to give a good solid hit to the right while running at top speed without slowing down and pivoting to the right. The difficulty is the same as in receiving the ball from the right—a lack of upper body twist with feet continuing in a forward line. The weak hit results from not having the body behind the ball and a lack of wrist snap.

To aid in correcting these difficulties, a slight circular movement of the stick preparatory to the hit is suggested. The player runs forward with the ball slightly ahead of her right foot, she continues running, overtaking the ball, and contacts the ball slightly behind her right foot. This is accomplished with a twist of the upper body so that the shoulders are at right angles to the hips. This twist and the necessary wrist snap on impact of the ball are accomplished by a quick clockwise circular movement of the stick and hands. The toe of the stick makes a slightly larger circle than the hands. This helps to get the shoulders around and cocks the wrists for the hit. As the player becomes more skillful, this should be accomplished as quickly as possible and with as small a circular movement as possible.

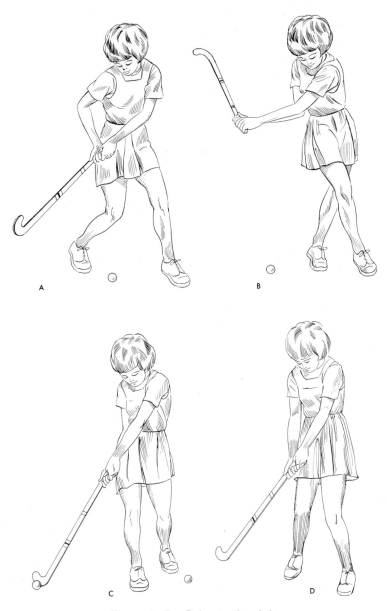

A

B

C

D

Figure 5–7.   Drive to the right.

Receiving the Ball on the Right.   Just as with the right drive, receiving the ball on the right is a difficult skill for players to master. Both skills are extremely important for those players on the left side of the field. Players who lack these skills will have difficulty in playing the left side.

As in the right drive, the upper body must be twisted to the right so that the shoulders are at right angles to the hips. How far this twist must go is dependent on the angle of the approaching ball. The toe of the stick, with a normal grip of the hands, should be pointed in line with the direction of the ball. This will help determine the extent of the twist. As the ball approaches, the player continues her run forward, gathering in the ball by her right foot, bringing it forward into dribbling position or getting it ready for a pass, dodge or shot.

Figure 5–8.   Receiving on the right.

Reverse Stick Hit.   In recent years, the increasing popularity and effectiveness of the reverse stick hit has been observed. It has always been permitted by the rules, but for many years interpretation of the rules in this country led officials to call obstruction every time the skill was used. As a result of observations of continental European teams, the reverse stick hit has now been accepted as a useful skill. The biggest dangers in its use are the chance for obstruction and the possible overuse due to lazy play and footwork. One of the main causes of obstruction with the reverse stick hit is that the ball can be played on the left side of the body when players are accustomed to avoiding committing obstruction on their right sides. The fact that the right shoulder is brought forward results in easily obstructing an opponent on the right.

Figure 5–9.   Reverse stick hit.

The reverse stick can be used for a pass, dodge or shot. The stick is either simply turned counter-clockwise with the wrists rotating in the same direction or the stick is turned within the left hand grip until the reversed blade is forward and the right hand then grasps the stick with the palm on the flat portion of the shaft. The first method of simply rotating the wrists is a quick maneuver but not a strong position. The second method may take longer and more practice, but a stronger hit or push can be executed.

From these positions, the player can hit the ball to any angle on the right, including a direct flat pass; play the ball ahead from the left side of the body or dodge a player directly in front of her. A scoop-dig type action

Figure 5–10.   Reverse stick hit.

from close to the left side produces an unusual shot for goal. In this stroke, the stick is placed directly behind the ball and the right hand pulls the stick up and forward, directing the ball toward the goal. This skill could also be used as a scoop-dodge past an opponent (Figs. 5–9 and 5–10).

Players should master the basic skills before learning reverse stick skills. Otherwise, the reverse stick can be used incorrectly causing heavy fouling and ensuing rough play.

Bibliography

Barnes, Mildred: *Field Hockey: The Coach and the Player.* Boston, Allyn and Bacon, 1969.

Barnes, Mildred J., et al.: *Sports Activities for Girls and Women.* New York, Appleton-Century-Crofts, 1966.

Delano, Anne Lee: *Field Hockey.* Dubuque, Iowa, William C. Brown Co., 1966.

DGWS: *Field Hockey/Lacrosse Guide.* Published every two years.

Crowley, Diana: "The development of forward play." 1966–68.

Hunter, Joyce: "Defense play in the circle." 1968–70,

Pepper, Eleanor: "The 1963 International Conference Matches." 1964–66.

Robertson, Grace: "What is your C.Q.?" 1966–68.

Shillingford, Jenepher P.: "The art of goalkeeping." 1968–70.

Volp, Anne: "Coaching a varsity team." 1970-72.

DGWS: *Selected Field Hockey/Lacrosse Articles.* AAHPER, 1963.

Rylands, Barbara: "Conditioning for field hockey."

———: "Has your team a sound defense?"

Shillingford, Jenepher Price: "How about trying out for goalie?"

Strebeigh, Barbara: "Roll-ins."

Taylor, Eileen: "Coaching for the advanced school player."

Volp, Anne M.: "Coaching forwards."

———: "Developing attack play in the circle."

Westervelt, Anna: "Emphasis on attack."

Lees, Josephine T. and Shellenberger, Betty: *Field Hockey.* New York, Ronald Press Co., 1957.

Mackey, Helen T.: *Field Hockey, An International Team Sport.* Englewood Cliffs, New Jersey, Prentice-Hall, Inc., 1963.

Meyer, Margaret H. and Schwartz, Marguerite M.: *Team Sports for Girls and Women.* 4th Ed., Philadelphia, W. B. Saunders Co., 1965.

Miller, Donna Mae and Ley, Katherine L.: *Individual and Team Sports for Women.* Englewood Cliffs, New Jersey, Prentice-Hall, Inc., 1955.

Mushier, Carole L.: *Team Sports for Girls and Women.* Dubuque, Iowa, William C. Brown Co., 1973.

Vannier, Maryhelen and Poindexter, Hally Beth: *Individual and Team Sports for Girls and Women.* 2nd Ed., Philadelphia, W. B. Saunders Co., 1968.

Pamphlets

Do's and Don'ts. Oxford, England, Pollard Publications Ltd.

Playing Hockey by a Team of Internationals. Oxford, England, Marjorie Pollard Publications Ltd.

Taylor, Eileen: *Coaching Hockey in Schools.* Oxford, England, Marjorie Pollard Publications Ltd.

West, Barbara: *Practices for Hockey Players.* Oxford, England, Marjorie Pollard Publications Ltd.

6

Lacrosse

Lacrosse enjoys its greatest popularity on the Eastern seaboard of the United States and in Great Britain and Ireland. As a competitive team sport it is showing continuous growth across this country every year. This growth is most obvious in the Central and North Central sections but other areas are joining in, as the number of competent teachers and coaches of lacrosse increases.

The sole organization concerned with the development of instructional and competitive programs in lacrosse is the United States Women's Lacrosse Association in cooperation with the DGWS.

Individual Skills Necessary for Competitive Play

As in any sport, a player well grounded in the basic skills of the game is a good prospect for beginning competitive play. The basic skills include the throw, catch, cradle and pick-up. These may not be polished at the beginning of the competitive season, but this is the job of the coach, and they will develop through properly conducted competitive play. Dodging, body checking, crosse checking and shooting are certainly important, but the true realization of these skills is difficult if competitive play has not been experienced.

In addition to stickwork skills, the player with potential for competitive play is the one who possesses speed and agility. In a running game such as lacrosse, speed and agility cannot be overemphasized for they are vitally important. Although not a substitute for good stickwork, they can make the difference between the average and superior player.

Competitive drive and determination are necessary in lacrosse as in all competitive sports. These aspects of play are considered in Chapter Three. A top level player should ideally be and have:[1]

1. Stickwork (catch, pass, pick-up, score)
2. Body movement
3. Speed of stick and feet
4. Quick reactions
5. Alert, get the ball, stay in the game
6. Neatness of play
7. Agility
8. Dash into open spaces
9. Passes to get there faster
10. Helpful to teammates
11. When marking and body checking, keeps opponent out
12. Tackles back

Selection of Players

Certain general qualities are necessary for all positions; these have been mentioned previously. There are, however, certain qualities particular to specific positions. The following suggestions may help in determining the better player of two being considered for a position or may be helpful when considering changing a player from one position to another. After the name of each lacrosse position, similar positions are listed as played in field hockey.

1. Homes
   First Home—(center forward in field hockey)
   a. Good tight stickwork.
   b. Particular dodging ability.
   c. Agile.
   d. Variety of shots close to goal.
   e. Quick spurt.
   f. Ability to move in very small area.
   g. Keeps front of goal clear—opens spaces for other attacks to shoot.
   h. Quick shot.
   i. Knows when to cut for pass and when her cut would congest scoring area.
   j. Ability to pass to free player when double teamed.
   k. Quick to retrieve missed shot behind goal.
   l. Ready for follow-up shot should the ball rebound off the goalkeeper's pads.
   m. Tackles goalkeeper if she comes out of the crease.

[1.] Oswald, Jane: "What Makes One an All-American Lacrosse Player?" Letter to members of USWLA Selection Committee, May 1967.

Second Home — (inner in field hockey)

a. Ability to set up play as well as score.
b. Central player on the attack.
c. Variety of shots.
d. Quick spurt.
e. Ability to distribute play.
f. Particular knowledge of defense interchange and moves accordingly.
g. Good dodging ability.

Third Home — (combination of forward and halfback in field hockey)

a. Assists in getting the ball through the middle of the field as a connecter.
b. Good variety of shots including long bounce shot.
c. Sharp, quick accurate pass.
d. Interchanges with center, attack wings or second home when necessary.
e. Distributes play.
f. Does not crowd first and second homes.
g. Ready to intercept on opposing defense clears.

2. Attack Wings — Center

Attack Wings — (wings in field hockey)

a. Ability to make fast long runs without rest.
b. Good long shot and crossover shot.
c. Varies play with the ball.
d. Acts as link between attack and defense.
e. Accurate passing to marked players.
f. Shows good judgment regarding when to pass and when to shoot.
g. Accurately receives long and short clears from goalkeeper and defense.

Center — (center halfback in field hockey)

a. Ability to run continuously.
b. Attacks as well as defends, although her primary duty is to mark opposing center.
c. Does not crowd homes.
d. Goes on attack if space is there and gets back quickly.
e. Link between attack and defense.
f. Good draw.
g. Distributes play.

3. Defense Wings — Third Man

Defense Wing — (side halfback in field hockey)

a. Ability to initiate attack as free player.
b. Speed and ability to sustain long runs — stamina.
c. Particular knowledge of her role in defense interchange and positions accordingly.
d. In general, marks attack wing in center of field.
e. Goes for the ball on the draw or is ready to drop back if it goes to opposing wing or other side.
f. Aware of interception opportunities.

Third Man — (halfback in field hockey)

a. Ability to initiate attack through center of the field.
b. Distributes play.

    c. Particular opportunities for interception.

    d. Good body checker.

    e. Tackles free player coming down center of the field.

4. Cover Point—Point—Goalkeeper

Cover Point—(fullback in field hockey)

    a. Quick, sound thinker.

    b. Good judgment.

    c. Exceptionally good at body checking.

    d. Steady, reliable, shows initiative.

    e. Often initiates defense interchange by tackling free player.

    f. Excellent marking ability.

Point—(fullback in field hockey)

    a. Exceptional marking ability.

    b. Does not block goalkeeper's view.

    c. Excellent body checker.

    d. Excellent crosse checker.

    e. Calm, sound player.

    f. Tackles player taking free shot at goal.

Goalkeeper

    a. Excellent catching ability.

    b. Excellent concentration and anticipation.

    c. Long accurate throw.

    d. Very agile.

    e. Courageous and determined.

    f. Exceptional reaction and movement time.

Combining Individuals for Team Play

As mentioned in Chapter Three, evaluating competitive spirit and the effectiveness of certain combinations of players, and assessing team attitudes are always difficult. It is one thing to select the top players, quite another to combine them effectively. General methods for selecting players and squads are also mentioned in Chapter Three.

One method of selecting the team is to pick (regardless of position) the best eleven field players, and then try to organize them into positions. This presents certain difficulties for there may be many more offense than defense, more defense than offense or possibly more than eleven good field players. The tendency therefore is to select the best player from each position. Many players, however, can play other positions equally well or better than the one they have landed in and to make matters more complicated, some positions may be overloaded with the better players. A combination of the two methods is indicated, evaluating each player in terms of the requirements for each position. This will give a number of possible line-ups. Each of the possible offensive and defensive line-ups must play against the same opposing combination in order to make fair comparisons of individuals and combinations of players. This becomes a long process if there are more than two possible line-ups.

In observing the different combinations of individuals on offense and defense, the following should represent the best combination:

Offense

1. An awareness of the positioning, capabilities and abilities of teammates.
2. Unselfish play for the best effort of the team.
3. A potential scoring threat in each position.
4. Ability to adjust to the play of others for the best team effort.

Defense

1. A cohesive unit working together.
2. Individual defensive skills good yet smooth, effective teamwork as in the defense interchange.
3. Adjusting quickly to offensive play and moving the ball to their attack.

Practice Sessions

General Conduct.   All practice sessions must be alive and meaningful to the participant. Indoor practices can contribute greatly to skill development and conditioning if the drills are of a demanding nature and require the participants to be working at top speed while performing skills.

Naturally the first practices will require more frequent rest periods during which time change of pace drills can be used which require less energy. The intensity of practices should increase each week.

In general, the basic skills should be stressed; these should be combined into more demanding situations as the season progresses. Cradling, catching, passing and picking up are most important and each player should feel entirely confident in their performance. It is amazing how much can be accomplished by players who are proficient in just these four skills. Shooting is nothing more than accurate passing. Dodging is a form of cradling combined with agility and timing.

The coach must take an active part in each practice session, drill and scrimmage. She should not take a stick and play, but the players should feel her presence in everything they do through her comments, criticisms, motivation and reinforcement of good performance.

Too many coaches try to teach and coach everything at once. It is better to have a few key points of a general nature for everyone to concentrate on in drills and scrimmage. Key words can be helpful, such as:

"Accelerate!" — meaning every player whether cutting, passing, picking up, dodging or shooting should accelerate rather than slow down while performing.

"Go to goal!" — meaning every player with the ball, whether point or

first home, should move on a line toward her goal while looking for team-mates cutting to receive the pass.

"*Adjust!*"—meaning both attack and defense players constantly adjust to the ball, opponent and goal and are prepared to anticipate the next situation.

Scrimmaging is important and should be introduced early in the outdoor practice sessions. The danger to avoid is allowing all practice sessions to become scrimmages and nothing more. The actual game situation should point out weaknesses and strengths both of a team and of its individual players and provide motivation for more intensive skill and strategy practice. Before the first match it is advisable to have full scrimmages of longer periods than the players will experience in a match, i.e., 35 minute halves.

Division of Time

1. *Warm-up*—10–15 minutes. Individual and group work on skills typical to the game, building up to top speed, is the best use of the warm-up period. A general pattern should be established so time is not wasted.
   a. General throwing and catching starting at a trot and working up to a run.
   b. Picking up in twos and threes on the move.
   c. Attack and defense players combining on dodging and body checking ending with a shot or defense clear.
2. *Skill drills and scrimmage*—60–80 minutes.

Most of the practice time should be devoted to basic skill drills during the first of the season. Later one or two skills should be selected for special work each day.

Each basic skill offers unlimited possibilities for development (e.g., passing: (1) basic fundamental of the throw; (2) passing to a moving player—coming toward passer, running parallel to passer, running diagonally toward and diagonally away from passer; (3) direct flat pass; (4) long hanging pass; (5) catch and immediate pass; (6) passing when marked and (7) passing to a marked player). Certainly these could not all be accomplished in one day but might be the emphasis for a week, two weeks or a season! Passing has been used only as an example, but it is of major importance in team play and generally the weakest element. The drills used to accomplish improvement of passing will, by necessity, involve catching, cradling, cutting, marking and picking up. So it is difficult to isolate a specific skill. This is probably good because drills which involve a combination of skills will more closely approximate the game situation.

One area most often neglected as a part of the practice session is the tapering off or cooling down period. Players who have been engaged in vigorous physical and mental work should have five to ten minutes of less intensive work in which to let down gradually. This practice will help prevent muscle soreness and mental and emotional let down. Some of the same type of activities as used in the warm-up may also be used, such as simple drills that do not require all out activity, or individual or small group work on specific weaknesses.

Specific Conditioning.   The type of endurance necessary for lacrosse is not developed by endless running at slow or even moderate speeds. Since lacrosse involves bursts of speed over 25 minute intervals, the training should approximate the game situation.

There are two commonly accepted methods of achieving this endurance: (1) through a physical conditioning program and (2) through more and more demanding skill drills designed to promote the necessary conditioning while simultaneously improving skills. No matter what method is used, it must cause the participant to be able to play two 25 minute halves at top form. Some specific suggestions for each method follow:

Physical Conditioning Program

1. Warm-up exercises — 3–5 minutes. Calisthenic exercises, jumping jacks, alternate body twists, sit-ups, running in place.
2. Endurance and muscle tone — 10–15 minutes. Wind springs, 25 yard sprints, bench stepping, skipping rope, long distance running, alternating running and jogging.

Conditioning Through Skill Drills. The following drills lend themselves easily to conditioning when conducted in small groups if performed with little rest and at top speed.

1. Footwork drills.
2. Dodging and body checking drills.
3. Picking-up drills.

Drills.   Certain generalizations can be made about using drills for the development of advanced ability and employing these in game situations. First and foremost, the drills must fit the needs of the players and the situations. The standard, common drills that are used with great success to teach beginners are not sufficient when used over and over with the intermediate and advanced player. They must be challenging and meaningful or the players will simply "go through the motions." The best person to devise drills for her situation and her players is the individual coach. Only she knows exactly what is needed at a given time for a given player or players.

The following section includes some suggestions that will assist the coach in devising her drills. Suggestions are made for selected specific skill development drills and situational drills, and sources are given where the reader can find further drills.

Skill development drills for intermediate and advanced players should include all possible situations in which the skill is used. Three specific skills of passing, dodging and body checking and shooting follow as examples:

1. *Passing*—pinpoint accuracy of all types, with and without opponents, always at top speed; high catch, low catch, catch behind on both sides while running forward.
2. *Dodging and body checking*—footwork, against different opponents, using acceleration, requiring different combinations of skills before and after dodge or body check.
3. *Shooting*—high soft shots, wrist shots, underarm shot at all levels, shot while level with goal right and left, against one or two opponents.

It is possible and helpful to combine several skills in sequence, e. g., pick up — pivot — pass — catch — dodge — shoot.

Specific skill development

1. *Footwork*—can be used for warm-up purposes and for stressing dodging and the footwork involved in body checking.
   a. Change of direction stressing quick small steps. On command, the group moves left, right, forward or back and continues until next command.
   b. Same as (a) using a stick as if body checking an opponent. Stick is held in a forward position no matter in what direction the feet are moving.
   c. Moving backward as in body checking, switching lower part of the body from a run on the right to a run on the left (see description of body checking in advanced skills section of this chapter).
2. *Passing*—(of necessity the catch will also be involved)
   a. Four even lines of players in the approximate positions of center, third home, second home and first home. All players in the center's line have balls. Working with the first person in each line, the center passes to the cutting third home, who pivots, goes to goal and passes to a cutting second home. Second home pivots and passes to cutting first home who then shoots. Players rotate from line to line.
   b. Same as (a) adding one, two, three or four defensive players.
   c. Pass to parallel cutter — (see description and uses of parallel cutting in offensive strategy section).
      Player 1, with her back to her defense (player 2) executes a pick-up or catch, pivots left or right and begins to dodge player 2. Player 3 then cuts to the same side as player 1's dodge to receive the pass (Fig. 6–1).

Figure 6–1.   Passing drill 3.

    d. Four players in a line spaced approximately 15 to 20 yards apart. Player at one end has the ball, runs forward and passes to cutting player next in line. Player pivots, accelerates and passes to next player and so on through the four players. End players should switch with middle players periodically. Further stress can be put on the pivot by permitting only the pivot to the right or left during the drill, and on the cut by specifying the type of cut as parallel, either side or double back.

    e. Player 1 with the ball and without a defense (later add a defense player) runs forward and passes to player 2 or 3, whichever is free, as they cut diagonally toward her. Player 4, as a defense player, may go either with player 2 or player 3 or hover in between for an interception. The important thing is that player 1 can spot the free player and pass to her (Fig 6–2).

Figure 6–2.   Passing drill 5.

3. *Picking up ground balls*
    a. Partners face each other ten to 15 yards apart; place a ball directly between them on the ground. At top speed, one player runs forward, picks up the ball, pivots, accelerates and replaces the ball in the middle. Her partner then repeats the pattern. After each set the players move toward each other two steps and repeat the pattern. As they move closer together, the pick-up and pivot must be executed in a smaller space. Emphasize top speed execution.
    b. Working in groups of three, two players stand side by side with the third ten yards away with a ball in her hand. The ball is rolled in any direction at any speed. On the release the other two players both attempt to pick it up.

4. *Interception Drill*—players 1 and 2 execute a pass from a stationary position. Players in lines 3 and 4 time their run to intercept the pass to the player closest to them. All lines move back after each player in lines 3 and 4 has attempted the interception in order to increase the distance of the pass and the run for interception (Fig. 6–3).

X₁
  ₃OOO

OOO₄
  X₂

Figure 6–3.   Interception drill.

COMBINATION OF SKILLS DRILLS

1. Working in groups of three, this is a fine endurance drill, similar to one used in basketball involving passing, catching, cutting and body checking.

   Player 1 passes to player 2 and then moves to body check player 2 as player 2 passes to player 3 who cuts in any direction. Player 2 now moves to body check player 3 as player 1 repositions cuts to receive the pass from player 3 (Fig. 6–4). The movement is continuous. Stress can be put on one type of cut to be used.

X_3
X_1

Figure 6–4.   Combination drill 1.

X_2

2. Passing, catching, cutting, marking, intercepting and crosse checking are involved in this drill.

   Player 1 with the ball passes to player 2 while cutting away from the defense, player 3. Player 3 either attempts an interception or is in position to crosse check player 2's stick the moment the ball enters (Fig. 6–5). (See defense strategy section in this chapter for description of the options of the defending player.)

X_1

Figure 6–5.   Combination drill 2.

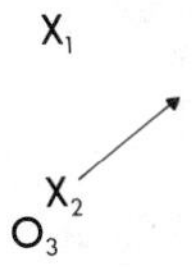

X_2
O_3

3. Picking up or catching, dodging, body checking, shooting with possibility of crosse checking and double teaming are involved in this drill. It is similar to the one-on-one drill in basketball.

   Attack players are arranged in a semi-circle around the front of the goal approximately 20 to 25 yards from the goal line. Each attack player has a defense player facing her about five yards away. Each couple takes a turn with the attack player first picking up the ball or catching a self-toss and going to goal. The defense player attempts to body check and crosse check, preventing the shot. The attack player attempts to get off a good shot whether or not she is still being body checked. After each couple has had a turn, the attacks move one space to the right to have a different angle on the goal and a new defense player. After a full round rotate the defense players so they are defending on a different angle. To make this drill even more challenging, station two extra defense, one on each side of the goal, to double team the attack player no matter which side she takes or to be a second defense if the attack eludes the first defense. The attack must get her shot off before she is double teamed.

4. Passing, catching, cutting, marking and defense interchange are involved in the following drill.

Worked in groups of three. Player 1 is a free attack player going to goal. Player 2, also an attack, pulls to one side or the other to draw her defense away and make the interchange difficult. Player 3, the defense, must go with player 2, and then time her tackle, coming off on to player 1. As player 3 commits herself to player 1, player 2 then cuts toward goal and receives the pass from player 1. This approximates the game situation quite accurately and provides practice in timing the defense interchange and the pass to the resulting free player.

GAME SITUATION DRILLS

1. *Half Field*—set up specific situations for the attack or defense as follows:
   a. Attack must pass in the following order
      1. LAW—3H—LAW—1H—shoot
      2. RAW—3H—1H—RAW—shoot
      3. C—2H—3H—shoot
      (there are infinite variations)
   b. Defense clear in the following order
      1. G—CP—LDW
      2. P—RDW
      3. P—3M—LDW
   c. Free attack player with the ball going to goal forcing the defense interchange. Use different attack position as free player. Stress that attack player closest to the free attack should not cut into her path but should pull away, making the interchange difficult. This closest player can make a parallel cut or double back toward the goal, but she should be ready to be the next free player if her defense player tackles the free attack. Other attacks should keep moving to keep the defense moving, being ready for a possible pass. The defense must mark closely until the interchange must occur. The free attack must accelerate toward goal.
2. *Full Field*
   a. Place just one team on the field starting with the ball in the goal or in the possession of a defense player and work the ball down the field.
   b. Two teams on the field as in a normal scrimmage. The players are to pass every time they hear the whistle. This drill keeps the attacks moving and looking for spaces. Do not continue too long or use too often as players must learn to think and react for themselves.

SELECTED SOURCES FOR FURTHER DRILLS

DGWS Field Hockey/Lacrosse Guides. AAHPER (years indicated after title)

Barrett, Kate: "Progression: key to development of motivating
    practices." 1964–66.
Dendy, Elizabeth: "Lacrosse stickwork practices." 1958–60.
Fetter, Mary: "Drill variations for basic skills." 1962–64.
Oswald, Jane: "How to develop a lacrosse team." 1962–64.
Russell, Enid: "Borrowing secrets from a U. S. player." 1970–72.

Scrimmage.   Scrimmage plays a most important role in pointing out individual and team weaknesses in skills and strategy and provides a learning
situation for play. Obviously one of the best ways to learn to play the game
is to play the game. This learning does not occur by simply "putting in
time" on the field in a specific position. It is the coach's responsibility to
make the scrimmage a learning experience. Some suggestions toward this
end are:

1. Have one general objective for all players on the field to concen-
    trate on (e.g., acceleration). Players will need reminders to ac-
    complish this.
2. Have further general objectives for attack and defense (e. g., at-
    tack—short, quick passes; defense—marking to within one or
    two feet of opponent at all times except during interchange).
3. Comments on these general objectives can then be made to the
    entire field.
4. One or two specific objectives for each individual should be de-
    veloped daily, weekly or for the entire season.
5. There is a great temptation for the coach to talk too much. If too
    many directions and comments are given they lose their impor-
    tance. Use concise words and short phrases that identify the sit-
    uation.
6. It is often necessary to stop play in order to review a situation or
    provide instruction. Care must be taken not to disrupt the flow
    and pattern of play too often or to concentrate attention only on
    one end of the field or on certain players.
7. Some players thrive on constant individual coaching, others do
    not and may feel bogged down by it. Know your players!
8. The tendency is to coach attack play to the exclusion of the
    defense. This is understandable since the attack most often must
    initiate the play the defense is to defend or interrupt. The good
    coach achieves a balance between attack and defense and is able
    to analyze both while play is going on.

The practice scrimmage must not be limited to one particular style of
play. For example, the attack must be able to play against a tight or loose
marking defense, even a zone. They must be able to cope with a situation
where their most aggressive and highly skilled player meets her match in
her opponent. The pattern of attack play must change in these different situations, and it will be far easier if the players have experienced them
before, and have been coached in how to cope with them. Defense players
must have played against: (1) an opposing team where the strength on attack is situated in the attack wings with one or both constantly initiating the

attack or eluding their defense player; (2) the strength and initiation coming from the center, the third home or the second home; (3) a free opposing defense player constantly initiating the attack as a free player; (4) an opposing attack, that as a whole, is faster and more skillful than the defense.

In most cases it is suggested that the coach not attempt to officiate the scrimmage as well as coach. If a manager or other appropriate person trained for this purpose officiates the scrimmage, it leaves the coach free to observe the play and speak to individuals or small groups without stopping play on the entire field.

In a squad situation decisions must be made as to what amount of scrimmage time will be spent with the top offensive group playing against the top defensive group (strength against strength) and how much time will be spent with each group, top and lower, playing as a team against each other. Much can be said about both types of practice. Playing strength against strength is the most challenging practice for the top group and therefore must be done. There is also the necessity of playing as a team for continuity of play, so this also must be done. The strength of the lower group will be a determiner as well for, if this group is close to the ability of the top group, there is not as much concern about playing strength against strength. In most cases a combination of these two types of line-ups for each of the groups is best, provided the lower group is also challenged and does not feel that they are of secondary importance.

Strategy

OFFENSIVE STRATEGY

Basic Beginning Pattern of Offense.   The usual basic pattern of offense is included here since it is a good general guide to use when players are just beginning their playing experience and because it is typical of what players have been exposed to if they have had some previous experience.

Beginners customarily are coached to believe that attack wings move like field hockey wings, remaining in the alleys except when going to shoot for a goal. This tends to keep them out of the middle of the field where they cannot crowd the homes. Centers defend against the opposing center, connecting play between the attack and the defense, seldom, if ever, coming into the territory of the homes. The homes move more horizontally than the other attacks, with first and third homes pulling to one side, and second home to the opposite side. In this way it is usually the third home who makes the decision as to which side the individual homes will move. As the ball progresses down the field, the third home either cuts toward the ball or pulls away, allowing the second home to cut toward the ball.

This system of attack can become very stereotyped, easy to defend against and *can leave wide gaps between players* because of the lack of options and difficulty in filling vacated spaces. It does keep individual players out of the way of the others when their competitive knowledge and experience is limited.

Figures 6–6 and 6–7 show two examples of the basic type of attack play:

Third home cuts toward player with the ball. First home pulls to same side as third, while second home pulls to opposite side (Fig. 6–6).

Figure 6–6. Basic attack play.

Third home, even with the player with the ball, has pulled away and second home cuts to receive the pass (Fig. 6–7).

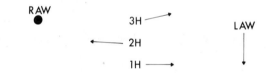

Figure 6–7. Basic attack play.

Competitive Patterns of Attack. The strategy of having all players maintain their own relative positions is a good way to give beginners a basic pattern but it is not totally adequate for competitive play. As a team practices and is coached together, players must begin to adjust and adapt to the moves of the other attacks in relation to the ball without concern for the territorial boundaries of specific positions. As players cut and pull away, they are replaced so that possible gaps in attack do not result. The following diagrams (Figs. 6–8 and 6–9) show this flexible attack play in action. It

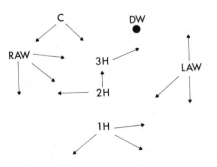

Figure 6–8. Competitive patterns of attack.

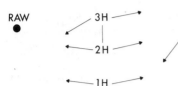

Figure 6–9. Competitive patterns of attack.

should be noted that some of the possible cuts of players will be the same as in the beginning attack pattern but with more options possible.

Developing Attack Play.   Good attack play is difficult to develop because there are very few definite moves or cuts that are all right or all wrong. Lacrosse attack play must be creative yet effective, orthodox (expected, anticipated) yet unorthodox (the unexpected, a change of pace or style) and at all times have one aim in mind—to score a goal.

An attack player must be able to get the jump on her close marking defense player in order to be free to receive a pass. There are a number of ways that this can be accomplished:

1. Short, deceptive movements with body and stick before the actual cut—similar to the fake in basketball.
2. Begin a full cut in one direction and cut sharply in another direction.
3. Hold fast until the last moment and then dash in the desired direction.

It is important to remember that a defense player cannot mark an offense player on all four sides at once, so there must be freedom to move in some direction.

CUTTING.   The type of cut to make depends on each individual situation. Several types of cuts and their uses are:

1. *Connecting*—the player making this type of cut is referred to as a "connecter." A connecter is any player cutting away from her goal to receive a pass. This is particularly useful in moving the ball down the field. Centers, third homes and attack wings will make many connecting cuts and all players will make them at one time or another when the situation demands that they move toward the ball and away from goal. There are many possible angles that a connecter may take in her path away from goal.
2. *Cutting Toward Goal*—the player making this type of cut is referred to as a "cutter." In this case the cut is made so the player receives the ball to shoot on the way to goal. It may or may not be a cut toward the ball. This type of cut would be the usual for a free player without the ball who wishes to receive a pass, or for one or more players when the ball is held behind their goal.
3. *Double back or drop back*—in this case the player cutting usually

fakes a connecting cut drawing her defense player up and then turns and cuts back, usually away from the ball, to receive a pass over the head of her defender. The player cutting must be careful on her double back cut not to be moving on a direct straight line with the potential passer as this makes for a very difficult pass and catch. The pass must be extremely accurate to get over the defender's stick and yet be manageable enough for the attack to catch. This is not a cut to be used by beginners, as it encourages their natural tendency to cut away from the passer. This cut is often used by the second home as her cover point tackles a free player.

4. *Parallel*—this cut implies that the player cutting is moving on a parallel line with the passer. It also means that she cuts toward the side of her teammate's body to which the stick has been pulled in anticipation of the pass. This is particularly useful when the passer is being body checked and has pulled to one side. The player should then cut to that side to avoid forcing the passer to pass through her opponent.

Some hints for cutting:

1. The player with the ball should immediately go to goal. If she has received the ball on a connecting cut, she should immediately pivot and accelerate to goal. This pivot and acceleration should be the signal for others to cut, as the player with the ball can now see the players and determine her pass. It is senseless to cut when the player with the ball has her back to the cutting players.
2. Keep the path open directly in front of a free player with the ball. If a player cuts into this space she brings a defense player with her who can easily tackle the free player.
3. Cut at top speed, do not drift into a space.
4. Keep moving, making spaces or cutting.
5. The cutting player should indicate with the stick that the ball should be passed to her on the side away from her defense player.
6. There should be at least two options for each passer, preferably three. If only one person cuts to receive the ball, this leaves little doubt as to the direction the ball will go and, furthermore, the cutting player may find herself closely marked.
7. A flat cut, one in which the cutting player cuts at a 90 degree angle to the player with the ball, is dangerous and should be discouraged unless the cutting player is well ahead of her defense. It permits an easy interception by the closely marking defense player.

POSITIONING DURING ATTACK.   The ability of attack players to adjust to one another is the most important single factor in offensive strategy. This means that the players must not only be aware of the ball and their opponent, but their teammates and their teammates' opponents as well. Two attack players should not arrive at the same place at the same time. Nor should a position area be left vacant because that player has made a cut somewhere else. If an attack wing makes a cut into the center of the field, her position area should be filled by another player. This might be the center, third home, second home, first home or even the other attack wing depending on what has happened in the preceding moves, the position of the player and the ball. Players are not encouraged to have one attack wing dash to the other side of the field to fill the position of the other attack wing, but it is possible that this might be correct in certain situations.

At this point, it may seem that no suggestions have been made as to specific cuts by specific players at specific times. Lacrosse, by its very nature, presents this interesting challenge to players and coach because of its unstructured form of attack play.

DEFENSIVE STRATEGY

The basic defense strategy in lacrosse is a player-to-player defense. Marking on defense implies being within one to two feet of the opposing attack player. If each defense could maintain this position, then the game would scarcely be as exciting as it is, and attacks would always be forced to pass to a marked player. In no game is the defense completely successful in marking every player all the time. With this in mind, the advantages of the player-to-player defense over other possible systems are:

1. Constant close pressure on all attacks at all times. The opponent, no matter how skilled, is a human being and will make mistakes.
2. A definite pattern of defense so that covering for each other in an interchange is more smoothly and effectively accomplished.
3. A positive form of play. The defense is always ready and in a position to intercept and gain possession of the ball.

Other systems of defense may appear to have certain merits, but the disadvantages are greater than the advantages. These other defenses include:

1. Loose player-to-player or defense sloughing off to a position of ringing the goal.
   Reason it occurs—inexperience on the part of the defense and lack of positive coaching. A defensive style of play used when opponents are superior in speed and/or skill.
   Disadvantages—permits attack to play with the ball outside the reach of the defense; dangerous shooting may result since defense are ringing the goal. This method of defense can hold the score down but encourages rough play near goal.
2. Zone—similar to shifting zone in basketball.
   Reason it occurs—defense is outclassed in general or specifically in speed. Attempts to hold down scoring by attacks but permits their free play with the ball.
   Disadvantages—completely defensive play, attack players are

relatively free with no individual pressure. Difficult for this defense to initiate the attack.

Marking. Once the player-to-player defense is established, individual defensive skills must be considered. Marking implies being only one to two feet from the opponent. The best marking position will depend upon the position of the attack player, the ball and the goal. In general, the defense player should be in such a position that she can attempt to intercept any pass given to her opponent. If this is not possible due to the speed or agility of her opponent or the accuracy of the pass, then the defense player should be in a position to be able to stick check her opponent at the moment the ball enters her crosse. Attack players find this most disconcerting. If interception or stick checking is not possible, then the defense player must be in position to body check her opponent. This requires being between her opponent and her goal. Good body checking is difficult and there are a number of theories concerning its execution. For this reason, body checking is covered as an advanced skill in this chapter.

As soon as a defense player gets possession of the ball, she becomes the first attack on the team, even if she is the goalkeeper. Her role now becomes that of moving the ball quickly down the field and into her attacking area. This is usually best accomplished by a series of passes rather than by long runs. The ball travels faster in the air than in the stick. When the defense gains possession of the ball, each defense player becomes an attack and makes appropriate cuts to receive the ball. If the ball is close to goal these cuts should angle away from goal to prevent a disaster in the event that the attack intercepts. At times, defense wings or the third man can effectively initiate the attack by carrying the ball into the attack and drawing an opposing defense player to tackle her, thus leaving a free attack. While this is effective, it can be overused, and will lose its value if a teammate does not cover for this defense player and the ball is intercepted by the opponents. The player responsible for this covering would be an attack wing or center not involved in the attacking play.

Defense Interchange. The defense interchange occurs when an attack player has passed her opponent and is approaching the goal unmarked and free. The cover point, as the pivot of the defense, is the usual player to take this free attack player. As the cover point tackles, the defense wing on the opposite side of the field from the free attack moves into position to be able to intercept a pass to the second home or body check second home should she receive the ball. It is very important that each defense player mark closely until the last moment, and then move definitely, so that all players can time their moves at the right moment. The free defense must get back into the defense as soon as possible, taking on the free attack player resulting from the interchange. The interchanged defense should remain with these attack players until the particular attacking move is over, either by a goal scored or a defense clear executed.

The following diagrams show examples of the defense interchange.

Left attack wing has passed her opponent (RDW) and is moving to goal unmarked and free. Cover point is moving to tackle LAW while LDW moves to mark 2H (Fig. 6–10).

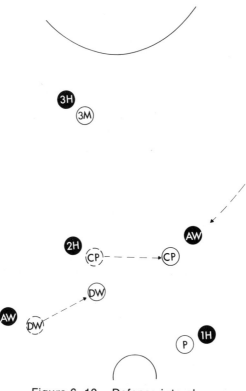

Figure 6–10. Defense interchange.

Center has passed her opponent and is moving to goal unmarked and free. Rather than waiting until cover point can tackle, third man, if she is in position to do so, will leave third home at the last moment and tackle the free center. The defense wing closest to third home will mark third home (Fig. 6–11).

Point, at the last possible moment, will move to check an otherwise free shot by an unmarked player, in this case second home. First home is marked by the defense wing on the same side as first home (Fig. 6–12).

The defense must be careful not to anticipate the defense interchange by marking loosely and thereby leaving a number of attack players relatively free. The defense should anticipate that a good attack will use the

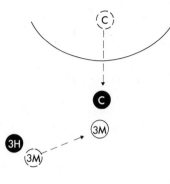

Figure 6–11.   Defense interchange.

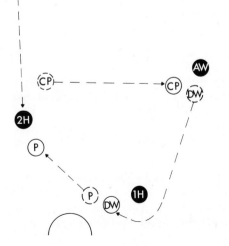

Figure 6–12.   Defense interchange.

free attack and once an interchange is forced, the resulting free player must be covered quickly. Until the "lost" defense regains an opponent, the attack will have one free attack player and an excellent chance to score. The strategy of the interchange is to slow down the attacking move and force as many passes as possible. The more passes the attack must make, the more chances for interception, for bad passes, for dropped balls and more time for defense recovery.

Defense players should be impressed with the fact that crosse checking must be done firmly. This does not mean dangerous or rough checking, but firm, well-controlled crosse checking. The skilled attack player will not be disturbed by a light crosse check. In some cases a check from under the stick (the so-called "up check") is the only way to dislodge the ball from a skilled player's stick.

Defense players observing an attack player close to goal who tends to hold the ball while working for a good shot rather than shooting quickly or passing, should make every effort to double team this player.

In general, the defense player should have one major thought in mind before she steps onto the field, "My opponent will not touch the ball during the game."

Coaching the Game

Pregame Warm-up.   Probably the greatest benefit from warming-up procedures results when the procedures closely simulate the game itself. The captain should be in charge of this warming-up period. It can be organized to follow the procedure used before practices, or individuals can be allowed to warm up at their own pace by themselves or in small groups. It is very important that the goalkeeper also warm up, familiarizing herself with the goal cage, footing in the crease and the surrounding ground from which balls may bounce on shots. Several players should assist in her warm-up by shooting long bounce shots and then working in until they are taking short shots close to goal.

Pregame Instructions.   It must be remembered in coaching a game like lacrosse that it is somewhat like conducting a choral group. The intense practice goes on before the performance, not during, although the performance in and of itself will be a learning experience. In a game where players go on the field for a 25 minute half with no time-outs and no substitutions, the coach has little immediate control.

Key words used in practice ("accelerate," "go to goal," "mark closely") are useful as general statements before the match. Reminders to individuals and the team as a whole as to specific objectives for the game will help to stimulate the necessary concentration. Care should be taken to settle down those players inexperienced in competition.

During the Game.   Once the team is on the field, the captain is in charge of field play. The rules do not permit substitution (except at half time in schools and colleges) and so the coach cannot communicate with players on the field. The coach should keenly analyze the play of both teams. Comments can be shared with those players not on the field to increase their awareness and readiness. At no time should the coach shout and coach during play.

Half Time Procedures.   The main purpose of the ten minutes between halves is rest. The players should be permitted to catch their breath before any coaching comments are made. If possible, the entire squad should be involved in the half time comments, although they all should not participate in the discussion. The coaching comments can be handled in a number of different ways depending on the level of skill, the maturity of the players and the game situation. The coach can do all of the talking, telling the players what the problems are and how they can be solved. This is a very disciplined approach and does not allow for any contributions from the players. In a second method the coach indicates the problems and weaknesses and then asks the team for solutions. This method does permit student participation but the coach has structured the situation. In a third method the coach permits the players to develop both the problems and the solutions to the problems. The discussion must be guided and directed carefully. Different situations and participants will demand different methods and there are times when all three will be used. The ten minute half time does not permit a full exploration of matters; therefore, expediency may be the major concern, leaving the more democratic approaches for the next practice session when more time is available. In any case, the coach must know her players. Some will respond well to direct comments and others may become overly concerned with constructive criticism. Each player is an individual and must be treated as such.

End of Game Comments.   The end of the game does not permit any lengthy discussion or analysis. It is not the time to dwell on past mistakes. Players are very sensitive to the sincerity of statements made at this time. There is always some positive comment that can be made about the play. It is just as upsetting to a player to be told that she has played well when the reverse is true as it is to be degraded in an emotional moment. A simple "well done" or "well tried" can be most meaningful when players know it is sincere.

Charting and Statistical Evaluation of a Game.   Charting a lacrosse game has been primarily limited to comments written as play continues or to some coach's own method of recapturing play. (Figure 6–13 illustrates one example of how a lacrosse game can be charted and statistical evaluation made.)

TEAM	TEAM
SHOOTING: Percentage First Half ____ Second Half ____	SHOOTING: Percentage First Half ____ Second Half ____
1H	1H
2H	2H
3H	3H
LA	LA
RA	RA
C	C
LD	LD
RD	RD
3M	3M
CP	CP
P	P

1, shot taken; (1), shot made; –, shot wide of goal | 1, shot taken; (1), shot made; –, shot wide of goal

POSSESSION OF BALL BY:

First Half	Second Half
_____ Interception _____	
_____ Bad Pass _____	
_____ Check _____	
_____ Poor Skill _____	

POSSESSION OF BALL BY:

First Half	Second Half
_____ Interception _____	
_____ Bad Pass _____	
_____ Check _____	
_____ Poor Skill _____	

COMMENTS:

Figure 6–13. Charting a lacrosse match.

Care should be taken to differentiate between a shot taken that would have entered the goal except for a save by the goalkeeper and a shot that simply missed the goal. The same is true in differentiating between a clean interception and one caused by a poor pass. Poor skill would refer to a player dropping the ball and the other team retrieving it and gaining possession.

Advanced Skills for Competitive Play

Several aspects of play have been chosen for further discussion. These skills may or may not have been taught in a beginning class, but they are necessary for competitive play. In some cases new approaches or modifications of the skills are presented. This section does not diminish the importance of the basic skills but aims to contribute to the competitive player and team.

Goalkeeping.   Goalkeeping and goalkeepers have been neglected for many years by teams and coaches. How many teachers and coaches teach goalkeeping or have studied it to the necessary degree? Good goalkeepers do not just happen, they evolve as players like anyone else, through hard work and coaching.

The first step is the selection of the goalkeeper. She should be agile, have quick reactions and excellent catching skills, be able to make a good long clear, have courage and the desire to be a goalkeeper. This is not an easy person to find!

Include goalkeepers in stickwork drills, sometimes in their pads so they become accustomed to moving in the equipment. Make sure the equipment protects the player well and is comfortable. Special practice for the goalkeeper will be necessary—not just standing in the goal while attack players practice *their* shooting. Most squads, particularly those of varsity and junior varsity teams, have more than one goalkeeper. The two or more goalkeepers can work together on their specific skills. The following are specific goalkeeping practices:

1. Hand thrown ball at different speeds from all angles.
2. Using two or more balls—hand thrown as in #1 allowing only enough time for one save before the next ball arrives.
3. Long bounce shots from all angles—progress from one person shooting to two in rather quick succession.
4. Close shots from all angles.
5. Crossover shots, underarm and overarm—goalkeeper coming out on the stick of the shooter about to execute an underarm.
6. Clearing the ball accurately, as far as possible, to a cutting player.
7. Picking up the ball quickly and passing at top speed with all equipment on.
8. Smothering a ball that has rebounded from the pads and keeping it within the crease.

Figures 6–14 to 6–20 illustrate approximate positions the goalkeeper would assume when the player with the ball is at the apex of the triangle in each figure. Note that the goalkeeper moves on an imaginary half circle from goal post to goal post. As she moves, she must take quick small steps.

Figure 6–14.   Very small angle. Likely to be a high or low corner shot. Vulnerable on non-stick side which makes it more difficult. From Burke, Karen: "Goal Keeping." DGWS Field Hockey/Lacrosse Guide, AAHPER, 1966–68, p. 93, 94, 95. (Used with permission of AAHPER.)

Figure 6–15.   Must be ready to move in either direction. Hard bouncy shot is very effective at this angle. Apt to aim for high or waist-high left side, as it is very hard to get the stick there and the left catch is usually a weak spot. (From Burke, Karen: "Goal Keeping.")

Figure 6–16.   Could be a difficult shot. Could go to either side, high or low. Consider who is shooting, how she is marked, and be ready to move either way at any height. If out far enough, look for a bouncing shot. (From Burke, Karen: "Goal Keeping.")

Figure 6–17.   Could be a hard shot to stop. Must try to outsmart the attack. Be on toes, alert, and ready to move into the ball. Keep eye on the ball, it may be any type of shot or an attack may come in close for a soft, high shot or shovel. (From Burke, Karen: "Goal Keeping.")

Figure 6–18.   Similar to No. 2 except vulnerable side is now the stick side, a little easier to handle. On both these angles be careful not to overpull (i.e., cover too close to the goalpost) as this leaves too big a space to shoot into. (From Burke, Karen: "Goal Keeping.")

Figure 6–19.   Just a little away from the post: most vulnerable side is stickside, high or low. Be sure not to pull too far over to the post; it gives too much room. (From Burke, Karen: "Goal Keeping.")

Figure 6–20.   It is fairly safe to cover to the post. Only place left to shoot is stick side, high or low. If close enough, it will often be high and soft. Don't give room between you and the post. Don't overpull beyond post, as it makes the shot possible at a larger angle. (From Burke, Karen: "Goal Keeping.")

One question that must be considered is, "Should a goalkeeper come out of the crease? And if so, when?" When a goalkeeper has achieved confidence in her position, she should be ready to field any ball that she can get to before an opponent does, within a ten yard radius of the crease, provided a teammate cannot get to it more easily. This is positive aggressive play to gain possession of the ball, which is the key to winning the game. Once the decision has been made to come out of the crease, it should be done without hesitation. Hesitating may give the opponents a few extra seconds that may put them in possession of the ball. The goalkeeper is also in an excellent position to intercept a long pass to an attack player in front of the goal. The attack player cannot see the goalkeeper and this places her at a disadvantage. This move on the goalkeeper's part takes confidence and good timing in order to arrive when the ball does.

Once the goalkeeper is out of the crease, her defense must move quickly to receive her pass. If she is being checked by an opponent, she will want to give a short pass. If the goalkeeper fails in her attempt to get the ball, the defense should mark closely rather than attempt to cover for the goalkeeper in the goal. Covering for the goalkeeper leaves a player free, may confuse the defense as to who shall cover, may make it difficult for the goalkeeper to return to the crease and leaves the covering player in a dangerous position without protective equipment.

A highly skilled goalkeeper will carefully evaluate her opposing attacks, their favorite shots and any habits that give clues as to when and where they will shoot. Her most important job is to follow the ball, even when it is in the opponent's crosse, rather than the distracting movements of the attack player's body. A highly skilled goalkeeper may purposely leave openings for shots so as to draw shots where she can control them. This is not possible when the attacks are beginners and are not sure where the proper place to shoot is or where the ball will go after they release it.

Goalkeeping is a fascinating position and a very important one. A good goalkeeper can make the difference between a confident or an unsure defense, a winning or losing team.

Shooting.   Although shooting is very accurate passing or throwing, it deserves special attention. To be absolutely topnotch in shooting, a player must spend many seasons practicing to perfect her skill. Basically, shooting is putting the ball where the goalkeeper isn't and cannot reach. Against a good goalkeeper this means accuracy within an inch! The attack player must learn "where" the goalkeeper will be "when." Unfortunately this is not enough. An inexperienced goalkeeper may not be where she should be and the experienced goalkeeper, seeing the attack doing the obvious, may position herself accordingly. Therefore, the attack player must have her eyes on the goalkeeper at all times when shooting. She must convince the goalkeeper that she is going to shoot anywhere but where she intends to shoot. This can be done by body position, head position, stick or even eyes if the goalkeeper is following them. A free attack shooting at goal should score 95 per cent of her shots if she is skillful. Quite an incentive for acquiring this skill!

To be more specific about shooting, the following types of shots and their effectiveness are discussed below: long bounce shot, crossover shot and wrist shot.

The *long bounce shot* is typically used by attack wings and third home to a greater degree than by the other attacks. It should be a very hard shot directed to bounce just over the crease. The shooter should get her entire body and shoulder behind the ball. Because of the potential speed and the bounce, it can be a difficult shot to stop. It is possible, by turning the stick slightly on the release, to put a spin on the ball so that it bounces slightly left or right. This shot is affected by the condition of the ground inside the crease. If the ground is exceptionally hard or exceptionally soft, the ball must be aimed close to the goalkeeper's feet so that it will not bounce over the goal cage or bounce sluggishly and therefore become an easy save.

The *crossover shot,* in which the shooter is moving at some angle across the goal, is designed to make the goalkeeper move. The more the goalkeeper is forced to move, the more vulnerable she is. No attempt is made here to analyze the basic underarm or overarm shots but a few advanced possibilities and options are presented. With the knowledge that the goalkeeper will come out onto the stick of a player about to do an underarm shot, the shooter can fake an underarm and, as the goalkeeper comes out, put a soft overarm shot over her head into the goal. If the goalkeeper does not come out, then the shooter can continue with the underarm shot. Players usually hold the ball until midway or further across the goal, shooting back into the space left by the goalkeeper. As the goalkeeper learns to expect this, it has been observed that a lever type underarm shot performed sooner than expected can fool an experienced goalkeeper. This shot is hard and fast, entering the goal about waist height on the non-stick side of the goalkeeper.

The *wrist shot* is not often seen, even among highly skilled players. It is a most effective shot and can be learned, with practice, by most players. Basically, the wrist shot comes from a simultaneous snap of both wrists with little wind-up or follow through. Because there is no preparatory movement, the ball can be released at almost any point of the cradle. A high cradle makes this shot easier and perhaps more effective. The shot is not an exceptionally hard and fast one but it can be developed to pinpoint accuracy to enter any part of the goal cage (Figs. 6–21, 6–22). It can be executed at any point close to goal and is particularly effective when the player is level with the goal line, using a motion similar to the "round-the-head" shot in badminton.

There are many other variations on shooting that different players

Figure 6–21.   Wrist shot.

Figure 6–22.   "Round the head" shot.

may develop. An unorthodox shot as a surprise maneuver can be very effective. Shots that are created by batting or slinging the ball are poor at best, since there is little or no accuracy and a goal will result only through luck.

Body Checking. Body checking is a basic defensive skill but many players find it difficult to master. Good footwork is of prime importance and players must practice body checking at top speed to discover the proper timing and footwork. First of all, the body checker begins to move backward in the same direction as the attacker. At this point the body checker should extend her stick at the attacker as far as possible, placing the head in line with the attacker's shoulders. This prevents the attacker from getting too close and therefore being able to outmaneuver the body checker. As the attacker makes a definite pull to one side, the body checker will turn the *lower* half of her body to the same side in order to run with the attacker. At this point she is still between the attacker and her goal and is forcing her off path. It is most important that this pivoting from the waist occur so that a normal run can be made, yet the body checker is still facing her opponent with her stick, attempting to check as well. It is impossible for someone running backward to run as fast as someone running forward. Therein lies one of the major problems of players attempting to body check—they fail to point their feet in the direction in which they want to run. It must be remembered that a successful body check can cause the attacker to deviate from her path, force her to pass or be stick checked and lose the ball as a result (Figures 6–23 and 6–24).

Dodging. Just as body checking is a basic defensive skill, dodging is a basic attacking maneuver. The major faults of players attempting to dodge are slowing down instead of speeding up or using a change of pace, being obvious as to the side they will pull and not protecting their stick from a stick check as they dodge. Accelerating or a change of pace can be most effective against a body checker. The attack should attempt to get close to the defender before making a pull to one side or the other to avoid giving the defender time to adjust. This cannot be accomplished if the attacker slows down, for then a body checking function has been accomplished by the defense. The attacker who can "wrong foot" her opponent and take advantage of it by accelerating, should be able to dodge most any player on the field. This is a difficult concept to teach, since the opportunities to wrong foot happen at top speed and the attacker must sense when they occur.

Wrong footing refers to the situation when the defender has her weight on her left foot when turned to the right or on her right foot when turned to the left. In this position (and it must happen on every other step) it is very difficult for the body checker to follow a player who suddenly pulls to the opposite side. She has her weight committed to the wrong foot and

Figure 6–23.   Body checking.

Figure 6–24.   Body checking.

therefore cannot make a quick change of direction and still face her opponent. She will then either be behind her opponent or will have to turn her back to her in order to reposition herself. In either case the attacker or dodger has gained the advantage (Fig. 6–25).

Figure 6–25.   Wrong footing.

As the dodger pulls to one side when first initiating the dodge, she must pull well around to avoid a stick check. Too many players *think* they have pulled far enough but in reality have not. If a dodge is successful, the stick must quickly be brought to the normal cradling position, since a "hanging" stick will invite a check from the rear.

Bibliography

Boyd, Margaret: *Lacrosse, Playing and Coaching.* London, Nicholas Kaye Limited, 1959.
Crosse Checks. Published annually by the United States Women's Lacrosse Association.
    Barrett, Kate: "Knowing how to play your position isn't enough." 1963.
    Demars, Janet: "Are you fit to play lacrosse?" 1965.
    Fetter, Mary: "Marking." 1963.

Longstreth, Barbara: "Attack play in general." 1962.

Mushier, Carole: "Top hand for top notch lacrosse." 1965.

Smith, Nathalie: "Get the ball!" 1965.

Delano, Ann: *Lacrosse for Girls and Women*, Dubuque, William C. Brown Co., 1970.

DGWS: *Selected Field Hockey/Lacrosse Articles*. AAHPER 1963.

Stevenson, Ruth: "Beginning coaches and players."

DGWS: *Selected Field Hockey/Lacrosse Articles*. AAHPER 1954.

Boyd, Margaret: "How to build a sound defense."

Haydock, Kathleen: "Building an attack."

Richey, Betty: "Playing attack."

Shellenberger, Betty: "Attack in lacrosse."

DGWS: *Field Hockey/Lacrosse Guide*. AAHPER. Published every two years.

Barnes, Mildred: "Cutting and timing for offense play." 1962–64

Barrett, Kate: "Progression: key to development of motivating practice." 1964–66.

Burke, Karen: "Goalkeeping." 1966–68.

Dendy, Elizabeth: "Lacrosse stickwork practices." 1958–60

Dunn, Gertrude: "Let's maintain the spirit of the game." 1966–68.

Fetter, Mary: "Drill variations for basic skills." 1962–64.

Lamb, Susan: "A sound defense." 1958–60.

Oswald, Jane: "How to develop a lacrosse team." 1962–64.

Pitts, Jackie: "Shooting with variety." 1968–70.

Reeson, Joan: "Shooting." 1956–58.

Sanderson, Judith: "Close marking vs. zoning." 1962–64.

Schuyler, Gretchen: "Buliding for good attack play." 1958–60.

Smiley, Judith and Boehringer, Sandra: "Wing defense" 1966–68.

Mushier, Carole L.: *Team Sports for Girls and Women*. Dubuque, Iowa, Wm. C. Brown Co., 1973.

Vannier, Maryhelen and Poindexter, Hally Beth: *Individual and Team Sports for Girls and Women*. 2nd Ed., Philadelphia, W. B. Saunders Co., 1968.

7

Softball

Softball continues to rank as one of the most popular amateur team sports in America. The official game is governed by the International Joint Rules Committee on Softball. The Amateur Softball Association of America is the primary governing body in this country.

Competitive softball demands that each of the nine players possess the defensive skills of efficient catching and accurate throwing as well as the offensive skills of batting and baserunning. The skills of pitching and catching are unique to selected players and are coupled with defensive team effort through seven innings of play.

Individual Skills Necessary for Competitive Play

There are six essential skills which a player must bring to a competitive softball team. An individual's speed, agility, hitting, throwing accuracy, fielding ability and speed of throw, as well as her attitude, will determine her ability to play and the position for which she is best suited. Some of these skills are developed prior to joining a team and others will be refined under proper supervision of the coach. A pitcher must display the same qualities as all other players, although the degree may vary, in addition to the unique skill of pitching.

Speed and agility are of utmost importance in offensive and defensive skills. A player's ability to accelerate, maneuver one's body and display good running speed affects the execution of other skills. Hitting is an obvious necessity, for games are won only by runs scored. Competitive teams cannot depend on errors by opponents or pitching inadequacy to force players around the bases. Rapid, strong and accurate throwing ability together with aggressive and sure fielding are fundamental to the *automatic out* — the play wherein the ball is caught and thrown accurately, resulting in an out. The automatic out is the defensive basis of softball.

All of these physical skill essentials become meaningful only to the extent that the player's attitude allows her involvement. Her ability must be reinforced by her desire to play softball and her willingness to "hustle" through practice sessions, learn strategy and improve individual skills.

Selection of Players

In addition to the skills mentioned, there are both general and specific defensive skills of each position. The coach looks for these specific movements in identifying the best possible person for the position. Generally, all players must be able to diagnose the type of offense and defend against it. This includes the ability to read and respond to defensive signals. Perhaps the key is the Golden Rule of softball — "Play as if every ball is coming to you; know what you are going to do with the ball before it is hit."

It is obvious that when two equally effective players are vying for a defensive position, the coach must select the best hitter and base runner for total team effectiveness.

The following defensive skills are specific to each position:

Pitcher
1. Accuracy and control in delivery.
2. Good fast ball (minimum requirement).
3. Curve ball (should be developed early in her career).
4. Change of pace pitch.
5. Physical strength and stamina as well as emotional stability.
6. Ability to recover to fielding position after delivery.
7. Knowledge of hitter (be able to read the hitter and remember the pitches she hit or swung at from prior times at bat).

Catcher
1. Catch all deliveries of the pitcher and follow the flight of the ball as it is pitched and when hit.
2. Ability to analyze the batter and call for a pitch.
3. Good stamina, good flexibility.
4. Agile and strong legs.
5. Serve as the defensive leader (change defensive fielders' positions).
6. Ability to "snap throw" to the bases.
7. Spark plug of the team.

1st Base
1. Height is helpful as full extension makes a good target.
2. Speed and quick footwork; ability to coordinate footwork with catches.

3. Ability to stretch and reach and catch all kinds of throws while positioning the lower body to make contact with the base.
4. Ability to cover her territory.
5. Ability to catch and throw accurately to any base.

2nd Base

1. Agility in covering first or second base (she is always in on a double play situation, either fielding or covering a base).
2. Ability to throw quickly and accurately is more important than strength of the throw.
3. Ability to field to left or right with equal speed.
4. Ability to tag a sliding runner and maintain balance to throw.

3rd Base

1. Height is an asset when catching line drives.
2. Ability to catch and throw rapidly and accurately. Strength of throw is important, as many throws must travel to first base.
3. Ability to tag a sliding runner and maintain balance and composure.
4. Ability to judge and catch fly balls.
5. Ability to come in fast on a bunt.

Shortstop

1. Fastest player on the team in many cases; many hits go through this position.
2. Ability to get a "jump on the ball" at the instant it is hit.
3. Accuracy and near perfect timing in fielding balls and throwing.
4. Throws the underhand whip as well as the overhand.
5. Possesses many of the qualities of 2nd baseman.

Outfielders

1. Have excellent ability to visually track the ball as it is hit.
2. Speed.
3. Good throwing arm.
4. Ability to field all kinds of ground balls.
5. Ability to field all flies.
6. Quick to adjust to batters' strengths.
7. Ability to think constantly and stay ready.
8. Ability to get a jump on the ball and react quickly.

An outfielder must know her position relative to all other players at all times and know the ability of each of the players in handling a ball in "fringe areas." The center fielder should be the fastest player in the outfield and one of the best throwers. She may be designated to call all plays in the outfield. Theoretically, a left-handed player in right field and a right-handed player in left field protects the areas between these respective positions and the center fielder most effectively.

Advanced Skills Necessary for Competitive Play

Advanced skills are built upon a thorough understanding and ability to perform basic techniques. Development of the advanced skills indicated below distinguishes the competitive player from the recreational softball player.

Batting.   Observation and increasing research evidence in baseball suggest that there is a wide variation in grips and stances among strong hitters. Evidence indicates that improved strength and placement skill result when a player:

1. Selects a bat of medium to thin handle for a free swing. She may select a thicker handle for the choke grip. The maximum length and diameter are governed by rules, but within these constraints select the proper length, weight and style for body build and swing pattern.
2. Places the hands on the bat firmly to avoid recoil and loss of power. Players with weak wrists can compensate by choking the bat or spreading the hands. Maximum velocity of the bat is attained when the middle knuckles of both hands are aligned. (This grip also allows greater range of motion in the wrists.)

Mechanical analysis of batting in baseball indicates a basic sequence of body movements even though various preliminary movements may precede the swing. Effective hitters execute a short stride, rotation of the body at the hips and shoulders, rapid extension of the forearms and rapid uncocking of the wrists.[1] A cinematographical analysis of batting styles of six great baseball players disclosed:[2]

1. The center of gravity of the body followed a fairly level plane throughout the swing.
2. The head was adjusted from pitch to pitch to get the best and longest possible look at the flight of the ball.
3. The leading forearm tended to straighten immediately at the beginning of the swing, thus resulting in a greater bat speed.
4. The length of stride was essentially the same on all pitches.
5. After hitting the ball the upper body position was in the same direction as the flight of the ball, thus transferring the weight to the front foot.

The *stride* increases the body momentum and increases the force of the hit. A short stride is desirable as the rotary action of the hips is somewhat dependent on the stride. (Too great a stride may result in locking the hips and the body falls away from the plate). The stride is timed with the release of the ball by the pitcher.

The *stance* should be both comfortable and functional. Preference is

---

[1]Reiff, Guy G.: *What Research Tells the Coach About Baseball.* AAHPER, 1971, p. 2.
[2]Breen, J. L.: "What makes a good hitter?" *JOHPER*, 38:36, April 1967.

for the compact stance with the bat held in a near vertical position and arms comfortably away from the body. The batter stands at a distance from the plate that enables her to reach over the far side of the plate with the end of the bat without unduly stretching. The rear foot points toward the plate and the forward foot is turned slightly toward the infield so the body is angled slightly to view the pitcher. While in this stance it may be helpful to take a few preliminary swings to release muscular tension and to verify that the hitting surface of the bat covers the strike zone. Only correct swing patterns should be executed; it is relatively valueless to try to decoy the pitcher by swinging high or low and it may alter a desirable swing pattern.

The body should rotate dramatically and powerfully for effective hitting. The hips begin the motion while the shoulders remain stationary or rotate slightly backward to overcome the inertia of the bat and increase the arc of the swing. The shoulders and hips are level and the head stays relatively level throughout the swing. The pivot opens the hips and as the hips come around the arms and hands follow with each successive member of the body increasing in speed until optimum speed is attained.

As the hands reach the hitting area, the lead arm is straight and the speed of the hands through the hitting area is increasing or at maximum velocity. Contrary to general opinion, the impact of the bat on the ball is reached with wrists square and unbroken. Power is applied before the wrists roll. The wrists roll after the ball has left the bat. (Right wrist rolls over left for right-handed batter and left over right for left-handed batter.)

The importance of visually tracking the ball is unquestioned, but the distance and time one can track the ball is controversial. The speed of the ball's flight may prohibit a player from tracking it up to point of contact with the bat; however, only by watching the ball can the batter make a choice as to movement pattern. Skillful batters seem to react to a pitcher's release as an "alert" reaction and the movement action follows when the ball is midway from the pitcher.

Bunting. Present strategy of softball requires that all players be able to bunt. Young players prefer to "hit away"; consequently, the coach must carefully plan practices to assure technical perfection of bunting fundamentals.

SACRIFICE BUNT. In executing a sacrifice bunt there is no need to conceal the intent to bunt because the batter is willing to be put out to advance the base runner. The batter pivots from her normal stance and faces the pitcher just prior to the release of the ball. A batter who crowds the plate should pivot by placing her lead foot to the outside and bringing her rear foot parallel to it. Feet are spread well apart. The batter who stands away from the plate pivots by turning the lead foot and bringing the rear foot parallel to the lead foot (Figs. 7–1, 7–2). Her body must be parallel to home

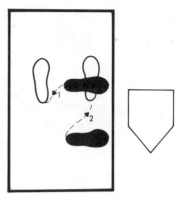

Figure 7–1.   Bunt pivot for the batter who stands close to the plate.

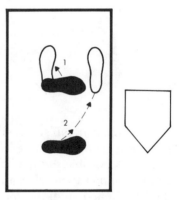

Figure 7–2.   Bunt pivot for the right-handed batter who stands away from the plate.

and the bat square to the infield so that the bunted ball will land in fair territory. She should frequently be reminded that an out will result if she steps on the plate or out of the batter's box. As she pivots she slides her top hand on the bat up to the trademark area and grips the bat firmly between thumb and forefinger. The remaining fingers are clenched into a fist and held under the bat, knuckles facing the infield. The hand gripping the handle serves as a guide and holds the bat loosely to lessen the impact of the ball on contact. Gripping the bat too tightly leads to a hard bunt. The bat should be kept level and high to work down on the ball, as pop-ups often result in double plays. Arms are well extended with the bat out in front of the plate. The hand on the handle guides the angle of the bat and the extended hand acts as a fulcrum for directing the angle of rebound. The bunter does not push the bat to the ball nor pull the bat back as the ball approaches. The *ball hits the bat* with a slight recoil often taking place. If the ball is low the batter bends her knees, keeping the level plane of the bat (Fig. 7–3).

Figure 7–3.   Sacrifice bunt stance. The bat is held high and level. Feet are parallel with the body squared toward the pitcher.

DRAG, PUSH AND SLASH BUNTS.   The drag, push and slash bunts are attempts to get on base. In execution the intent to bunt should be concealed as long as possible so the pitcher cannot change her mind and the fielders cannot commit themselves until they are certain of the batter's intentions. The fundamentals of the *drag bunt* are similar to those described in the sacrifice with the exception that the batter's feet remain in a batting stance position as the body pivots toward the pitcher with the bat in front of the body. At the instant the ball is contacted, the batter runs for first base. An attempt is made to place the ball down the third base line but a well-placed first base line bunt is often successful.

The *push bunt* is also an attempt to get on base. The positioning is similar to that used in the drag bunt. An attempt is made to push the ball past the pitcher on either side of the mound.

The *slash bunt* is not frequently used in softball but a player capable of executing the bunt is a constant threat to the opposition. It is most successful against a slow pitch, especially a curve ball. The batter assumes her bunting stance and as the ball approaches, the bat is brought back to the shoulder and the hands move slightly together in an exaggerated choke grip. The swing is downward and directed toward the third or first baseman.

Sliding.   Sliding is controlled advancement while lowering the body from the running position. It serves four purposes for the advanced player: (1) to stop momentum in the quickest and safest manner; (2) to escape injury from contact with a fielder who is attempting a tag; (3) to avoid being tagged out and (4) to break up a play or consume time to protect another base runner. Once a player commits herself to advance or return to a base she must immediately condition her thinking to a slide. Once a decision to slide has been made, it must be completed for the safety of the player.

HOOK SLIDE.   The hook slide is the most frequently used "all purpose" slide. The side to which the runner slides is determined by the direction of the throw to the infielder making the tag and the tagging position the infielder takes. Always slide away from the direction of the ball and the tagger. Basically, all slides are initiated the same way. The takeoff is approximately two body lengths from the base, with the direction of the slide determined by the takeoff foot and the side of the body on which the slide will be executed. For example, in going to the right side of the base the right foot is normally the takeoff foot and the left foot (inside foot) will hook the base. As the takeoff occurs, the arms are thrown up, the upper body is extended backward and the feet forward. The body lean should be in the opposite direction from the takeoff foot. The player lands on her buttocks and then turns so the slide is on one side. The hands are off the ground to prevent abrasions and the back is arched and parallel to the ground. The head is back but raised enough to see the base and the player making the tag. Upon landing, both feet are extended toward the base. In the hook slide the toe of the inside foot contacts and hooks the base as the knee bends. The outside foot continues past the base.

BENT LEG SLIDE.   The bent leg slide is used when the base runner feels she is certain to be safe if she slides. A player can regain her footing quickly in the event of a bad throw and extra bases can be taken. The slide is made directly toward the base; the takeoff foot is the same as the side on which the runner slides. After the takeoff the runner lands squarely on her buttocks and the takeoff leg bends under the other leg which remains slightly flexed but extended to touch the base.

STRAIGHT IN SLIDE.   A straight in slide begins about ten feet from the base. The execution is similar to the bent leg slide except both legs remain extended toward the base. This is a natural slide and easily executed by young players.

HEADFIRST SLIDE.   The headfirst slide is relatively dangerous but it is a natural response for the "scampering return" of competitive players. Justification for teaching this slide is to avoid injury, even though the coach may not encourage its use. It is used when a player lacks momentum to execute a traditional slide or lacks confidence in other slides, or when an injury prevents another slide. With her limited forward momentum the base runner bends forward and dives low. She lands on her chest, head up with hands outstretched to the base.

Combining Individuals for Team Play

Every coach eventually develops her own techniques, objective and subjective, for evaluating individual skill and combining players into an effective team. These procedures should enable the coach to place players in their most effective positions and to plan a training program which improves their skills and strategic abilities in these positions.

Very early in the tryout period a coach makes decisions which may involve moving a player from a position she desires or is accustomed to playing. Players frequently come with a preconceived idea of "my position" and one of the first challenges the coach faces is that of convincing each player that all nine positions are essential to team play. Many times a player can become more skillful in a new position because of her basic abilities and the team needs.

As previously stated, the player must have both offensive and defensive skills. Although it is a truism that the game is won by the team scoring the largest number of runs, it need not be true that many of these runs result from a defensive team's errors and poor strategy. Many high school and college coaches who are aware of the importance of effective offensive skills feel that an opponent will afford several runs by errors and poor judgment and that the real coaching challenge is to develop one's own team to prevent errors and unsound strategical moves. Those holding this point of view place vast importance on fundamentals and the execution of them with confidence in the team's strategic decisions.

It is far easier to evaluate a person's skill at a given time than to estimate her potential and speed of improvement. For this reason the coach is constantly alert to the "emerging" player who is maturing in strength, speed and basic skills. Information can be accumulated if records are gathered periodically on players' performance. The following simplified form, using a 1, 2, 3 scale of effectiveness, is helpful when position decisions must be made:

Batting

1. Effectiveness
2. Placement
3. Distance
4. Bunting (as directed)
5. Wrist flexibility
6. Smoothness of swing
7. Grip
8. Stance
9. Stride
10. Pivot or turn
11. Swing pattern
12. Judgment of pitches

Running

1. Speed
   a. 1st base
   b. 1st to second
   c. All bases
2. Slides

Rating
(1 – good; 2 – fair; 3 – poor)

(times may be added)

Defensive ability reflected in a player's mobility, quickness in maneuvering, catching skills and fast, strong, accurate throws can be determined during practice with infield and outfield players. A player may be rated on:

Fielding

1. Maneuverability
2. Getting the jump on the ball
3. Judgment of ball position
4. Footwork
5. Speed
6. Ground balls
7. Flies

Throwing

1. Selection of style
2. Speed
3. Strength
4. Accuracy

Rating
(1, 2, 3)

Only through practice games is the coach able to evaluate a player's drive, cooperative team attitude and her ability to resist the stress of competition. As players improve or hit plateaus of performance, the positioning and ranking of players should be subject to change.

Practice Sessions

Practice sessions must focus on:

1. Developing individual player's physical condition.
2. Developing individual skills.
3. Developing offensive and defensive patterns and strategies.
4. Building team morale and a competitive spirit.

Prior to tryouts players should be advised to begin a personal conditioning program that focuses on physical conditioning and reviewing fundamental techniques. In climates where outdoor opportunities are limited, the personal program is easily modified for indoor facilities. Players may work independently on physical conditioning but should work with a partner on technique improvement. The areas discussed below should be considered in recommending a program.

In conditioning for strength, flexibility and cardiorespiratory endurance, activities might include:

1. Jogging and running (one-half mile to two miles a day).
2. Rope jumping.
3. Shuttle and agility runs.
4. Neck, shoulder, wrist, trunk and leg flexibility exercises.
5. Stride jumps for reach, extension and flexibility.
6. Weight training program or isometrics for developing arm strength and wrist strength. (Push-up, modified if necessary, and squeezing a rubber ball are examples of suitable exercises.)*
7. Throwing a weighted ball.

Partner drills are designed for technique improvement. The drills can be done independently or in a timed circuit following the exercises outlined above.

1. Ball conditioner drill. Two players—one with two softballs. One player rolls the balls from one side of the fielding player to the other, causing her to move farther and more rapidly. Change positions after a given period of time.
2. Bunting drill. Two players—one player is the pitcher and the other the bunter. The pitcher must field the bunts as quickly as possible. Alternate positions.
3. Covering first base drill. Pitcher rolls the ball to a field position so the first baseman may play the ball (as in a bunt). Pitcher covers first base and receives throw from first baseman. Alternate positions. (Although this is not a game situation drill, it is recommended to increase speed of both players.)
4. Weighted bat drill. One player swings a properly weighted bat two minutes. Partner checks swing and body position. (See the advanced skills section of this chapter for description.)
5. Batting tee drill. One player hits from the batting tee for two minutes. Her partner observes and checks as above.

One of the coach's major concerns is keeping the squad actively involved in worthwhile activities during the practice session. Practices should be carefully organized so that time is allotted for each area of concern and all positions. The softball season is short and the weather is such a factor

---

*Research relating to improvement of throwing and batting performance by strengthening of selected muscle groups is limited. General conditioning for strength and endurance is generally accepted as most desirable for physical and psychological readiness.

that each day must be used to advantage. Many drills can be improvised so that they can be used indoors if necessary.

Individual offensive drills will be used early in the season as the coach concentrates on basics. Later they will be incorporated in situational drills simulating the situation and speed of game play. The following baserunning drills can be practiced individually or in groups with players following one another.

1. Hit and accelerate—to improve footwork and develop rapid start from home.
2. Hit and run—to improve form and speed in running to first base.
3. Swing and go—to teach technique of rounding first toward second. Player should practice taking second and returning to first as if she were cut off.
4. Takeoff drill—emphasis on footwork and power of takeoff from first base as pitcher delivers.
5. Sliding drills—these often neglected drills are imperative to skillful play. Straight, hook and bent leg slides are used by collegiate and amateur teams.

Team Drills.   The following drills are designed for use during practice sessions. They afford a meaningful practice of skills that are frequently used in play. Varying the group selected assures interesting practices. Stress the importance of "hustling" through all drills, that is, practicing them at the speed at which they will be played. Each group drill requires one softball field and a rather large squad, and allows the group activities to be carried on simultaneously.

Group I. Each pair of players has a softball for warming up and practicing accurate throws. Infielders throw to each other, outfielders throw to outfielders. The catcher warms up the first pitcher who will throw batting practice or drill work. Other catchers and pitchers organize "pepper games" in which several hitters, 30 to 35 feet from fielders, hit ground balls in rapid sequence off fielders' throws. Infielders and outfielders increase throwing distance, and practice throws they must make from their positions.

Group II. A catcher, pitcher, first baseman, second baseman and shortstop assume their positions. All other players serve as base runners at first base or batters in turn. The pitcher delivers and the base runner breaks for second base. The batter may attempt to hit the ball. The objects of the drill are (a) pitcher practice; (b) catcher practice throwing to second base; (c) base runner sliding or scampering back to first base; (d) first baseman practice receiving throws and tagging; (e) shortstop and second baseman practice receiving throws from catcher and tagging base runner.

Group III. Infield set up as in II but including third baseman. Base runners are on second base initially and later on both first and second bases.

Group IV. Infielders and catcher in position. Place one, two or three pitchers near the pitcher's plate. Pitchers follow one another in the drill. The coach stands in batter's box with a softball in hand. The pitcher delivers and as the ball is caught at the plate by the catcher the coach may:

(a) toss the ball on the ground in front of the plate or down either base line just as a batter would bunt.

(b) throw the ball on the ground in the vicinity of first base. The first baseman fields and throws the ball to the second baseman who is covering first base.

(c) throw the ball on the ground directly to the pitcher or to either side of her. Players not participating in the drill are placed as base runners. The coach announces the score, inning, number of outs and bases occupied. The group drill is designed to give pitchers, infielders and catchers practice on infield and bunted balls.

Group V. (1) Shortstop and second baseman assume their positions. The coach stands near the pitcher's plate and throws ground balls to either the shortstop or second baseman. The player receiving the ball throws to the other one who covers second base and she, in turn, throws to the first baseman to complete the double play. (2) One player hits fly balls to the outfield from a position in back of either first or third base. Other players organize bunting practice at home plate. Players take turns fielding bunts. This group practice is planned to give (a) shortstop and second baseman practice fielding ground balls and executing double plays; (b) first baseman practice stretching to catch throws from second base; (c) outfielders fielding practice; (d) pitchers, catchers and third baseman bunting practice.

Group VI. Infielders pair off on the infield and throw ground balls to each other. Outfielders engage in bunting practice at the plate. Pitchers go to the outfield and take fielding practice. These drills give (a) infielders practice in fielding ground balls; (b) outfielders bunting practice; (c) pitchers practice fielding fly balls and an opportunity for general conditioning.

Group VII. Outfielders, infielders, catchers and base line coaches take their respective positions. Other players act as base runners. The coach is at home plate and after she announces the score, inning and number of outs, she hits the ball to the outfield. This practice is designed to drill (a) outfielders fielding flies and ground balls and making plays to the bases; (b) pitchers and other players running bases; (c) infielders receiving throws from the outfield, relaying throws,

tagging runners and making cutoff plays; (d) catchers receiving throws from the outfield and tagging
base runners and (e) baseline coaches directing base
runners.

Group VIII. Third baseman, second baseman and first baseman
take their positions. Outfielders, catchers and shortstop have bunting practice at the plate. Pitchers organize pepper games. Purposes of the drill are to give
(a) third baseman practice fielding ground balls and
starting double plays; (b) second baseman practice on
double plays beginning at third base; (c) pitchers drill
on timing at bat.

As the season begins a coach should follow a well-organized plan for
each practice session. Each session will present some new ideas and review
the old, but opportunity for theory and strategy, individual and team
skill development and scrimmages should be provided. Rate of progress
is naturally dependent upon individuals' skill and experience but the
topics listed indicate reasonable expectations from a collegiate or amateur
team:

   I. Policies — team and coach
      A. Care of equipment, uniforms
      B. Practice procedures
      C. Training and conditioning expectations
      D. League and game schedule, travel, etc.
  II. Sportsmanship as a team member
 III. Knowledge and review of rules
 IV. Batting — theory
      A. Purpose of practice
      B. Batting order
      C. Analysis of batting form and placement
      D. Signals
   V. Bunt plays
      A. Sacrifice
      B. Bunt for hit
 VI. Analyzing pitchers
      A. Tracking the delivery
      B. Timing the swing
VII. Baserunning
VIII. Offensive plays (Hit and run, squeeze, bunt, etc.)
 IX. Defensive plays
      A. Shifting infielders according to score, outs, inning, batter
      B. Shifting outfielders
      C. Breaking up bunt, hit and run, squeeze
      D. Coordination of infield and outfield on fly balls
      E. Double plays
  X. Duties of base line coaches

Division of Time.   Practice sessions should rarely exceed two and one
half hours and frequently two hours is adequate for accomplishing the

purposes of the session. No matter what the length, each minute must be used efficiently to avoid boredom and loss of interest by team members. Early in the season more time will be spent on individual skill development, conditioning and basic strategy. Later more time is spent in situational drills and games. Practice games should not be neglected early in the season but the coach should avoid turning every practice into a "game situation" within the squad or with opponents.

Practice games should point up the individual and team strengths and weaknesses and serve to inspire more intense and meaningful practices. The following example is for a two and one-quarter hour practice for a collegiate team several weeks into the season.

15 minutes — Individual warm-up and skill drill (Group I drill).
30 minutes — Fungo practice to outfield; fungo hitting to infield. (Individual coaching is given at this time on catching, running, etc.)
30 minutes — Group III drill with outfielders having batting practice initially; later infielders come in for batting practice.
45 minutes — Situational practice (as described in Group VII drill); game situation with base line coaches.
15 minutes — Team meeting to discuss strategy or theory of a skill for next practice session. (Open discussion and questions should be encouraged.)

Strategy

The most important strategic weapon a team possesses is its desire to win. A winning attitude is a personal matter among the team members and coaches. It may develop through mutual faith and trust, individual skill and knowledge of strategy or it may form around the spirit of a team "spark plug" in the form of a player or coach. The winning attitude is usually laced with superstition and symbols that generate cooperative competition. It is not uncommon to find some players wearing the same pair of socks or insisting on the same seating arrangement in the dugout during a winning streak. Symbols produce a feeling of faith and belief; the team towel, stuffed animal, mascot or a piece of equipment may be the unifying item for the entire team. No matter what the superstitions and symbolic meanings the idiosyncrasies of the team emerge into the winning spirit that must be nurtured.

Strategy is simply *playing the percentages* for success in a given situation. When a coach states the percentages of a certain maneuver, she is describing the chance of a successful event occurring. The chance element is derived by dividing the total number of times an event has occurred into the total number of times it was successful. Batting averages reflect the number of hits divided by the number of times at bat. A player with a .300 average has hit successfully 30 per cent of the times at bat. Similar calculations are made with hit and run, stealing, sacrificing with no outs or one out and many other plays.

In recent years the probabilities of virtually all game situations have been calculated for major league baseball. Some of the findings seem to question traditional strategies of offensive play. One must draw cautious inferences for softball and for the less skilled players, but some findings worthy of consideration are noted throughout the next section.*

OFFENSIVE STRATEGY

Standard Offensive Procedures. A team with basically sound skill begins with traditional standard offensive procedures.

BATTING ORDER. The placement of batters is part of the total offensive technique of organizing for the most effective hitting, bunting and baserunning. Cook's findings suggest that the batting order should be arranged so that the most productive hitters appear in descending sequence of ability. The probability behind this is that the best hitters come to bat more often. Critics of the theory argue that players may get on base but this order does not afford the best chance of being advanced. It is obvious that this plan considers only batting ability to the exclusion of other offensive skills.

Some coaches feel it is wise to spread the hitters throughout the lineup to deceive the pitcher who thinks she is past the good hitters and then tends to relax. Spreading the hitters has merit in games in which the opponent is unfamiliar with the batting ability of the other team's players. Not only is the pitcher prone to mistakes, but infielders may misplay, expecting weak hitters.

The most common theory of arranging batting order is that of bunching hitters. Basically, those players who can get on base and have good speed should be ahead of strong hitters. The last three players include the less dependable hitters. Pitchers are eased in the last one third and inexperienced batters gain poise and confidence in these positions. Some criteria for placement are:

Lead off batter should be a fast runner and consistent hitter, although not necessarily a long ball hitter. A left-handed hitter has a one step advantage toward first base. She should be a good drag bunter.

*For more details see Cook, Earnshaw and Garner, W. R.: *Percentage Baseball.* Baltimore, Waverly Press, 1964.

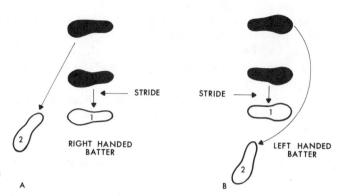

Figure 7–4. A, Footwork of a right-handed batter starting from home. B, Footwork of a left-handed batter starting from home.

Number two batter should be fast and a good bunter, although not as reliable a hitter as number one. She should be capable of base stealing and should be a threat for the hit and run situation.

Number three batter should be the best hitter on the team with adequate speed to score on long hits. Left-handed hitter has some advantages.

Number four is the "clean up" batter and is the clutch hitter of the team. She can single or hit the long ball. Speed is a real asset.

Number five should be a long ball hitter and even though she may not be consistent she must be a potential threat.

Number six should be an adequate clutch hitter. She often comes to bat with runners on base. She should be a better hitter than number one but not necessarily as fast.

Numbers seven, eight and nine are usually the weakest and most inexperienced hitters. Usually the pitcher is in this group and frequently the catcher. Although they may be good hitters they are not called on to slide or steal.

INDIVIDUAL HITTING HINTS.   Mental and visual perception are important for effective hitting. The batter must realize that good hitters do not wait for the perfect pitch through the middle of the strike zone; they are ready to hit all strikes in the area. The first concern is to visualize the total zone and realize the size of the area she must protect.

Anticipating the pitch, the batter bears in mind the number of runners on base, score, inning, number of outs, count, position in the batting order, play that is on and the wind conditions. In addition she should reflect on the tried and true hints passed down by successful batters:

1. Have a positive and confident attitude and a definite thought in mind.

2. Know the best pitch and be ready for it.
3. Avoid guessing as to the pitch that will be delivered.
4. The first pitch is usually one that can be hit (normally a straight ball if no one is on base). A batter may swing at the first pitch; however, taking this pitch in a game may refresh the batter's memory of the pitcher's speed and delivery and allow her to "feel" the pitcher's tempo while getting settled. It is advisable to take the first pitch if the previous two batters have hit it and have been put out.
5. Never try to pull an outside pitch. On a change-up think of hitting to the opposite field (this holds the swing up and allows the batter to hit the ball). Most left-handed pitchers naturally pitch their fast ball outside to right-handed batters and inside to left-handed batters. Left-handed pitchers use their curve ball more against left-handed hitters because the ball starts at the hitter and breaks away from her.
6. Be prepared to swing on every pitch. Avoid becoming a hitter who looks for "base on balls" rather than a hit.
7. The count on the batter is a clue to whether a good strike can be expected. When the count is two and one or three and one chances are good for a fast ball. When one and one, or zero and one, the pitcher can work the batter and anything can be expected except a ball down the middle. With two strikes and less than three balls, the batter should protect the plate (perhaps choke the bat) as a curve is a good possibility. With the count three and two, the batter can expect a strike and probably a fast ball.
8. Check for instructions from the coach before leaving the circle. Check for hit or take signals when the count is two balls and no strikes and three balls, one strike. Percentage calls for the batter to take on the three and 0 pitch unless the batter is very capable and her strength is needed to advance runners. "Hit" means to go after the pitch if it looks like it is in the strike zone; "take" means do not go after it.
9. If a hit and run is called, do *everything possible* to try to hit the ball (even if it is a pitch out, wild pitch, etc.) to protect the runner.
10. When the batter is not ready for the pitch, she should request time out from the plate umpire and step out of the box.
11. Acknowledge all signals given by the bench, even if they affect only the base runners.
12. *Always* run out a hit in or near foul territory.

PITCHING STRATEGY.* This is important to the batter if she intends to be more than an occasional lucky hitter. She must train herself to think as the catcher and pitcher. For example:

1. When runners are on base, the batter can expect more "stuff," for pitchers know most hitters are better fast ball hitters than breaking ball hitters.

---

*Also see Defensive Strategy, Pitching, in this chapter, p. 184.

2. In a tight spot, pitchers throw more curves and slow balls.
3. More fast balls are thrown when there are no runners on base.
4. When the score is close, fewer fast balls are thrown unless the pitcher is behind in the count. With two outs and no one on base the batter may see a fast ball at a slower pace when the defense is not in trouble.
5. Relief pitchers usually have more stuff on the ball because they do not have to pace themselves and can put more energy into each pitch.
6. Lead off batter and players sixth or below in batting order can usually expect more fast balls than curves unless a batter shows weakness against a particular pitch. Third, fourth and fifth batters are usually given curves and breaking pitches.
7. When the hitter has the wind at her back, the fast ball is slower and the curve ball has a bigger break. The contrary is true when pitching with the wind, i. e., the curve ball breaks less and the fast ball is slightly faster.

BASERUNNING STRATEGY. Running bases correctly can add innumerable runs during the season. Runners must remember that the focus is to reach a point by the shortest distance in the least amount of time. When going to first the runner should run hard and touch the outside (foul line side) of the base and then cut to foul territory. She slows down only after crossing first base. If extra bases can be run, the first base coach will call the runner on. Approximately 20 feet from first base the runner curves out of the base line and starts the turn by leaning to the right then cutting back left at first base, touching the inside corner of the bag with the left foot while driving to second with the right foot. When crossing second base the runner touches the inside corner with the right foot; at third base she touches the corner with the left foot.

The runner should go directly for the base and slide on close plays at all but first base. A slide is an efficient way of stopping a run without losing speed through early deceleration. A sliding player also presents a smaller target in a difficult position for a tag by the baseman.

Suggestions for runner on first base:

1. Run out all ground balls and get a ruling as to fair or foul after reaching base.
2. Hold first base on pop-ups to the infield.
3. When a fly ball is hit to the outfield, go approximately halfway to second base and hold to see if the ball is caught or dropped. (An individual's speed will determine exactly where she must stop; she must be able to advance or return, beating the fielder's throw.)
4. On a double play ball, slide to second base unless it is clear that the runner has the play beaten. If the baseman is off base and attempts a tag rather than a force out, try to stop and retreat toward first to delay the play and allow the batter to reach first safely. If the throw is made for first, dig hard for second.

5. When a steal signal is given with base runners ahead, do not go all the way without checking to see that the runner ahead is also trying to advance.

Suggestions for runner on second base:

1. Run on all grounders hit to the right side of the infield.
2. When a ground ball is hit to the left side of the infield, advance to third only when the ball is hit behind the runner unless forced by a runner from first base. Hold at second if the runner at third does not attempt to score.
3. On a ball hit ahead of the runner, advance only as far as to allow a safe return to second. If fielder fails to drive the runner back, advance to third if it is open.
4. On flies hit to right or center field, tag up at second and advance after the catch.
5. On flies hit to left field advance about half the distance on a long fly or one-third the distance on a short fly. If the coach has found a weakness in the fielders' throws she may call for an advance after a tag-up at second.
6. On all fly balls, check the base coach for signals and instructions after taking the normal position.

Suggestions for runner on third base:

1. Run from third base to home down the foul line to avoid the possibility of a put-out by being struck with a batted ball in fair territory.
2. With less than two outs tag up on all flies, both fair and foul, for a possible advance after the catch.
3. With none out, do not risk scoring on ground balls that seem certain to be fielded cleanly. With one out, attempt to score on any ground ball that goes past the pitcher. (Some coaches may hold the base runner in anticipation of a good hitter coming to bat.)

General Offensive Strategy. Each time a team comes to bat players must focus on strategic moves to get players across home plate. Strategy used early in the game may differ from that used later. Obviously, the score of the game is a major determinant for the pattern of offensive play. Some considerations for the coach are discussed below.

A team's offensive pattern is no stronger than each individual's ability to carry out her duties. The offense is controlled by score, number of outs, speed of the player, ability of the hitter and the opposing team's strengths and weaknesses.

Try to score early in the game. An early lead somewhat limits the opponent's strategy and if they are two or more runs behind and need three to win they tend to play cautiously and may lose momentum. At high school and collegiate levels most coaches plan on two unearned runs, so by gaining an early lead the team can concentrate on good defense and protect the lead.

In college and high school softball when the first and second batters get on base, bunt the next batter. There is always the risk of hitting into the double play.

It may be wise to bunt two batters when there are no outs and the good hitters are coming to bat. From the fifth inning, if the score is tied or there is a one-run difference, play for one run whether ahead or behind. Avoid playing hunches. Know the percentages and play them for consistent winning. Know your players and adjust the style of play to their abilities.

A good hitting, poor running team will use the hit and run since this type of play permits the batter to protect the inability of the runner. Because players hit the ball often, the double play potential is increased.

Except when the offense is trailing and the runner or runners on base represent less than the tying run, the good hitting batter may be left free to swing at a three ball, no strike pitch when there is:

1. Runner on second; runner on second and third with two out.
2. Runner on third with one out.
3. No one out and a good batter up with weaker ones to follow.

Good hitting teams rarely use the squeeze play nor do they take in hopes of walking unless the pitcher is very wild. They *can* afford to take strikes waiting for a better pitch.

The *poor hitting team* has a major problem of getting on base. Players must attempt to walk; to do this means more than waiting for the pitcher to deliver four balls. The batter should:

1. Take more pitches forcing the pitcher to throw more and perhaps tire.
2. Avoid swinging at pitches on the fringe of the strike zone.
3. Avoid swinging when ahead of the pitcher who is pressured to throw a strike.
4. Never let a pitcher become aware of the intent to take a pitch.
5. Bunt occasionally for a hit with two strikes.

The poor hitting team must use sacrifice bunts and run and hit plays and variations to advance base runners. When the batter is a capable bunter and the runner a good base stealer, bunt for a hit rather than a sacrifice.

The aggressive baserunning team employs delayed steals, attempts to take the extra base and always uses speed and agility as offensive strengths designed to exploit opponent's weaknesses.

BASIC TACTICS.   The following offensive tactics are basic and every team may find them used in a normal game situation. Aside from mastering the execution of the patterns, a team must learn to defend against them as well.

1. Sacrifice bunt is used to advance runners to scoring positions or to score through the squeeze play.* It should not be used by a team which is more than two runs behind. The sacrifice bunt is usually executed when there are no outs but is used occasionally with one out.
   a. Runner on first: The sacrifice bunt is executed whenever one run is necessary to win, tie or score an insurance run. Frequently used when the eighth or ninth batter in the line-up is first on base. Seldom used with one out and then only in desperation (e. g., late in the game with a slow runner on base and a poor hitter at bat). The bunt should be placed toward first to prevent a force out at second base.
   b. Runner on first and second: The sacrifice is used unless the team is so far behind that there is little benefit from the two runs possible. Early in the game the fourth batter can hit but later in the game if a run is needed to tie or win the game, she should bunt. The bunt should be directed so the third baseman must field the ball.
   c. Runner on second base only: When the offense has one or no outs and the hitter is capable, a bunt to the third baseman may advance the runner. She could then be in position to score by the squeeze, sacrifice fly (one out), error or passed ball. Generally this tactic is used late in the game when the offense needs one run to tie or win.
2. Suicide squeeze bunt should be used as an element of surprise or when a run is desperately needed. It is a difficult play to execute and is not considered a wise move with no outs. It is most frequently used late in the game with one out and a runner on third, second and third or first and third. (It should not be attempted with the bases loaded, since a force at home and a double play at first are possible.) The runner breaks for home with the pitch and the batter must contact the ball to protect the runner. A soft bunt to either side of the pitcher or toward the first baseman is desirable.

The *safe squeeze* is recommended only for experienced players with speed, for it calls for split second decisions by the runner. In executing the safe squeeze the runner does not run until she sees that the ball has been bunted. The bunt should be to either side of the pitcher or toward first base.

---

*Reiff, reporting on Cook's findings based upon analysis of major league baseball games, states: "The sacrifice bunt actually and significantly decreases the chances for scoring. By eliminating it, except for weakly hitting pitchers, a team can score 63 more runs per season." (From *What Research Tells the Coach About Baseball.* p. 24.) No such information is presently available for women's softball but such conclusions indicate conservative use of the sacrifice bunt in softball.

Bunting for a base hit is a surprise move used when the offense has difficulty hitting the opposing pitcher. It is usually executed by fast runners when the bases are empty, against a slow third baseman and a slow fielding pitcher.

Stealing is an important tactic that gives the offense the advantage of making choices in strategy rather than depending on the straight away hit. A steal is usually attempted by a runner on first in an effort to reach second base. A successful steal obviously puts the runner in scoring position and avoids the possibility of the batter hitting into a double play. Stealing third base is rarely attempted, for the risk is usually too great unless the pitcher or infielders are careless. A runner should score from second base on a hit; however, in desperation a steal to third may be attempted so that the runner might score on an error, squeeze play or long fly ball. A fake bunt may pull the third baseman in so that a runner on second can steal to third.

It is possible to steal anytime on a pitcher with poor technique, and base runners must study her movements to minimize the risks. A weak catcher makes the steal even more possible. A steal is best effected when a curve ball is thrown (count on the batter may give a clue to the type of pitch to be delivered) and ideal when the batter is left-handed, for she hides the runner on first. Stealing second is often possible with runners on first and third. The defense cannot afford to let the run score and will doubtless cut off the throw to second and permit the runner to advance.

The *delayed steal* by a runner on first is possible when the catcher lobs the ball back to the pitcher, when neither the shortstop nor second baseman have gone all the way to second base to cover after the pitcher's delivery.

A *steal of home* by a runner on third is always a threat with a fast runner but it is rarely attempted unless there are two outs and the base runner is capable of an effective slide. The batter should crowd the plate to screen the runner from the catcher. The batter does not swing or move after the pitch.

Double steals with runners on first and third base are frequently used with two outs. The runner on first serves as a decoy to score the third base runner against a weak and inexperienced defense. Two perfect throws, one by the catcher and the other by the fielder covering second, are necessary to protect against the first base runner advancing and the third base runner scoring.

The *hit and run* play is used to move a first base runner and avoid a double play. It is imperative that both the runner and batter know the play is on. The runner breaks for second at the instant the pitcher releases the ball. The batter protects the runner by swinging at the pitch no matter where it is pitched. If possible, execute the hit and run when the batter is ahead of the pitcher. If the batter gets a good pitch it should be hit to right field, thus necessitating the long throw to third base by the right fielder. When developing a young team, the coach may find the hit and run strategy helpful in encouraging aggressive batting.

The *run and hit* play differs from the hit and run in that the batter hits the ball only if it is a good pitch. Should the batter take the pitch or miss, the runner is on her own. Obviously, the base runner must be a threat as a base stealer.

The *bunt and run* and the *slash bunt* are two variations of the hit and run strategy. In executing the bunt and run, the batter attempts to bunt to the third baseman. If the bunt goes some other place the base runner must hold up at second base. The slash bunt is most effective when the third baseman and first baseman are charging in to field an anticipated bunt. The batter swings from a bunt position and slashes at the ball. Any hit on the ground toward first or third should result in a base hit. If successful, it breaks up double plays and results in both runners being safe. Occasional use of the slash bunt keeps first and third basemen cautious in bunt situations.

Offensive Signals.   Signals are a means of communicating between coach and players. Signals begin the execution of surprise plays and since there is a defense for every offensive tactic, secrecy is important. The team coach directs play from the bench or third base. The most direct method is from third base. Some teams prefer that the right-handed batter get signals from the first base coach as it is easier to look in her direction. Signals must be clearly visible and understandable. They must be natural simple body actions. They include touching parts of the body or uniform, positioning of hands, arms and feet or a combination of these. Complicated systems are difficult to steal but they are also equally hard to read by the offense. The number and difficulty of signals depend on the age, experience and number of offensive tactics players can perform. Three basic plays require a signal: the bunt, steal and hit and run. An additional sign for the "brush off" or "take off" is necessary so that the coach can call off any play previously called for and also inform the player that no play is on. Such a signal assures the batter or runner she is on her own. The take sign is frequently used when the coach wants the next pitch to go by. As teams become more experienced and skilled they add signals for squeeze, special steals and particular bunt tactics.

Signals should be given after a pitch when the ball is returned to the pitcher. At this time the batter can concentrate on the signal and acknowledge the sign by a simple act of touching the right sleeve, shoulder, etc., to indicate that everything is understood. If a base runner is involved, the signal is timed so that she can receive it as she returns to base.

DEFENSIVE STRATEGY

The defense must be prepared to handle the three major offensive maneuvers of hitting, bunting and baserunning. A team's defense is comprised of three distinct yet cooperative units of the battery, infield and outfield. Assuming each individual has the basic techniques needed for her position, the following tactics must be developed before game play will be defensively successful.

The Battery.   A large part of a team's success depends upon the pitcher's knowledge and ability to put the ball where the batter cannot hit it. Assuming she has developed control and a variety of balls,* the effective use of her skill depends upon her knowledge of general batting characteristics and specific strengths and weaknesses of individual batters. A discerning pitcher will notice signs which indicate a batter's preference and then she can concentrate on the delivery of balls most difficult for the batter to hit. The following suggestions are general and do not encompass the many individual idiosyncrasies evident after a long period of careful analysis.

1. Batters who crowd the plate find inside balls difficult to hit; those who stand away from the plate have difficulty with outside balls.
2. The batter who crouches has difficulty with high balls; the erect batter has trouble hitting low balls.
3. Batters who stand toward the rear of the box prefer medium high balls of moderate speed. Low fast balls are good deliveries.
4. Batters with a rigid, fixed stance find it difficult to adjust to fast balls.
5. Batters with an open stance who stand in the front of the box prefer slow balls. Speed is of prime importance in the delivery whether the ball is high, low, inside or outside.
6. Batters who stride to the ball with good swing patterns are potential threats and the pitcher must avoid balls down the middle of the strike zone. Rely on change of pace balls.
7. Batters who consistently step away from the plate find slow balls and low outside balls difficult to hit. Players who step toward the plate should receive inside fast balls.
8. A long stride may indicate the batter loses height and would fail to hit high balls; whereas a batter with a short stride prefers high rather than low balls.
9. Batters who swing hard and take big cuts for the big hit prefer fast balls and may have their timing disrupted by a slow ball or a change of pace.
10. Weak batters prefer slow, high pitches and have difficulty with low balls of medium or fast speed.

*No attempt is made to present techniques of delivery in this chapter. The reader is referred to references in the bibliography.

The styles of straight away, pull and opposite field hitting indicate a preference for certain deliveries. A straight away hitter swings at the ball where it is pitched and hits through the center. A pull hitter contacts the ball early and in front of the plate (a right-hander pulls to the left of second base) and a right-handed opposite field hitter contacts the ball late and the ball travels to the right of second base. Straight away hitters are dangerous as they can shift for high or low balls. Their style calls for low outside and inside balls which they are less likely to hit solidly. Pull hitters find high fast balls difficult; opposite field hitters find fast balls difficult because of their late swing.

Certain situations call for analysis by the pitcher. With runners on base and less than two outs the pitcher should avoid throwing outside to right-handed batters or throwing a good pitch to opposite field right-handed hitters or left-handed pull hitters. The delivery should be one difficult to hit to right field.

With runners on third and less than two outs the pitcher should avoid throwing the fast high pitch to a good hitter as the ball can travel great distances on the fly.

When a bunt is indicated, a high fast ball is a sound delivery as contact is difficult and, if hit, a pop-up often results.

The pitcher's primary responsibility in the infield is to cover home plate on passed balls and to cover third base when the third baseman plays the ball. When appropriate, she also covers third base on shallow hits to right and center field. She moves quickly to cover home on a wild pitch or a ball passing the catcher with a runner on third. The faster the pitcher gets to home plate the more time she has to get set for the tag and the catcher has to prepare for the throw. Arriving at the moment the ball and base runner arrive is dangerous.

The double play initiated by the pitcher who throws to second base is often mishandled by the pitcher in her anxiousness. She must remember that the ball reached her very quickly and she has time to turn, get set and throw, allowing time for the infielder to cover the base.

The *catcher* should learn the batters' weaknesses, the pitcher's most effective pitch and her control pitch. By working with a pitcher she learns where each pitch should be thrown and how to set up the batter for certain pitches. She must set up a steady target for the pitcher; that is, immediately after the signal she assumes her catching stance and holds it. Some catchers find they can aid the pitcher who is having control problems by presenting an open target. She simply holds her hands up in front of their respective shoulders, palms facing the pitcher, to provide a wider target until the pitcher regains control.

The catcher should attempt to back up the first baseman on any ball hit to the infield and on shallow hits to right and center fields if there are no runners on base. When fielding a bunt the catcher should approach the ball so that it lies between her and the base to which she is going to throw. This eliminates the time it takes to turn, look for the base and set to throw. She also throws harder for she is moving in the direction of the throw.

The Infield.   The *depth the infield plays* from the batter depends on the range of the throws and the batter's hitting and running ability. Playing deep affords more time to judge the ball and to set for the throw. It also enables players to catch pop-ups otherwise out of reach. A more shallow position of the infield becomes necessary to prevent a runner from scoring from third base. Such situations occur when a critical run is on third with no one out or when there are runners on second and third with one out. When the offense has no more than one out with runners on first and third or on all bases and when the runner on third base represents the winning run, the infield may play a little deeper in anticipation of a double play, still allowing a play at home plate. Experience indicates that the infield plays shallow with first and second bases occupied and plays deeper with two outs, regardless of the situation on base.

Infielders serve as both cutoff and relay players for the outfielders. As the ball is hit to the outfield, the appropriate infielder lines up the throw by stationing herself between the ball and the base to which the ball is intended. The ball is thrown above the head level of the infielder so that it may be caught or cut off and relayed to another base, or it may be allowed to pass and reach the intended base on one bounce. In each case the baseman for whom the throw is intended determines and calls for the cutoff. The designated infielder reacts to her command. After calling "cut off" she may then name the base where the ball should be relayed. If she feels the throw is accurate and the ball will arrive in time, she remains silent.

The cutoff player to home plate should be the third baseman on all balls hit to left and center field and the first baseman in all other situations. The cutoff player assumes a position about even with the pitcher's mound

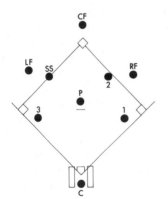

Figure 7–5.   Shallow defensive position of the infield.

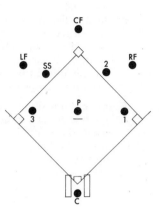

Figure 7–6. Halfway defensive position of the infield.

and in line with the path the ball would travel to home. The catcher gives the verbal command if she wants the ball cut.

When a ball is hit deep to the outfield and a throw to base is too long to be successfully made by the outfielder, an infielder must relay. The infielder runs to the outfield and becomes the middle player in the relay. The shortstop usually relays when the ball is hit to left, left center or center. The second baseman assumes the task when the ball is hit to right or right center field. Since the infielder's back is toward the infield when receiving the ball, she must be guided as to the place of her throw by the outfielder closest to, but not involved in, the play.

General defensive hints to infielders and the battery:

Pop fly:
1. On pop flies to the infield, the catcher designates who should make the catch. The pitcher should avoid catching them if another fielder is available.
2. On pop flies to the outfield when a base is deserted by an infielder attempting the catch, the pitcher should cover the base.

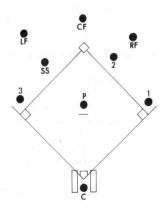

Figure 7–7. Deep defensive depth of the infield.

3. On pop flies in the catcher's territory but also within the reach of the first baseman or third baseman, the baseman should make the catch, as pop flies tend to move deep to the infield and are less difficult for the baseman. The baseman should attempt to face the infield when making the catch, as she is then in a better position to throw to the bases.

Common bunt situations:
1. When there is a runner on first base, the first baseman, third baseman and catcher move in to field the bunt. (Pitcher fields only if the ball is deep down the middle of the infield.) The shortstop covers second base and the second baseman covers first base. The pitcher and left fielder cover third base if the ball is fielded by the third baseman.

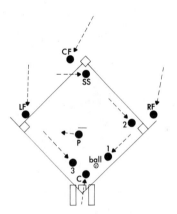

Figure 7–8. Infielders' positions for bunt defense with runner on first base.

2. With runners on first and second base the first baseman charges in to field any bunt on her side of the infield. The third baseman attempts to field all balls bunted to the third base side of the infield. The catcher protects home, the shortstop moves to cover third base, the center fielder covers second base and the second baseman covers first base. The catcher should direct the throw by verbal command to either first base for the most likely out or, if there is time, to third for the force out.

Common Defensive Play Situations

1. Runner on first, single to the outfield. When there is a runner on first and the batter hits a single to the outfield, the outfielder throws the ball on a line to second if a play can be made. If the runner is safe at second and holds, the outfielder may walk the ball in or throw to second. If the hit is deep and the runner goes for third, the throw is on a line to third so that it comes to the base after one bounce.
2. Runner on first, extra base hit to the outfield. The shortstop acts as a relay player on balls hit to direct center and to left of center;

second baseman serves as relay on balls hit to the right of center field. On hits over or between outfielders, the first baseman is the cutoff for the catcher.

3. Runner on second or runners on second and third, single is hit to the outfield. Whenever possible the outfielder tries for the base runner who is going to score. (With runners on first and third when a single is hit, the runner on third will no doubt score and the play should develop as if there were only a runner on first base.) First baseman cuts off on hits to right or center field and the third baseman is the cutoff on hits to left field and to left center field.

4. When there are runners on first and second and a single is hit to the outfield, the player fielding the ball must make a decision to play the lead runner at the plate or play the second runner. The shortstop acts as a cutoff player for the third baseman while the second baseman covers second base.

5. When there is a runner on second and a bunt is laid down, the defensive position is the same as when there are runners on first and second; however, the defense must be more alert and faster since the play at third is a tag rather than a force play.

Defensive Signals.   During the game it is often desirable for the coach to send messages to the defense. Such might occur with a runner on third and less than two outs. The infielders might want a coach's decision on whether to play in and attempt to cut the run off at the plate, play half way or play back and give up the run. Obviously, the score, inning and strength of the batter will influence the coach's decision. A commonly used set of responses for designating player depth is: play deep—coach raises both hands with palms toward the infielders; play midway—crossed forearms; cut off at the plate—hands up with palms facing the coach.

Other commonly used signals are as follows: (1) Intentional walk—The coach calls to the pitcher and points toward first base. The coach may give the signal directly or it may be relayed by the catcher. (2) Steal signal detected by the coach—The coach relays to the catcher who may call for a pitch out. (3) The catcher signals to the baseman to expect a throw to tag a runner who is taking a big lead and is slow to return to base after the pitch.

Highly skilled teams often rely on the coach to call pitches in close situations. A signal system is then set up with the catcher for the fast ball, curve and change of pace. In these situations it is helpful if both infielders and outfielders know the pitch to be thrown. Signaling is the job of the catcher. For example, after signaling the pitcher, the catcher touches the top of her mask to indicate a fast ball, middle of the mask for a curve ball and bottom of the mask for a change of pace. A coach may prefer that the shortstop catch the original signal from the catcher to the pitcher and relay it to the outfield by placing her hands behind her back and indicating various pitches by closed and open fists.

Coaching the Game

Each game day tests the organizational ability of the coach, her staff and student managers as well as the playing ability of the team members. The coach should develop a pregame checklist for both home and away games that covers the necessary items of game preparation.

A team's starting line-up and battery should be posted at least a day prior to the game so that each player can prepare her personal mental state for the event.

Pregame Practice.   The amount of time allotted for pregame practice is a major factor in determining practice patterns. Frequently a tournament schedule will permit only ten or 15 minutes on the field before play. In these cases players must conduct their personal warm-ups independently and with a partner in small areas surrounding the field. In single game events more time is usually available.

On arriving at the field the coach inspects the playing area for field conditions, general layout, temperature and wind velocity and direction. She passes pertinent information on to the players during warm-up or at a brief meeting immediately before the game.

Players begin warm-up exercises of arm windmills, body bends, stretching exercises and running immediately before or as soon as they enter the field area. Throwing and catching with a teammate for approximately ten minutes ends the general warm-up period.

The pitcher and catcher begin batting practice as soon as they enter the field while others are throwing. General batting practice follows the assigned order with each player getting four or five swings and at least two bunts. The battery working batting practice is not the one assigned to the game. While batting practice is in progress a fungo hitter places ground balls to the outfielders located away from the infielders.

A pattern of infield practice should be established. For example, during the first round of infield practice the ball should be hit straight to each infielder who throws to first for the imaginary out. The first baseman throws to the catcher who throws against an imaginary runner at second or third. The baseman then throws to the next base or home until the ball is returned to the catcher.

As time permits, the following patterns should be followed. On the second round the ball should be hit to the glove side of each infielder; the third round the ball is hit to the side opposite the glove hand. Patterns of throwing around the bases may be altered or the same plan followed as in round one. In the fourth round the double play throw is practiced and in the fifth time around the bunt recovery for double play or play at the plate is stressed.

As infield practice progresses to fielding bunts, the outfielders move to their regular positions with the fungo hitter near second base. Toward the end of the practice period outfielders should have an opportunity to make at least one throw to second base, third base and toward home.

Analysis of Opponents. The analysis of opponents begins during their warm-up period. The coach and players have an opportunity to search for weaknesses in throwing and fielding. During the game the scoresheet tells much about an individual's ability and the analytical eye of the coach continues to seek weaknesses in the defensive and offensive patterns. The following questions are designed to assist in team analysis.*

Pitcher:
1. Is the pitcher consistently wild?
2. Is her style unusual? Is her timing of release deceiving?
3. What is she throwing? Fast balls, curves, "stuff"? Is there a pattern in her delivery that indicates what she will throw?
4. Is she a good fielding pitcher? If her follow through limits her effectiveness in fielding, hits in her area may be indicated.

Catcher:
1. Is her technique sound or are there obvious weaknesses which indicate that a player might steal against her? Several points to check:
   a. Does she remain in a crouch with runners on base?
   b. Does she take preliminary steps in throwing to the bases?
   c. Does she throw to occupied bases consistently?
   d. Does she leave home plate unprotected?
2. Does she back up players at other bases?
3. Does she move well to bunts? Does she face the infield while fielding fouls?
4. Does she read the batter or call for a consistent pattern from the pitcher?

First Baseman:
1. Does she play too deep in a normal situation?
2. Does she adjust well for the bunt situation? Does she recover well?
3. Is she right- or left-handed? (This indicates her reach and how she may play a runner returning to base after a lead. A longer lead may be indicated with a right-handed first baseman and, consequently, more opportunity to steal.)

Second Baseman:
1. Is she alert to sense plays developing?
2. Does she cover first base on bunts to the first baseman?
3. Does she cover second base when the ball is hit to left infield?
4. Does she serve as cutoff player on throws from the outfield?

Shortstop:
1. Is she agile and fast?
2. Does she cover second base on balls hit to the right infield?

---

*For a more complete discussion, see Stringer, Pat: "Analyzing Your Opponent," *Softball Guide,* 1966–68, DGWS, AAHPER.

3. Does she cover second base on an attempted steal?
4. Does she back up second and third bases?
5. Does she move to serve as cutoff on throws from the outfield?
Third Baseman:
1. Does she play too deep at normal depth?
2. Can she adjust for the bunt situation?
3. Does she recover quickly?
Outfielders:
1. How strong and accurate are their throws?
2. Do they back up outfielders as well as infielders?
3. Do they move to the ball aggressively or do they play cautiously?
4. Do they show experience in judging wind conditions, field conditions and the action on the ball?

Analysis of One's Own Team.   This procedure utilizes the same methods and questions designed for opponent analysis. When playing defense the coach can observe and follow the charting of play just as one does the opponents. During a game each player should analyze her own play in terms of the critical role of her position.

Analysis of offensive play is admittedly difficult. The statistics of the game are usually the best indicator of offensive performance; however, no sound method has been found to evaluate one's role as the team's spark plug and play maker. Coaches are the best judges of a player's ability to follow signals, but teammates may be the most authoritative in determining field leadership. A wise coach involves players in self-analysis of each game performance in a postgame meeting of all players.

Game Strategy.   Game strategy may be plotted before play begins but the wise coach must be capable of flexibility. Strategy must always be adjusted to the progress of the game. The well-coached team has so rehearsed situational play that it responds with confidence. Coaches serve to remind players of possible offensive moves by the opponents through the use of defensive signals (see p. 189). A team's offensive play is enhanced by base coaches at first and third bases. These two coaches should be true students of the game and remain with the team throughout the season. The third base coach should be most astute in sizing up the game situation. To be effective, a team must adopt a simple signal system between player and coach which allows for a clear understanding of each signal and when, where and how it will be used. Some coaches use both voice and hand signals. Verbal signals should be given with the hands cupping the mouth so they can be heard above team chatter and crowd noise.

The *first base coach* positions herself in the front of the box with no runners on base, and parallel with the base and the runner with players on base. Her signals may include:

1. Circling arm on a ball hit to the infield encourages the runner to hustle to first.
2. A raised arm pointing toward second indicates that a turn can be made.

The first base coach's responsibilities include:

1. Encouraging the batter before every pitch.
2. Coaching the batter as soon as she becomes a base runner. Encourage her to run hard just as the ball is hit.
3. Directing the hitter to take her turn and watch the ball as it is fielded.
4. Reminding the runner during the 10 to 12 seconds while fielders get set and the pitcher receives her signal of the following:
    a. Score, number of outs
    b. Find the ball (to prevent hidden ball and to watch for mishandling and possible opportunity for advancement)
    c. Play situation and runner's responsibility
    d. Be alert for bunt, steal, hit or run, signal (depending on score and situation)
    e. Be alert for passed ball
5. Frequently assuring the runner "you're all right."
6. Watching shortstop with runners on second.

The *third base coach* is positioned in the box in line with second base before the ball is hit. She moves down the line toward home with a runner advancing toward home. Her signals include:

1. Circling left arm calls for the runner to advance toward third.
2. Raised right arm pointing toward home sends the runner on to score.
3. Both hands raised overhead, palms facing out stops the runner.
4. Forceful downward thrust of the hands indicates a slide. Direction of the slide is indicated by waving lowered hands in the direction of the slide.
5. When there is no need for the runner to slide, but the ball is coming into the infield or is cut off by the shortstop, the coach may point to the base indicating the runner should come to the base fast and standing up. It also means do not overrun, the ball is behind the runner.

The third base coach is responsible for runners on second and third base. Her responsibilities include:

1. Directing runner on extra base hits from first to third base, from second to home and from third to home.
2. Reminding the runner at second of:
    a. Holding the base and finding the ball
    b. Number of outs and score
    c. Possible play or signal
    d. Infielder position—in or deep
    e. When to tag on a fly ball
    f. Heads up for a line drive
    g. Heads up for a passed ball
    h. With no outs make the ball go through and take no unnecessary chances

    i. With one out, hold third if the ball is hit to third baseman, pitcher or first baseman

    j. Go for home if the ball is hit to deep shortstop, second baseman; hold if these players are playing in

    k. With two outs be alert for a passed ball or possible steal of home

Charting and Statistical Evaluation. The statistics of the game serve in analyzing past performance and in motivating players. A properly charted scoresheet of one's own team and the opponent is the most graphic record of individual and team performance. From the scorebook the coach can develop a data sheet that serves as a statistical compilation of individual players or the total team. This helps to indicate a player's efficiency in special situations and where both individual and team weaknesses lie.

The data sheet (Fig. 7–9) may be used to report a single game or serve as a summary of an individual's record or team record as they develop throughout the season. It also serves as a season summary. The information charted is self-explanatory, with symbols of H — hit, HE — hit into an error, HP — hit by the pitcher, W — walked, and I — interference used to indicate how a lead off batter got on base. Similar symbols are used to indicate how a player got on base when others were on base. Sacrifice hits are indicated by X — successful and F — unsuccessful.

Complete and accurate use of the scoresheet is imperative. Every team must have one person who is capable of proper statistical charting. Scorebooks with complete instructions for charting are available commercially. Basically, when one's own team is at bat, it is charted for offensive play and the opponents' defensive acts are recorded; with the opponents on offense, charting is identical. Players are numbered by position; that is, (1) pitcher, (2) catcher, (3) first baseman, (4) second baseman, (5) third baseman, (6) shortstop, (7) left fielder, (8) center fielder and (9) right fielder.

Abbreviations on the right side of the player's box of each inning indicate the method of getting on base. A mark through the appropriate symbol is all that is required of the scorekeeper. It is helpful in later evaluation of a player's placement or opponents' defensive strengths and weaknesses to draw a line from home in the direction and approximate distance of the hit. A base on balls, sacrifice hit or hit by a pitched ball does not count as times at bat in statistical tabulation.

Strikes and balls are recorded on all batters in the small frame in the player's box. An out made by the batter is recorded to indicate the way it was made and the player or players who were involved. For example, F4 indicates a fly to the second baseman. The type of fly ball, pop-up or long ball, may be indicated by an arc over the play recorded — pop-up, F9 or a long fly $\overline{F9}$. An unassisted play, such as the first baseman fielding a ball and stepping on base, is recorded as 3U.

GAME OR PLAYER _____ POS. _____

     OR

SUMMARY THROUGH _____GAME

Players or Games																							
AT BAT																							
RUNS SCORED																							
HITS 1B																							
2B																							
3B																							
HR																							
PUT OUTS																							
ASSISTS																							
ERRORS																							
SACRIFICE ATTEMPTS S/F																							
WALKED																							
STRUCK OUT S/C																							
INNINGS PLAYED																							
RUNS-BATTED-IN																							
STOLEN BASES																							
DOUBLE PLAYS																							
LEAD-OFF HITTER																							
GOT ON BY																							
FIRST ON BASE BY																							
WITH PLAYER ON BASES HITS																							
BB																							
SH																							
HE																							
HP																							
FAILED WITH PLAYER ON																							
BATTING AVERAGE																							
FIELDING AVERAGE																							

Figure 7–9.　Softball coach's data sheet.

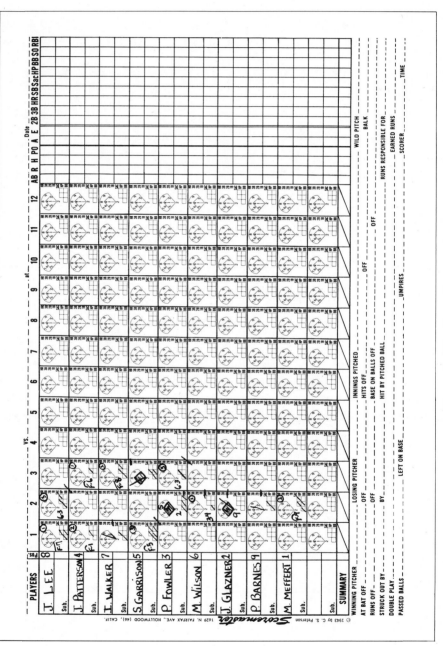

Figure 7–10.   Sample scoresheet.

An example of scoring three innings of play for one team when at bat follows:

Lee, centerfielder, hits a long fly ball to left field. The count was two and one. Out number one is recorded.

Patterson, second baseman, pops up to the pitcher. Two outs are now recorded.

Walker, left fielder, gets a hit driving the ball past the second baseman into right field.

Garrison, third baseman, pops up to the third baseman with a full count of three balls and two strikes. The side is retired.

In the second inning, Fowler, first baseman, takes first base on balls.

Wilson, shortstop, sacrifice bunts to the first baseman who throws to the second baseman covering first for the out. Fowler advances.

Glazner, catcher, hits the pitch delivered for a double to deep right field. Fowler comes home.

Barnes, right fielder, gets a hit past the second baseman to right field. Glazner scores.

Meffert, pitcher, pop flies to short right field. The second out is recorded.

Lee hits to the shortstop who throws to first on a fielder's choice for the third out of the inning.

Patterson leads off in the third inning. She pop flies to the shortstop for the first out.

Walker hits a long fly ball to the center fielder for the second out.

Garrison hits a home run beyond the left fielder.

Fowler hits to the shortstop who throws to first for the third out.

Bibliography

Adams, G. L.: "Effect of eye dominance on baseball batting." *Research Quarterly*, 36:3, March 1965.

Allen, Archie P.: *Baseball Coach's Handbook of Offensive Strategy and Techniques.* Englewood Cliffs, N. J., Prentice-Hall, Inc., 1964.

Allen, Archie P.: *Coach's Guide to Defensive Baseball*, Englewood Cliffs, N. J., Prentice-Hall, Inc., 1960.

Amateur Softball Association of America: *Softball Coaching and Playing Techniques.* ASA, 4515 North Santa Fe, Oklahoma City, Oklahoma.

Bender, J. A., Kaplan, H. M. and Johnson, A. J.: "A conditioning program for baseball." *Athletic Journal*, 45, March 1965.

Brace, David K.: *Skills Test Manual: Softball for Girls.* AAHPER, Washington, D. C., 1966.

Breen, James L.: "What makes a good hitter?" *Journal of Health, Physical Education and Recreation*, 38:36–39, April 1967.

Brose, Donald E. and Hanson, D. L.: "Effects of overload training on velocity and accuracy of throwing," *Research Quarterly*, 38:4, December 1967.

Division for Girls and Women's Sports: *Softball Guide.* AAHPER, Published every two years.
    Atwater, Anne Elizabeth: "The overarm softball throw," pp. 23–32, 1968–70.
    Kuenn, Harvey: "Your strategy at bat," pp. 30–33, 1970–72.
    Neuser, Jean A.: "The ideal batting order," pp. 26–29, 1970–72.
    Riley, George A.: "Competitive softball," pp. 42–44, 1964–66.
    Safrit, M., Pavis, Joanne and Pavis, Adele: "Overarm throw skill testing," pp. 39–43, 1968–70.
    Sisley, Becky: "Check your form," pp. 18–22, 1968–70.
    Sisley, Becky: "The coached game," pp. 40–42, 1966–68.
    Stringer, Pat: "Analyzing your opponent," pp. 43–45, 1966–68.
    Temple, Ina G.: "Establishing specific objectives in bunting," pp. 20–26, 1966–68.

DeGroat, H. S.: *Baseball Coaching Aids.* Springfield, Mass., Springfield College, Rev. ed., 1946.

Irace, S. Charles: *Comparative Baseball Strategy.* Minneapolis, Minn., Burgess Publishing Co., 1967.

Kitzman, Eric W.: "Baseball: electromyographic study of batting swing." *Research Quarterly*, 35:166, 1964.

Luebke, Laura L.: "A comparison of the effects of varying schedules of mental and physical practice trials on the performance of the overarm softball throw." Unpublished Master's Thesis, University of Wisconsin, 1967.

Michael, Ernest, Skubic, Vera and Rochelle, Rene: "Effect of warm-up on softball throw for distance." *Research Quarterly*, 28:357 December 1957.

Miller, Robert G., and Shay, Clayton: "Relationship of reaction time to the speed of a softball." *Research Quarterly*, 35:433, October 1964.

Neuberger, Tom: "What the *Research Quarterly* says about warm-up." *Journal of Health, Physical Education and Recreation*, October 1969, pp. 75–77.

Race, D. E.: "A cinematographical and mechanical analysis of the external movements involved in hitting a baseball effectively." *Research Quarterly*, 32:394, October 1961.

Reiff, Guy G.: *What Research Tells the Coach About Baseball.* AAHPER, Washington, D.C., 1971.

Seymour, Emery W.: "Comparison of base running methods." *Research Quarterly*, 30:321, October 1959.

Smilgoff, James: *Winning High School Baseball.* Englewood Cliffs, N. J., Prentice-Hall, Inc., 1956.

Vannier, Maryhelen and Poindexter, Hally B. W.: *Individual and Team Sports for Girls and Women.* Philadelphia, W. B. Saunders Co., 1968.

8

Volleyball

Since its inception as a passive indoor recreational game requiring limited skill and physical conditioning, volleyball has matured to a power competitive team activity of Olympic status. As one of the most popular sports in the world, it is played in more than eighty countries with international competition in such events as the Pan American Games, European Championships, Championships of North and Central America and the Caribbean, Asiatic Championships, World Games and the Olympics. In recent years the attempt to draw the United States Volleyball Association (USVBA), DGWS and International Rules together has resulted in major rule changes affecting the nature of the entire game.

The term "power volleyball" describes the highly competitive game and denotes advanced individual skill and highly refined team strategy. It is truly a team game where each player has specific duties to effect well-planned offensive and defensive patterns. Each player, in each court position, has offensive assignments of passing, setting or spiking and defensive duties of blocking or defending against the dink or spike.

Individual Skills Necessary for Competitive Play

The offensive and defensive strategy used by a team dictates the degree of specialized skill needed by each player; conversely, the individual skills of the members dictate team strategy. In either case, there are basic techniques which each individual must bring to the game situation. The term "techniques" as used throughout the chapter refers to the technical elements of position (fundamental or ready), moving or shifting in the playing court, the volley or underhand pass, the low pass, dig or underhand pass, the roll, serve, spike, block, dink and net recovery. Each of the techniques when properly executed by a highly skilled player takes on her personal style.

The skills of agility, speed, lateral mobility, flexibility and jumping are limiting or expanding factors in developing game techniques. There is little question that a player's basic talents can be enhanced by coaching and directed practice. Even with diligent efforts, however, not all six players will develop with equal skill in spiking, blocking or back court digs, but each must acquire a balance of strength, speed and endurance as a basis for technique development. As a point of departure, players must move quickly and be prepared to move again, or recover to the next set of movements. Direction of this movement requires perception and quick physical adjustment to the visually perceived situation. All must be able to jump and reach, some well above the net level. Training in game skill and learned strategy prepare the player for team play.

Selection of Players

The coach must look to two forms of evaluation in selecting players: (1) the individual skill as reflected by some form of evaluation and (2) a player's performance record in competition. Evaluating one's potential for technique development is essential, for the coach must know the skill level of each player in considering team assignments and she is better able to design workout schedules for ultimate individual development. Four basic skills should be appraised soon after players report to the team.

1. *Height of Jump.* A standing vertical jump and reach test and a running vertical jump and reach test are indicative of potential. A number of jump boards are available and techniques vary. A simple method is to lower the board to the normal reaching height of the player, she then jumps and touches the one inch slat suspended on chain or nylon cord to indicate her jump height beyond her normal reach. From this information a coach easily discerns that a 5' 10" player, with a standing reach of 7' 3" and a jump reach of 26 additional inches has the basic skill for executing an effective spike from two feet above the net.
2. *Speed and Agility.* The combination of these two skills, so necessary for responding to game situations, can be generally evaluated by a timed shuttle drill between two lines, ten feet apart. The player begins by touching one line and on signal, runs in a cross step or side shuttle to touch the other line. The shuttle should be repeated several times during one timed trial. This evaluation can be expanded to include a roll, a bump or other techniques.
3. *Mobility at the Net.* With the net raised six to 12 inches above normal height, a player begins at the side line near and facing the

net. On signal she jumps and touches the top of the net with both hands, runs to the other side of her court and touches the net. This should be repeated several times during a single timed trial. This can be modified by having the player begin in mid-court on a marked spot and, on a verbal signal of "right" or "left," move to touch the tape at the side, return to center mark and await another verbal signal.

All of the above evaluative techniques will also indicate an endurance factor with each player. All of the test results can be improved if the coach teaches the specifics of the test. The general conditioning program may be designed to stress the components in the test which the coach feels are integral skills of volleyball.

After a coach determines the level of skill her players bring to the team, she proceeds with technique and style development. Many successful teams stress fundamental techniques, well described in textbooks for the beginning player. The following statements on basic techniques serve to reinforce the need for developing and drilling on fundamentals.

Basic Techniques. The *serve* is a team's first offensive move and the one time in the game when a single player is in complete control of the action of the ball. In power volleyball the serve is more than a means to put the ball in play. It is an important offensive skill. Of the many styles of service, the overhand floating serve is the most commonly used by highly skilled players because of its accuracy and unpredictable flight. Similar in action to the knuckleball in baseball, the floater does not spin, but ducks and weaves in flight resulting in a swerving path that frequently finds the receiver unprepared. The server's body faces the net with feet in forward stride position with weight equally distributed. The ball may be held high or "lifted" (with no spin) just above the head and in front of the hitting arm and shoulder. As the ball begins to drop, the hitting arm is extended overhead with the elbow slightly bent. The body weight transfers forward and the striking arm snaps powerfully forward. The elbow leads and the heel of the open hand contacts the center of the inert ball. It is important that the ball be struck in the center to avoid imparting spin. The wrist is firm with limited follow through. To float effectively, the ball must be compressed at contact so that the flexibility of the ball results in distortion and weaving action. To gain maximum compression, the smallest possible area should be used while still assuring good control. A few players use the side of the hand or base of the thumb to get increased compression and weaving action.

Both the overhand serve and the roundhouse, executed with an overhand throwing motion, travel with overspin and drop quickly and forcefully. Spin serves, resulting in balls curving in flight, are less deceptive and serve primarily as a change of pace.

Soft underhand spin or floater serves may gain an occasional point against a deep defense, but are generally used only by players who have not perfected a more effective offensive skill.

Fundamental position is the position the player assumes before volleying the ball. The body position may be high, medium or low; however, the medium position is considered "ready position" from which a player moves. The player's legs are apart in a forward stride position with knees flexed. The body weight is forward over the balls of the feet and toes and well balanced on both legs. A player on the right side of the court should advance the right leg; on the left side of the court, the left leg, so that her body is open to the court and a volley can be easily directed to the other players.

Ankles and knees are flexed to carry the hips lower; the body leans forward slightly curving the back. In the ready position the arms are extended forward, elbows close to the body.

Many times a player does not have time to shift and assume a fundamental position but must play the ball kneeling in an oblique position or in any of a number of unexpected postures. To arrive at her position she must shift from an assumed court position with rapid short steps. These may be well anticipated and require only a close shift to cover an unguarded court opening or require a burst of speed to cover a greater distance. Shifting is generally made with short steps, adding a jump to the side or forward for additional speed in covering longer distances. A half step, while in motion, is part of the shift technique. This "shuttle" is started by a step with the foot pointing toward the desired direction: the other foot is quickly brought parallel in a comfortable side stance. Legs never cross. This movement is used for lateral shifting near the net when preparing for the block.

The *volley*, or *pass*, is the controlled movement of the ball from one player to another. The techniques of volleying, passing and setting are the foundations of the entire game. The forearm pass is used to receive serves and spikes. As opposed to the chest pass, use of the forearm increases the time a player can follow the ball's trajectory before playing it, and increases the range of the player. The speed and trajectory of the ball determine the use of forearm: as a pass or a dig with one or both arms or hands to the front, laterally and with or without a roll. From a ready position, one hand is firmly extended with thumb in the palm facing upward, as the other hand clasps that hand. The thumbs are on top and close together (Fig. 8–1). Some players may prefer hand positions of (1) interlocking fingers with palms pressed together; (2) double fist or (3) hand in hand with thumbs joined on the surface.

Ideally, the ball should be contacted below the waist close to the floor. The arms are rotated outward so that ball contact is directly in front of the body on the fleshy portion of the inner forearms above the wrists. The arms are fully extended, elbows straight prior to, during and after ball con-

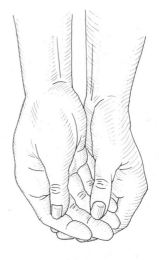

Figure 8–1.   Hand position for two arm, under-hand volley.

tact. At the moment of contact, the wrists snap downward, elbows are firm-ly extended and the follow through is an extension of the entire body with arms swinging upward from the shoulders (Fig. 8–2).

When there is not enough time to take a correct position, a low lateral hit or a dig is possible. The ball is contacted with both arms if close, otherwise, one arm is extended to the ball. The key to effective execution is that the inside of the forearms be placed in the direction that the ball should travel rather than upward so that contact results in upward or backward flight of the ball, making an offensive play difficult.

Good hands refer to the skill a player displays in volleying the ball with

Figure 8–2.   Body position for two arm, underhand volley.

proper direction, lack of spin and desirable height so that the next player has the opportunity to play the ball without readjusting for error.

Setting is the technique that determines the direction and structure of play. Once the basic hand and body positions are mastered, minor movement variations are needed to accomplish any set. With the body in fundamental position, the setter's hands are raised to provide a target of contact and to get the body balanced and poised. The body is nearly erect, yet relaxed with knees slightly flexed (Fig. 8–3). The hands are in front of the

Figure 8–3.   Body and arm position when setting.

face with thumb and index and middle fingers forming a triangle. The wrists are extended back and fingers cupped. As the ball approaches, wrists and fingers hyperextend and upon ball contact the arms extend and wrists and fingers snap upward and forward to impart force. Ball contact is made by the thumb and pads and second joint of index and middle fingers. The other two fingers of each hand serve as guides and as additional force. The trajectory of the ball is determined by the contact of force on the ball. (See Fig. 8–4.) The distance of flight is determined by force imparted by arm extension.

By adjusting the hands and body position, a setter can back set, flick, high or short set.

The lateral set and jump set should be attempted only by experienced players. As a deceptive maneuver, the lateral set is used to confuse blockers when the ball is at the net and cannot be set in the usual manner. The ball is set over the side of the body with body and arms extending up and sideward toward the direction of the pass or the follow through. A jump set is executed by an offensive net player feigning an attack. The body extends,

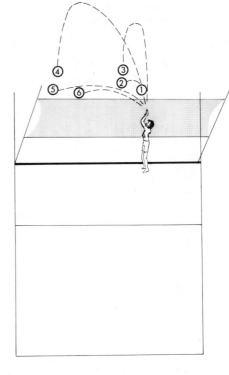

Figure 8–4. Basic set patterns: (1) Short set, executed after the attack player has jumped; (2) Low, short set. Spiker leaves the ground immediately after ball is set; (3) High, middle standard set; (4) Regular, side set; (5) Low, sideline set; (6) Low set, halfway between setter and sideline.

as in a basketball jump shot, and from the extended position the contact is made with the ball in front of the setter's face.

Advanced Skills for Competitive Play

Virtually all basic individual skills of volleyball necessary for competitive play are taught in a typical intermediate level class. The possible exceptions are multiple blocks and rolls and recoveries. The inclusion of spiking and blocking in advanced skills is to emphasize their importance in strategic competitive situations.

Attack Skills. The attack is usually the third contact a team makes and it is intended as the culmination of all preparation. It is the technique that puts the ball away for a point or side out. The spike is the most common attack and when forcefully hit, it can travel nearly 100 miles per hour. Less powerful spikes directed with more finesse result in off-speed attacks made by changing only the force and follow through of the contact. The dink is a passive attack technique directed to the open court or to a defender who is prepared to return a spike. The dink is contacted with a closed fist by less skilled players, and with the pads of the fingers of one hand by the skillful.

SPIKE.   The spike is most effectively executed from a two foot takeoff, although there will be an occasional need for a one-leg attack (Fig. 8–5). A

Figure 8–5. Approaching takeoff position for the attack.

shift often precedes the approach from ten to 15 feet from the net. Two to five steps are taken with three steps most frequently used. Several styles of takeoff are seen among highly skilled spikers, but a smooth approach pattern that allows for balance and late body adjustments seems generally more effective than hop styles designed specifically to gain height. After the final step, the trailing foot quickly closes to the lead foot and the heels dig into the floor. As the legs are flexed to a squat, the body leans slightly forward as the head and eyes follow the ball. The arms swing forcibly backward as the heels contact the floor, then the arms swing forward and upward as the legs and body extend. The entire purpose of the approach and takeoff is to place the striking hand as high as desirable or possible. Consequently, the technique of converting horizontal momentum to vertical force should be clearly understood. The key is that the jump must reverse the direction of the approach, consequently, a slight backward angle of the jump to increase vertical height is necessary. A true vertical jump may not reverse the forward momentum enough to prevent fouling at the net or center line. Too much horizontal speed requires more reversal and the backward angle makes the takeoff difficult (Fig. 8–6).

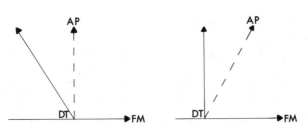

Figure 8–6. Reversal of body angle to gain maximum jump height. AP— Attack Position; FM—Forward Momentum; DT—Direction of Takeoff.

Once in the air, the attack must suspend herself and forcefully contact the ball while unsupported. The knees bend backward to aid the body lift as the arms swing upward. A right-handed player will throw the left arm over her head, as the right arm, elbow bent, is cocked in a throwing position with right hand near the right ear (Fig. 8–7). To achieve a suspended position, the legs snap downward and forward, creating a slight body pike. As the body extension is accomplished, the left arm is forcefully driven forward and down, reversing the shoulder angle and causing the right

Figure 8–7. The spike. A, Player suspended and adjusting her body prior to ball contact. B, Contact for the power spike.

shoulder to be rotated upward and forward. The elbow leads the upper arm forward, right arm extends upward to contact the ball. The ball is contacted by the heel of an open or cupped hand with base of fingers and pads quickly following if a wrist snap or roll is used to impart overspin. Follow through of the striking arm depends on the technique and attacker's position to the net. The elbow may remain extended in a full follow through or it may bend and pull the arm from the follow through path.

Advanced attack players should be able to place the ball anywhere in the opponent's court. From a regular set, the options are shown in Figure 8–8.

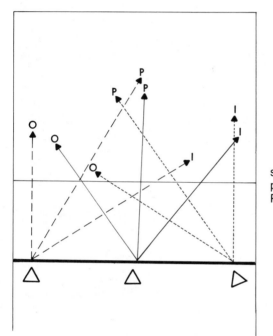

Figure 8–8. Angles of the spike from side and midcourt positions.   O—Outside;   P— Power; I—Inside.

The terms O—outside, P—power and I—inside represent the results of arm and wrist action of the spiker. The spiker must learn to hit angle shots around the defensive block. Most spikers develop a preferred wrist action and their power hit is off the inside or outside of the wrist. Right-handed inside wrist hitters find their greatest power hit right of perpendicular. They adjust in their jumps for this preference.

Angle hitting is used to hit inside, around or over the block when there is enough court to angle. It is also used to "wipe out"—that is, to hit off the outside blocker's hand when the block is set wide and the ball rebounds out of play.

To accomplish an outside hit by a right-handed player, the left arm pulls down and back causing shoulder rotation. The hand contacts the ball slightly to the right. The more angle needed, the more wrist she must use.

To hit inside the block that is set for the cross court power shot, the left arm pulls downward and across the body, limiting shoulder rotation. The left shoulder dips and the right moves back. The hand contacts the ball left of center and the wrist snaps to the right.

The recovery is made by a cushioned landing on both feet with the attack player turned toward the ball prepared for an immediate play.

The short vertical spike is the most effective of all spikes for it does not give opponents time to set a proper block. It requires cooperation and coordination between the setter and the spiker. The set must be close to the spiker as she sets the ball vertically from a low ready position. The set should rise just above the net level and the spiker, who has anticipated the set, jumps before the ball is set. The suspended spiker waits and hits the ball as it rises or at the moment its flight has ended.

BLOCKS. The block begins defensive play at the net; however, the rules of USVBA and FIVB (Federation of International Volleyball) permitting the block to be set across the net have resulted in blocking becoming a strong offensive skill. Blocking is intended to counteract the efficiency of the attack. Good blockers set the defensive pattern of the team. Individually or in multiple blocks, they must shift quickly in response to the opponents' strategy and jump in unison and to the same height.

Individual blocking skill is usually preceded by a short run and a lateral or oblique shift. Facing the net, the blocker leaves the ground with both feet, the arms aiding in the jump by their forward and upward thrust. While the blocker is jumping as high as possible, her arms reach upward past her face and forward until her hands pass over the net. The distance between the hands must be less than the diameter of the ball. Generally the palms face the opponent's court, but to cover spikes from any direction palms should be turned slightly inward.

The *attack block* is intended to score a point by contacting the ball prior to crossing or just at the net. It is used when the set is close to the net or on off speed spikes. The blocker's jump is timed so that she is descending as the ball is spiked. Reaching over the net with firm arms and hands the force is either a press forward or downward with hands fairly close together, or forward and inward with hands spread. Ideally, the ball is contacted by the heel of the hands.

The *soft block* is intended to deflect the ball to a teammate. The jump is later than in an attack block and timed an instant after the jump of the spiker so that the ball is contacted as the body is rising. The hands and arms are parallel to or slightly over the net. Hands and wrists are semirelaxed with ball contact on the palms or fingers rather than the heels of the hands.

Landing after the block should be easy over flexed knees. The player should be ready to return to game action.

Multiple blocks are those using two or three front line players. With the attacker's ball split between them, the blockers shift, stop momentarily at the spot from which they will jump and rise in a vertical jump simultaneously. When there are two blockers, the inside hands are parallel to the net and the outside hands face inward. In a three player block the hands of the inside player and the inside hands of the outside players are parallel to the net and the outside hands are turned inward.

Rolls.   In order to play difficult serves and attacks, it is often necessary to thrust the body in an off-balanced situation that necessitates a speedy recovery to playing position. For some years, Europeans have used a partial roll to get the midline of the body in line with the oncoming ball. The Japanese introduced the full roll as an important defensive technique.

The *partial roll*, frequently called a "screw under" because of the pivoting motion of the body as it falls, is used with an overhead pass or as a player extends a thrust or squats for a dig. The sequence begins with a body extension, pushing from one leg to a flexed support leg. As the ball is contacted, the support leg turns inward with toes pointing away from the direction of the body motion. The player sits down on the hip of the fully flexed support leg and rolls to her back. Rapid recovery follows by snapping the legs downward as the body rolls forward.

The *back roll* generally follows an overhead pass taken from a full squat position. The player sits down as she completes the pass and completes a partial roll on her back. Recovery is similar to the partial roll.

The *complete roll* is accomplished at high speed usually following a wide lateral move. If the ball is relatively close to the body and lateral speed is slow, the early movements are similar to the partial roll. If the player has gone to her right to play the ball, she twists to her left, rolling to her buttocks, rounded back and left shoulder. The feet and legs snap over and down with the left knee and toe making first floor contact. As speed of lateral movements is increased, there may be no time for the support leg to screw under the body. The knee, thigh and lower back of the squat leg touch the floor. The roll and recovery bring the player to a low ready position.

The *dive* is a forward thrust of the body to save a ball coming in front of a player when there is no time to shift to the ball, or when the ball changes direction suddenly. Women rarely use the technique except in zealous moments and last ditch efforts. It is not recommended for high school and college competition. The dive is taken from a low position with the front foot bearing the body weight. The body is thrust horizontally with arms outstretched. The hit may be with one or both hands or arms and immediately after contact the player touches the ground with the palms of her outstretched hands and arms, easing the body down. The head is held back as the body is lowered to chest, abdomen and thighs prior to recovery.

Combining Individuals for Team Play

As noted earlier, the coach looks at an individual's skills as well as performance records and psychological readiness for team competition. Volleyball is a game of both defense and aggressive offense and the minimum qualifications *all* team members must have are the offensive skill of serving and the defensive skills of passing from serve, spike or dink receipt. While all players must understand and be competent in conventional sets, one or more players designated as the setter in an offensive pattern must be capable of flat, low sets and the vertical short set. Height and jumping ability are unquestionable advantages for the spiker and blocker.

All players will have responsibilities of passing from serve and spike receipts during a rotation. Anticipation, speed and flexibility as well as rapid recovery are key factors in good passing. The passer must move and position herself so she can pass from any court position to the designated setter. She is fearless as she tracks the ball and reacts to its trajectory at the last possible moment. She becomes so conditioned through skillful practice that the response is automatic.

A setter must have all the game skills and must display intelligence and game sense as well as complete knowledge and ability to execute the type of set the attack desires. She can be of less height than the key spikers, but she must be able to effect the spike and block when needed. As the play maker she evaluates the opposition to give the attack player the best opportunity to score against the opposition's weaknesses. As designated set she must have great speed and agility to place herself in proper position to receive the pass. The body balance is the most important factor for a proper set. Psychologically, she is the team's spark plug; with calmness and control she sets the tempo of team play. She can do much to overcome weak passing and make an average attack exceedingly effective.

Spikers are frequently tall and strong with a jumping ability that lifts them at least 18 to 20 inches above the net. Effective spikers must develop the ability of controlled suspension while aggressively spiking over the block. Shorter spikers must substitute deception for limited jumping and reaching height. The success of the spike is dependent upon timing, precision and direction of the force imparted to the ball. Although the most effective spikers are strong and aggressive, they are alert to quick strategy change of a lay-off spike or dink to meet the defensive situation.

Blockers have many of the physical qualifications of spikers. They must shift quickly and time their jumps with the offensive play and their teammates. Good blocking sets the pattern for the entire team's defense. There is no place for timidity in blocking and those with the physical qualities must be taught the joy of aggressive actions or they will fail their defensive responsibility.

Practice Sessions

Coaches have long been concerned about the organization and administration of practice sessions and the relationship between practice and learning. Research reinforces the assumption that practice usually leads to learning and although practice does not insure perfection, it enhances a person's ability to learn a motor skill and develop an optimum performance level. The length of practice sessions, their frequency in a given period of time and the work-rest ratio within a practice period are largely determined by the coach, the player's schedules and limited research relating to massed and distributed practice.

Most competitive volleyball teams at the high school or collegiate levels are limited in their practice periods by league regulations or availability of local facilities. The season is approximately 12 to 15 weeks with three or four designated practice days and one or two competitive events a week during the competitive season. National and international competitive teams adhere to a minimum of four practice sessions of two to three hours each throughout the year.

Practice sessions have three basic purposes: conditioning, skill development and psychological readiness. Each of these purposes has individual and team implications. The purposes and general plans of practice sessions should be made known to players. Daily practice plans should be written and include specific items covered, organization and time spent on each. At the close of the practice session a written evaluation should be made to note general progress, suggested changes for the future and individual player's strengths and weaknesses. Notes covering players' responses, attitudes and psychological state are helpful for planning future practices. Each practice session should be planned with consistency, skill progression and flexibility as needed.

Early in the season emphasis is given to general conditioning and individual skill development; during the middle one-third of the season the focus of practice sessions should be on achieving team balance and offensive and defensive skills and systems. The last portion of the season is devoted to maintenance of physical and psychological readiness and refining team skills and strategy.

The following list is indicative of the percentage of practice time a team might spend on various items over the entire season.

Per Cent of Practice Session Time Allotment Over Entire Season
Conditioning 5%
Serve.. 5%
Pass and Dig..35%
Set 10%
Attack...10%
Block...10%
Offensive Systems..10%
Defensive Systems 10%
Scrimmage 5%

Emphasis will vary each session and each week. As intensity and quality of play develop, specific individual skill practices may be combined and further combined in offensive and defensive pattern drills.

Conditioning. The purpose of a conditioning program is development of a balance of an individual's strength, agility, speed and endurance. During the past few years competitive teams have found that drill, scrimmages and competitive matches are not enough to push the individual to the level of fitness needed for demanding tournament play. A specific program should be developed which applies the overload principle for muscular and cardiorespiratory development. The intensity of the program should be sufficient to convince each team member that she is physically and mentally ready for any match.

The program should be designed so that (1) a player assumes some responsibility for her conditioning independent of the group and (2) team directed conditioning during practice is also included. The individual's program should focus on her assessed weaknesses and be designed by the coach and player. The use of weights and specifically the Universal Gym* has been found helpful in developing specific power. Strength should be developed in the legs and buttocks for jumping, shifting, passing and digging; in the wrists and fingers for setting; and in the shoulders and arms for spiking. The following suggestions are for an individual home training program.

1. Strength
   A. Legs
      (1) Jump rope (3 to 5 minutes—with and without leg weights).
      (2) Squats with weights (shoulders bearing weight on Universal Gym—do not allow calf-thigh angle to exceed 90°).
      (3) Stadium or stair climbing.
      (4) Repetitive jumping over two foot string (three sets, 15 jumps, one minute rest between).

---

*For information contact Universal Athletic Sales Co., 4704 East Hedges, Fresno, California 93703.

B. Hands and wrists
    (1) Squeeze tennis ball 50 times. Repeat with nondominant hand.
    (2) Wrist curls. Universal Gym or hand weight — set of ten. Repeat three times.
    (3) Isometric. Place hands together, fingertip to fingertip. Push hands together. Hold for six to eight seconds, release. Repeat ten times.
C. Abdomen
    (1) Back-lying position, knees bent, feet on floor. Chin tucked. Hands at sides. Lower back flat on floor. Roll shoulders slightly forward raising knees toward chest. Pedaling action in this position. Raise legs, feet toward ceiling. Pedaling action in this position. Return to floor with knees bent.
    (2) Sit-ups — bent legs (2 minutes).
2. Endurance
    A. Distance running — one mile per day on practice days; two miles on off days.
    B. Run in place, knees high, three minutes at 180 runs per minute.

The circuit training technique lends itself to a team conditioning program, for it can be adjusted to the ability of the team members and intensified by increased number of repetitions, increased time at each station or increased number of repetitions during a *decreased* time period. The player visits established stations in a planned sequence and spends a designated period of time at each.

The following circuit is an actual example used during the first three weeks of conditioning for a competitive collegiate team. The system has nine 20 second stations. A five second period of interchange is allowed.

Station 1 — Jump rope. Two leg takeoff, as many times as possible.
        2 — Wall push-away. The player stands approximately an arm's length away from the wall. With arms extended, place fingertips against the wall. Bending elbows only, allow body to move to the wall, bearing weight on the fingers. Push body away from the wall to original position. Repeat as often as possible.
        3 — Running shuttle. Player runs from a starting line to a point 30 feet away. She stops, touches the floor with both hands, turns, runs back to starting point, stops, touches the floor. Repeat as often as possible.
        4 — Set to self (or partner). Practice a high, controlled set.
        5 — Side-shuttle. Similar to Station 3, except lateral movement is substituted for forward movement.
        6 — Wall bump (or bump to partner). Practice accurate passing. Emphasis should be on taking the ball as close to the floor as possible.
        7 — Treadmill. In sprinter's position, interchange feet.

The back is straight as legs alternate reaching out and backward as far as possible.

8 — Jump. Jump vertically as high as possible, pulling knees to the chest and keeping back straight. (Avoid intermediate hops; jump immediately following floor contact).

9 — Wall spike. Ball is thrown up, spiked so it hits the ground close to the wall and rebounds from the wall. It rises and the player shifts to contact it in flight.

At the close of most practice sessions, one or both of the following patterns is suggested:

1. Wave drill. All team members begin by running in place, lifting knees high. On hand signal from the coach, players move laterally (left or right), forward or backward. On signal they shift and execute a half or full roll recovery. This pattern should continue two to three minutes.
2. Sprint-jog. Team members sprint one lap around the gymnasium, jog two, sprint one, etc., for two minutes.

Drills.* Drills serve to improve skill and physical conditioning. Early in practice sessions time is designated for individual skill drills, later moving on to situational drills. Repetition must be used to learn the skill and assure overlearning. Some skills must be done to exhaustion in order to aid in physical development and to prepare players for tiring tournament play. At some time skills should be performed while fatigued; for example, serving which is generally practiced early in the session should be performed after a full and demanding practice session. As soon as possible, drills should be performed at the speed and tempo required in play.

Serving drills

Purpose: To develop 100 per cent good serves.

1. Four to six players on each end line. One ball per player. Serve a minimum of 20 balls without an error.
2. For serving placement. Mark receiving area and have server place five serves in each designated area. Scoring systems for intrateam competition can be devised.
3. Serve 20 balls, alternating floater with fast overhead.
4. Alternating types of serves, alternate short (ten feet from the net) with deep serves (five feet from end line).
5. To develop low trajectory, place rope three feet above net. Serve ten balls between net and rope.
6. To develop accuracy, place a team in receiving position; server places the ball to the player who calls for it by raising her hands.

---

*There are many variations possible in devising individual and game situations. For further suggestions, see Cohen, Harlan: *Power Volleyball Drills.*

OVERHEAD PASSING AND SETTING DRILLS

Purpose: To develop passing and setting effectiveness from any court position; to develop judgment of where and to whom to set.

1. Pass to self
   a. Overhead.
   b. Pass over net (player passes, runs under the net, etc.).
   c. Jump pass.
   d. Pass while running court lines.
2. Partner pass (two players, one ball)
   a. 30 feet apart, parallel to net.
   b. Jump pass—20 feet apart.
   c. Kneeling pass—20 feet apart.
   d. Squat pass—20 feet apart. One partner passes to other's side, forcing her to pass and fall at the same time. Half roll recovery.
   e. Blind pass—player without ball turns her back to partner. As the ball is passed, call partner's name; she turns, locates the ball and passes it back, calling partner's name.
   f. Ball is thrown into the net by player, partner recovers with squat or kneeling pass overhead.
3. Group drills
   a. Clock drill—designed to teach rapid shifting for a set. In groups of six to eight players, one player is designated as "out man (O.M.)." The remainder of the group forms a line directly in front of O.M. approximately ten feet away. O.M. sets to the first person in line who sets the ball back to her. O.M. sets the ball to the 11 o'clock position. As the ball is contacted by O.M. (but not before) the first person in line moves to position herself, sets the ball back to O.M. and then goes to the end of the line. O.M. sets to the next person and the sequence continues. Once the entire line has gone through the drill, the O.M. sets to ten o'clock position. The drill can be done at three, two, and one o'clock on the other side (Fig. 8-9).

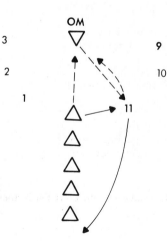

Figure 8-9. Clock drill.

b. Floating circle—designed to keep the setter alert to shifting for the set. In groups of six to eight, the players are positioned as follows (Fig. 8–10): Number 8 begins by setting the ball to Number 2 and leaving the circle at a point between Number 1 and Number 7. Number 2 sets the ball to the center of the circle. As soon as Number 2 *contacts* the ball, Number 1 moves to the center of the circle to receive the ball and sets to Number 3. Number 3 sets to the center and Number 2 moves to set the ball to Number 4. The pattern continues. Player in center exits on side of circle away from the set. She returns to her original position.

Figure 8–10.   Floating circle drill.

c. Shuttle drill—in groups of seven or eight players, one player (O.M.) faces the others in line. The drill begins with Number 1 setting to O.M. Then O.M. sets to Number 2 and follows the set, continuing to the end of the line. As O.M. touches the ball, Number 1 moves to replace her and receives Number 2's set. Number 1 sets to Number 3 and then goes to the end of the line (Fig. 8–11).

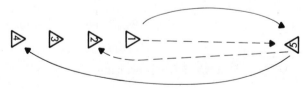

Figure 8–11.   Shuttle drill.

d. Back set and set—designed to improve back set. Number 1 sets to Number 2 who sets back to Number 1; Number 1 returns set and Number 2 *back sets* to Number 3. Number 3 sets to Number 2 who sets back to Number 3; Number 3 returns set to Number 2 who *back sets* to Number 1, etc. Each back set is preceded by three sets (Fig. 8–12).

▷ ⊲ - - - ▶ ◁   Figure 8–12.   Back set and set drill.

FOREARM PASS AND DIGGING DRILLS.   A large portion of practice time, perhaps as much as 60 per cent, should be spent developing forearm passing early in the season. Many of the overhead pass and set patterns may be used. The following are additional suggestions:

1. Bump to self
   a. Overhead.
   b. Over the net.
   c. Against a wall.
2. Partner
   a. Two hand bump.
   b. One hand bumps to the side.
   c. One hand digs combined with roll.
   d. Backward pass – player underhand passes to herself two times. She then turns her back on her partner and executes a backward underhand pass to partner.
   e. Player throws to partner facing basketball goal. She passes or digs attempting to place the ball in the basket. This drill should be practiced from varied court positions.
3. Group drills
   a. One player with many balls throws to players in defensive position. The balls are thrown with increasing speed so players have to pass from high, medium and low positions.
   b. As above, but throw so a one hand dig results.
   c. As above – player digs and rolls.
   d. Coach stands on a table and throws above the net level at players at midcourt from side to side. Alternate dinks and spikes. Players receive, bump and roll.
4. Combination pass and set drills
   a. Coach stands with back to the net and throws to one of two players in midcourt. The receiver bump passes toward the set position as her partner shifts quickly to set to the coach.
   b. Coach stands on table and spikes ball to defensive line-up. Ball is passed and set to spiker.
   c. Balls are served to defensive players who pass, set and spike, as above. Serves should be placed and tempo and style varied.

SPIKING DRILLS
Designed to develop technique, power and direction.

1. Spiker-setter drills
   a. Spiker hits 20 regular sets.
   b. Spiker hits 20 short, vertical sets.
   c. Spiker takes regular approach, as she jumps coach calls "outside, inside, power."
   d. Spiker varies approaches; that is, perpendicular, outside-in approach five feet from net, five or more feet outside court.
   e. Setter starts behind spiker; spiker tosses the ball to setter. Setter executes a short set as spiker jumps.

    f. Spiker shifts for deep sets, approximately ten feet from the net.

    g. Dinking short sets. Dink left, right, short and deep.

2. Spiking over obstacles. Recovering.

    a. The coach uses a broom to set a block on the spiker's hit.

    b. Three players stand on bench opposite spiker with their hands in blocking position. Spiker attempts to spike over the block (ten times). Spiker attempts ten wipe-outs.

    c. Spiker's shot is blocked in drill above; she must recover and pass to set.

Blocking Drills

1. Mock drills to improve timing, speed and jump.

    a. Two players jump and touch hands above the net. They move laterally several feet and repeat.

    b. Three blockers at the net. Coach calls "left, center, right"—players execute triple block, return to position and await call.

    c. Two players—one on a table placing the ball for blocker to contact.

    d. As above, blocker jumps up, reaches over the net in an attempt to knock the ball from first player's hands.

    e. Two players block a simulated spike; coach quickly throws second ball for recovery by blockers.

Combination drills

1. Spiking and blocking—designed to improve spiking placement, aggressive blocking and decisiveness.

    a. Two players, one on either side of the net. Coach throws ball over top of the net (or slightly over one side). Players should spike or block.

    b. One on one; two on one; three on one. Ball is set to spiker who attempts to block over one and two; wipe-out on three.

    c. Three blockers on one side of the net; passer, set and two spikers on the other. Ball is passed to set, who sets or back sets to a spiker. Center blocker should move to set a double block.

    d. Front on front. Three blockers against three spikers and a set.

    e. Offense-defense. A full team is set on one side of the net. Only a set and one, two or three spikers on the other. Defensive team attempts block or pass, set, spike sequence.

2. Setter-spiker decision drills

    a. Spiker and setter. Spiker passes ball to set, and moves to front or back of setter. Setter adjusts and passes to spiker.

    b. Two spikers and setter. One spiker passes ball to set, who sets between the two spikers eight to ten feet back from the net. Spikers call to play the ball. Both may replicate spiking movements.

3. Situational drills—designed to quicken responses.

    a. Players in normal receiving position. Server's delivery protected by sheets over the net. Receivers pass, set, attack.

    b. Players in normal spike defense position. Coach stands on a

table and spikes above net level. The defense should achieve
pass, set, attack sequence. Blocking is not attempted in this
drill.

Scrimmages.   Scrimmages serve to "put it all together" and evaluate
strengths and weaknesses. They evaluate individual physical and mental
preparation and are fun for team members. Each scrimmage should have
an objective—to test a new offensive pattern or blocking combination.
Teachable moments arise and the coach must be able to use them to reinforce a response or correct specific play. Constant talking by the coach dis-
tracts and minimizes the effectiveness of the important observations she
makes.

Scrimmages must be properly officiated, for lackadaisical habits of substitution, rotation, interchange and ball handling can be costly in competition. It is a truism that "we play to the level of officiating." The coach
should spend her time observing and making mental and written notes of
importance. The game should be charted by a team manager for further
information. Players are intensely interested in "how did I do?" and a
written evaluation is a clear summary of their play.

It is difficult to determine how much time should be spent with the better team playing against the lesser as complete units. Playing offensive
strength against defensive is more challenging to both, but team strategy
suffers in effecting total offensive and defensive patterns. Some teams are
fortunate to have defensive or attack specialists who play only designated
positions. These persons can alternate to strengthen either team at weak
rotation positions. The coach does well to remember that the "B" team
members may be starters next year and their importance should not be
minimized.

Strategy

As in all team sports, teams have both offensive and defensive roles.
The offense begins with the serve and is reinstated every time the ball
crosses the net from the opponents. An offense is only as effective as the individuals involved. A system should not be so traditional and inflexible that
it cannot be altered to fit the talent of the team.

OFFENSIVE STRATEGY

Four-Two.   The four-two offensive system is standard for high school
and college teams where players do not have equal ability to attack. Differences in height, ability and aggressiveness may dictate this system.
There is a minimum of exchange in positions, and slower teams find the

system results in fewer ball handling errors. Four players are attack and two are setters. All must have passing, digging and serving capabilities.

The rotation order places an attack on each side of a set, with two attacks between the sets. There is always a setter on the front line and if she is in left forward or right forward position, she switches into center forward position as the ball is served. Her teammates always try to pass to the center position so she can direct the attack from that point. The system is not deceptive and its success is dependent on the individual skill of setters and the attacks' ability to find weak spots in the defense. If the attacks are unusually tall and strong, the lack of a deceptive offense is minimized.

The four-two lends itself to covering attack players and switching from offense to defense easily.

Two basic formations are used to receive serves from the four-two. Both protect the setter from receiving the serve.

1. Star and crescent. The set is positioned near the net and the five remaining defenders assume a bowed line position about midcourt. The pattern assumes players can move forward and backward more easily than they can move laterally. It is most effective against straight, hard serves with consistent midcourt depth. If a weak receiver is in the line-up, she may be protected close to the net or deep in the court. The four strong receivers assume more lateral responsibility (Fig. 8–13).

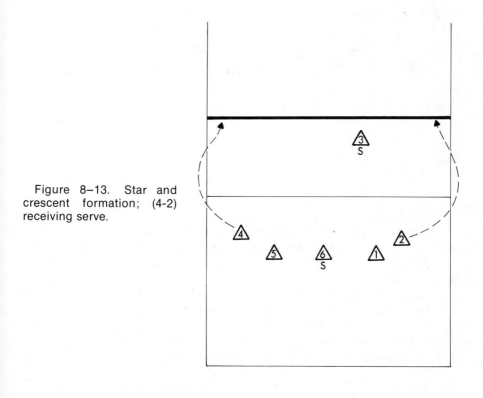

Figure 8–13. Star and crescent formation; (4-2) receiving serve.

2. W-formation assumes there will be a variety of serves, and players have the ability to move laterally as well as forward and backward. The setter is at the net and three receivers are approximately 15 feet in the court and the two deep receivers are about six feet in the court. Short receivers do not take serves above the waist or to the sides. The deep players have more time to adjust for receipt.

When the "W" is deepened — that is, the front receivers pull back approximately three feet — more protection is offered against deep serves and hard floaters, but it is vulnerable to a short serve (Fig. 8–14).

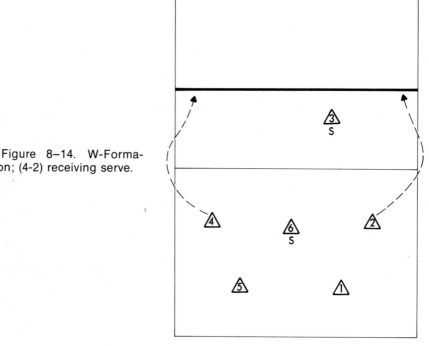

Figure 8–14. W-Formation; (4-2) receiving serve.

Five-one. The *five-one* offense is designed for teams with five attack players and one setter. It has the advantage of using three attackers at the net when the setter is in the back row. A four-two pattern is used when the setter is in the front row.

Six-0. The *six-0* system demands that all players have good skills and all have attacking ability. The individual skills of passing and mobility must be outstanding. The advantage of the system is that all three front court players can be potential attackers with the set coming from the back court. The attack patterns can be deceptive with frequent use of the short vertical set. Return to four-two is always possible if deception is unwise or unnecessary.

Multiple offensive patterns are often referred to as multiple "fakes." The intent is to deceive the defense by having three attackers at the net which results in blockers having to cover three areas until the last moment. This causes delayed or poorly formed blocks. Several options are commonly used.

1. The center forward (CF) moves on the pass and prepares for the short set at the net in midcourt. If the block does not form, the setter executes a 12 to 16 inch vertical set as the attack jumps. The attack must jump as the ball is set, not knowing if she will receive the ball. The other attacks (LF, RF) move in anticipation of a regular set.
2. Left front attack runs to center for a short set and center front goes outside to the side line. Play continues as above.
3. Setter moves toward right side. Center front comes forward for short set. Right front moves to the left of CF. Center front jumps and a low set to RF or higher set to LF are possible.

The five-one and six-0 serve receiving formations are similar when the setter of five-one is in the back court. When the setter is in the back row she is shielded from receiving the serve. She moves to front court as the serve is contacted. Her position will vary depending on the pass; ideally she sets from right of center court to at least two "on hand" spikers. A left-handed attack directly behind her in the front court presents a very strong offense.

From the right back position, the setter moves outside the right front attack to a position about ten feet from the right side line.

From center back position she cuts around the CF who shields her from the serve. She attempts to go to the right of CF, but may pull left if the serve is traveling in her path. When going left, she may receive the pass with her back to her LF and CF attacks and a back set may be necessary.

Another option exists to assure proper positioning of the set. The CF stays close to the net and CB pulls close behind. The serve defense remains with four players but the set moves easily into position and the CF is in excellent position for the short set.

The left back position presents the most difficult position from which to move. The setter moves as directly as she can, but frequently has to go left before hastening to the right front position. A high pass can give her additional time for positioning. Many six-0 offenses will not have the setter move from the LB position, but will have another player move from right back position if three attacks are used. Obviously a team using this pattern must have two setting specialists.

Serve receiving positions are illustrated in Figures 8–15 and 8–16.

Covering the attack is designed to recover the ball if it is successfully blocked by opponents and returns to the attacker's side of the court.

In a four-two offense, players position around the spiker and within

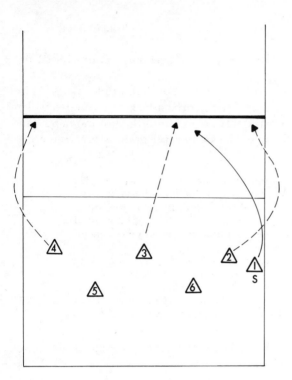

Figure 8–15. Serve receiving position for 5-1 or 6-0 with setter in right back position.

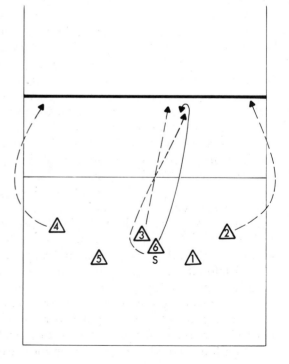

Figure 8–16. Serve receiving position for 5-1 or 6-0 with setter in center back position (line receiving pattern).

ten feet of the net. Figure 8–17 illustrates players moving to protect a left side attack. Right side coverage is reversed.

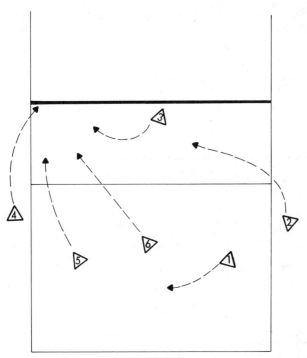

Figure 8–17. Covering the left side attack (4-2 offense).

1. Right back moves to her left to assume responsibility for the entire back court. A ball coming to this area is rarely hard driven.
2. Right front sees the set is not coming to her; she turns to cover the area vacated by the setter and to recover a rebounding block.
3. Center front follows her set and positions herself three feet from the net about five feet from the spiker. She plays sharp rebounds coming to the inside.
4. Left front is the attacker who should recover quickly to play a ball that comes directly back.
5. Left back pulls directly behind and inside the attacker. She is responsible for balls rebounding in back of the attacker and toward the outside of the court.
6. Center back moves between left back and center forward, seven or eight feet from the net.

When using five-one offense, court position to cover the attacker is the same as four-two if the setter is a front court player; it is similar to six-0 when three attack players are used.

The six-0 affords numerous possibilities for covering the attacker. When a feint or short set is used, Number 3 is unable to cover the court. A back line player is at the net as setter, leaving only two players in the back court (Fig. 8–18).

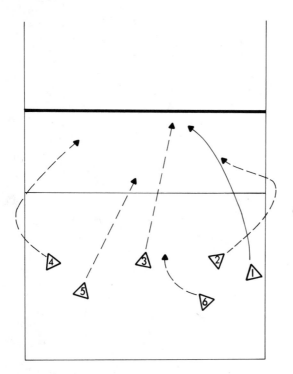

Figure 8–18.   Covering center attack (6-0; 5-1).

Number 1 is setter.
Number 3 is spiker.
Number 2 pulls behind and to the right of setter, six to eight feet from net.
Number 4 pulls to left of attacker, six to eight feet from net.
Number 5 follows the spiker and is directly behind her, approximately ten feet from the net.
Number 6 remains at midcourt to cover deep balls.

DEFENSIVE STRATEGY

Perhaps the most important factor to successful defense is the team's mental attitude that "no ball will touch the floor." Defense is imperative in winning play and is frequently neglected in team preparation. There are too few players to cover the court area; consequently, there is no perfect defensive pattern. There will always be weak areas and the key to success is reading the opponent's offense so the weak areas are not vulnerable. The instant the ball is controlled, the team begins its offensive pattern. Teams have two basic options in establishing defense systems: (1) play from a single system with minor variations or (2) develop a variety of defenses against an opponent's strengths. Beginning competitive teams are wise to play from a single system.

The first line of defense is the block; the second, the back court players. The back court players are effective only if they are positioned and coordinated in relationship to the blockers. Their individual readiness, as well as position, are based upon the knowledge of their own blockers' abilities and of their opponents' speed and style of attack. Players learn to assume defensive responsibilities for court areas.

The following patterns illustrate defense of a two player block against a right side and middle attack. Defensive positions for a left side attack are a reverse of the right side.

This defense (Figure 8–19) is successful against teams that do not dink or use off-speed spikes. It is frequently used when attack players are taller hitters than the blockers. The back court players must be skilled in executing digs, and blockers must go for the attack block.

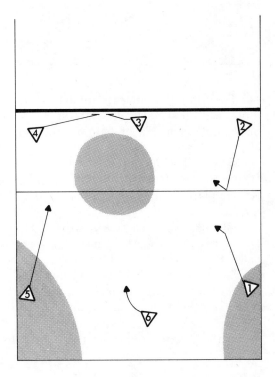

Figure 8–19. Two-player block and defense positions against middle attack (shaded area indicates vulnerable court area).

For middle attack, Number 2 and Number 5 are responsible for dinks and half-speed spikes (Figure 8–20). Player Number 1 covers the cutback and straight attack. Player Number 6 covers a ball deflected off the block or passing through a poorly formed block.

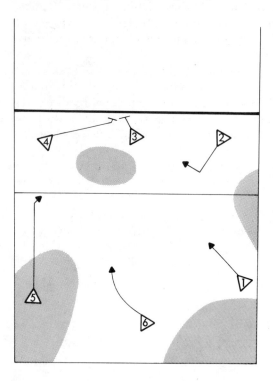

Figure 8–20. Two-player block and defense positions against middle attack.

For right side attack, Number 1 and Number 4 are responsible for dinks and off-speed spikes. Player Number 5 defends against a straight inside spike, and player Number 6 covers a deflection or missed block as above.

The following defense is used against teams that vary the attack (Figure 8–21). It is considered a good pattern for hiding one weak defensive player if the blockers are good and the other defense players very quick.

Blockers set area blocks to protect the middle of the court. Player Number 6, the weakest defensive player, is responsible for dinks and short balls off the block. In middle attack, Number 2 is responsible for off speed attacks or outside spikes. In side attack Number 4 has these responsibilities for covering dinks, off speed and inside spikes. Players Number 5 and Number 1 must be very fast and alert to an attack over the block (Fig. 8–22).

If there is no need to protect a weak defense player, player alignment

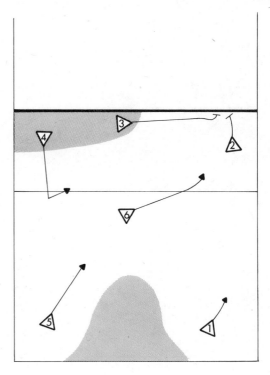

Figure 8–21. Defense and two-player block on side attack; used to hide weak defensive player.

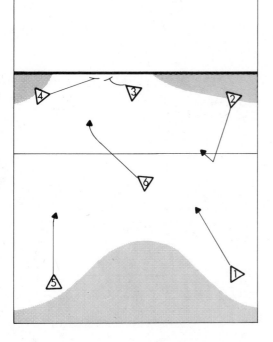

Figure 8–22. Defense against middle attack.

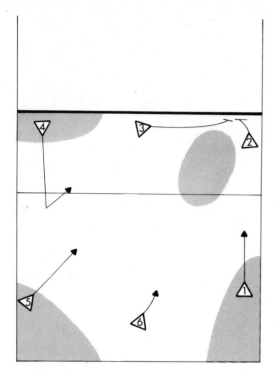

Figure 8–23. Defense and two-player block of side attack; strong defensive back court.

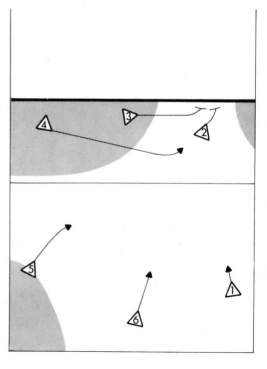

Figure 8–24. Defense of side attack; strong defensive back court.

(see Figures 8–23 and 8–24) serves to defend the same relative court areas.

A three player block can score very effectively or can give up points rapidly to dinks and off speed attacks in the vulnerable front court. This pattern is successful with predictable setting and attackers who do not vary the speed and angle of their shots (Figs. 8–25 and 8–26).

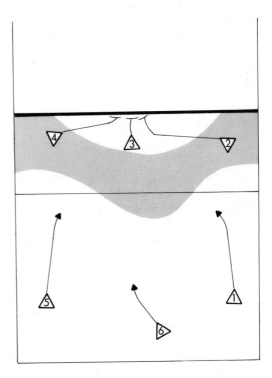

Figure 8–25. Three player block — middle attack.

Coaching the Game

The major responsibilities of the coach end prior to competition. The last practices before competitive events should stress individual and team weaknesses, review of substitution procedures, discussions of dress, conduct and protocol and the known strengths and weaknesses of opponents. Once at the game site, the coach assists in warm-ups, but thereafter she is relegated to a minor role and becomes an observer to witness the test of training and practice. She may call time-outs and make substitutions, but the team captain assumes large responsibility for game progress. The captain should have the confidence of both coach and team members. She helps determine the game plan and directs or alters it as situations arise. A captain, like a team, must mature through experience. Young players may need more direction from the coach than experienced players.

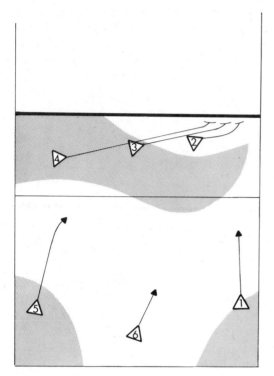

Figure 8–26. Three player block – side attack.

It is advisable to have a light workout at the tournament or game site prior to the competitive event. This is not always possible for the high school or collegiate team that travels to the game and returns the same day. The *pregame warm-up* becomes increasingly important, both psychologically and physiologically. Physiologically there is little evidence to indicate that muscles need warming up, but most players feel a readiness that comes only after executing skills. The mental aspect of adjusting to the court, lighting and crowd mood is best accomplished during the warm-up. Most teams find that a "minipractice," replicating familiar practice session patterns with a few dramatic executions of rolls or short spikes to attract audience and opponent's interest, prepares the team mentally. The following is a typical pattern for a 15 to 25 minute warm-up.

1. Modified circuit and wave drill.
2. Individual skills and drills with partner and small groups. Sequence of setting, passing, digging, spiking and blocking.
3. Spike-set warm-up at the net.
4. Spike-block combinations.
5. Serving.

Analysis of Opponents.   The term "scouting" denotes observing a team in a competitive situation in an attempt to evaluate individual weaknesses and strengths and the team's offensive and defensive patterns. Scouting charts are just now developing in volleyball with each coach designing her own. A team's own evaluation charts and sketches of offensive and defensive formations can be used with additional information designed to answer specific questions. These questions include:

1. What offensive patterns are used? The most common one?
2. What defensive patterns are used? Most common?
3. Who are the weakest players? Weak skills?
4. Is there a weak rotation pattern on serve defense?
5. Is setter (setters) deceptive? Does she have an established pattern? Favorite net position?
6. Who are the strongest attack players?
7. Do attacks have a variety of attacks—off speed spikes, dinks, etc.?
8. How effective is the short spike? Most effective player?
9. Are there weak blockers? What is each blocker's normal net position?
10. What are the patterns of substitution?
11. How does the team react to pressure?
12. Does play alter with a lead? When trailing?

Once in competition, the verity of the scouting report is evident. As the season progresses patterns alter and the coach and team must be alert to changes in play patterns and skill levels. New faces appear on the court and the tempo and style of the entire team may change.

Analysis of One's Own Team.   Charting during the game rarely gives an immediate feedback of a player's strengths and weaknesses. This must be evaluated after the contest. An astute coach and captain can spot weaknesses, general team slumps and players who respond adversely under pressure. Some of the tension of the first minutes of play will pass for an individual, if the team as a whole can continue its pattern play. Suggestions for charting and evaluating are noted below.

STRATEGY OF PLAY.   Competitors have clichés for all situations and two bear noting: (1) "Play with what you came with." A tournament match is not the time to change from a well-rehearsed offense to a weaker, more spectacular experiment. A weaker opponent may give the opportunity for some experimentation, but many teams are defeated by less skillful players using sound fundamentals. Learn from other teams but capture the new methods in practice sessions. (2) "Never change a winning pattern." This adage is generally true, but refinements and alterations of a winning style can be introduced. The score may not indicate that the opponents are reading the defense or the strongest attack, and that the lead is slowly dwindling.

When losing, the coach quickly seeks the causes. Are the serves 100 per cent effective with ten per cent accounting for aces and another ten per cent for opponent errors? If not, are the strong servers coming up in rotation order? Is a substitution needed?

If offensive and defensive patterns appear strategically sound, but individual technique is in error, it may be wise to make individual changes or correct a player's style at a time-out. Contrarily, if individuals are playing well, look to defensive patterns and the offensive patterns for the deficiencies. If, for example, the opponent's defense is reading the setter's pattern, a change, perhaps temporary, should loosen the blockers.

Time-outs and substitutions are two valuable aids to a team. Time-outs are used to:

1. Change offensive or defensive alignments.
2. Correct individual technique errors.
3. Break a rally or tempo of opponents.
4. Pass information concerning pattern or technique change by opponents.

Substitutes are increasingly important in volleyball. A strong defense player or a server with a record and reputation of aces can be a real and psychological lift for a team. Substitutes are called upon to relieve fatigued players, players experiencing off games or a player who has lost her effectiveness because her style has been read by opponents.

Charting and Statistical Evaluation.   Charting should be as simple as possible and be the task of a manager or nonplaying team associate. A coach cannot devote herself to total game analysis when she is tabulating.

The two examples below are typical of charts presently used. They serve only as guides for development of a coach's personal design.

The Game Scoring Chart is a running tabulation of how each point and sideout are won or lost by one's own team. If comparable information is needed on opponents, a second chart should be used. Each time a point or sideout is awarded, an abbreviation of the cause is recorded:

S — spike	E — error	SE — serving error
A — ace	F — foul	AE — attack error
D — dink	PE — passing error	DE — defense error
	RE — receiving error	

For example, Figure 8–27 shows State College playing State University at State College Gymnasium on October 21. College serves and scores the first point with an ace by RB Number 24. In the next play a sideout is called due to a passing error (PE) by CB Number 16. University scores as LF Number 12 traps a block set too far from the net, thus a defense error (DE). This chart gives immediate information of a team's effectiveness, but it does not always indicate the player who caused the point or sideout to be made against a team. If this information is needed, a "point lost chart" may be

G A M E   S C O R I N G   C H A R T

STATE COLLEGE
Team

OCTOBER 21   STATE COLLEGE GYMNASIUM   Game No. 1   Score _____
Date   Place

STATE COLLEGE   STATE UNIVERSITY
First Serve   Opponent

Player Position	Points Gained	Player Position	Side Outs Gained	Player Position	Points Lost to Opponent	Player Position	Side Outs Lost to Opponent
1 RB-24	1 A	1	1	1 LF-12	1 DE	1 CB-16	1 PE
2	2	2	2	2	2	2	2
3	3	3	3	3	3	3	3
4	4	4	4	4	4	4	4
5	5	5	5	5	5	5	5
6	6	6	6	6	6	6	6
7	7	7	7	7	7	7	7
8	8	8	8	8	8	8	8
9	9	9	9	9	9	9	9
10	10	10	10	10	10	10	10
11	11	11	11	11	11	11	11
12	12	12	12	12	12	12	12
13	13	13	13	13	13	13	13
14	14	14	14	14	14	14	14
15	15	15	15	15	15	15	15
16	16	16	16	16	16	16	16
17	17	17	17	17	17	17	17
18	18	18	18	18	18	18	18
19	19			19	19		19
20	20			20	20		20
21	21			21	21		21
22	22			22	22		22
23	23			23	23		23
24	24			24	24		24
25	25			25	25		25

Figure 8–27. Game scoring chart.

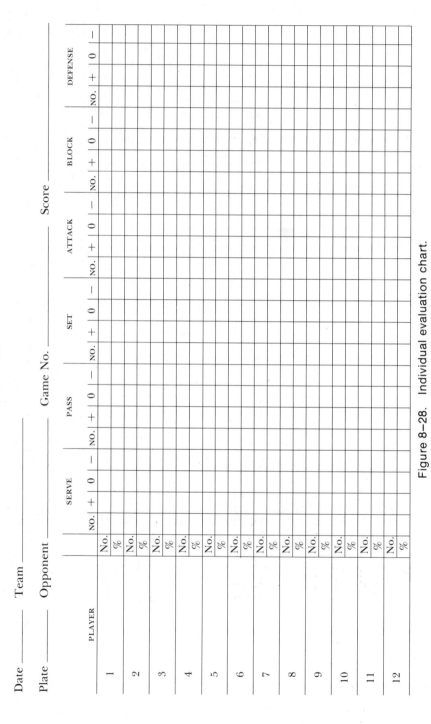

Figure 8–28. Individual evaluation chart.

used. Points are enumerated in a column with error columns following. The player causing the loss is indicated by number in the appropriate skill error column.

The Individual Evaluation Chart (Fig. 8–28) is most helpful after the game. A (1) tally is marked in the appropriate column indicating the quality of skill executions. A(+) = excellence; (0) = playable; (−) = inadequate or error in execution. Percentages are calculated by dividing each of the quality columns of a single skill by the total number of times the skill was performed.

The charts described are useful during scrimmages and when scouting other teams as well as during competitive matches.

Bibliography

American Association for Health, Physical Education and Recreation: *Proceedings at the Fourth National Institute on Girls Sports.* AAHPER, 1201 16th St. N. W., Washington, D. C., 1968.

Boyden, E. D., Burton, R. G. and Odeneal, W. T.: *Volleyball Syllabus.* United States Volleyball Association, Berne, Indiana.

Cherebetiu, Gabriel: *Volleyball Techniques.* Creative Sports Books, P. O. Box 2244, Hollywood, California, 90028, 1969.

Cohen, Harlan: *Power Volleyball Drills.* Creative Sports Books, P. O. Box 2244, Hollywood, California, 90028, 1966.

Cunningham, P. and Garrison, J.: "High wall volley test for women's volleyball." *Research Quarterly,* 39:486–90, October 1968.

Division for Girls and Women's Sports: *Volleyball Guide* Published every two years. AAHPER, 1201 16th Street, N. W., Washington, D. C.

"It's Power Volleyball." Published by United States Volleyball Association. Write Mrs. Betty Ann Ghormley, P. O. Box 514, Pacific Palisades, California, 90272, 1968.

Keller, Val.: *Point, Game and Match.* Creative Sports Books, P. O. Box 2244, Hollywood, California, 90028, 1968.

Laveaga, Robert E.: *Volleyball.* 2nd Ed. New York, Ronald Press, 1960.

Liba, M. R. and Stauff, M. R.: "Test for the volleyball pass." *Research Quarterly,* 34:56–63, March 1963.

McManama, J. and Shondell, D.: "Teaching volleyball fundamentals." *Journal of the American Association for Health, Physical Education and Recreation,* 40:43–50, March 1969.

Mushier, Carole L.: *Team Sports for Girls and Women.* Dubuque, Iowa, William C. Brown Co., 1973.

Schaafsma, Frances and Heck, Ann: *Volleyball for Coaches and Teachers.* Dubuque, Iowa, William C. Brown Co., 1971.

Schaafsma, Frances: "Teaching progressions for game-skill development." *Volleyball Guide,* 1969–71, pp. 45–53, DGWS, AAHPER, Washington, D. C.

Shick, Jacqueline: "Effects of mental practice on selected volleyball skills for college women." *Research Quarterly,* 41:1, 88–94, March 1970.

Singer, Robert N.: "Sequential skill learning and retention effects in volleyball." *Research Quarterly* 39:1, March 1968.

Thigpen, Janet: *Power Volleyball for Girls and Women.* Dubuque, Iowa, William C. Brown Co. 1967.

Trotter, Betty J.: *Volleyball for Girls and Women.* New York, Ronald Press, 1965.

Vannier, Maryhelen and Poindexter, Hally B. W.: *Individual and Team Sports for Girls and Women.* Philadelphia, W. B. Saunders Co., 1968.

Walters, Marshall L. (ed.): *Official Volleyball Rules and Reference Guide of the United States Volleyball Association.* Berne, Indiana, Box 109, USVBA Printer.

Welch, J. Edmund (ed.): *How to Play and Teach Volleyball.* New York, Association Press, 1969.

Wilson, Harry E. (ed.): *International Volleyball Review.* Encino, California, Harry Wilson Co., Box 554.

Index

Note: Page numbers in *italics* indicate illustrations.